Adapted Reading and Study Workbook

Science Explorer

PRENTICE HALL **Earth Science**

PEARSON

Prentice
Hall

Boston, Massachusetts
Upper Saddle River, New Jersey

ISBN 0-13-166592-8
8 9 10   11 10 09

Earth Science

Name _____ Date _____ Class _____

What Is Science? (pages 6–12)

Thinking Like a Scientist (pages 6–7)

Key Concept: **As scientists seek to understand the natural world, they use skills such as observing, inferring, and predicting. Successful scientists also possess certain attitudes, or habits of mind.**

- **Science** is a way of learning about the natural world.

- **Observing** is using your senses to gather information. Your senses are sight, hearing, touch, taste, and smell.

- **Inferring** is coming up with a reason for the things you observe. If you see people outside wearing coats, you might infer that it is a cold day.

- **Predicting** is saying what will happen in the future. If the sky is cloudy, you might predict that it will rain.

- Successful scientists are curious, honest, open-minded, and creative. They are also skeptical, or doubting. They doubt new ideas until the ideas have been tested.

Answer the following questions. Use your textbook and the ideas above.

1. Draw a line from each term to its meaning.

Term	Meaning
predicting	**a.** explaining the things you observe
observing	**b.** saying what will happen in the future
inferring	**c.** using your senses to gather information

2. Is the following sentence true or false? Successful scientists accept new ideas without testing them.

_____.

Scientific Inquiry (pages 8–11)

Key Concept: **Scientific inquiry refers to the many ways in which scientists study the natural world and propose explanations based on the evidence they gather.**

- Scientific inquiry begins with a question. For example, Benjamin Franklin asked "What is lightning?"

- The question is followed with a hypothesis. A **hypothesis** is a possible answer to a scientific question. Franklin's hypothesis was "Lightning is electricity."

- The hypothesis is tested with an experiment. To test his hypothesis, Franklin flew a kite in a thunderstorm.

- Data are collected in the experiment. Data are facts and figures gathered by observing. Franklin saw sparks of electricity in his experiment.

- The data are used to draw a conclusion. A conclusion is a decision about what the data mean. Franklin concluded that lightning is electricity.

- The data and other results are shared with other people. This is called communicating.

Answer the following question. Use your textbook and the ideas above.

3. The picture below shows steps in scientific inquiry. Circle the first step of the scientific inquiry process.

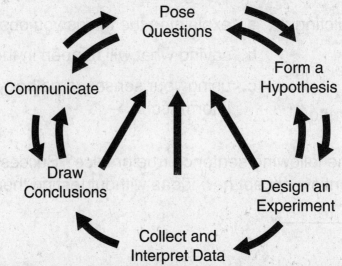

Introduction to Earth Science

Scientific Theories and Laws (page 12)

Key Concept: Unlike a theory, a scientific law describes an observed pattern in nature, but does not provide an explanation for it.

- A **scientific theory** is an idea that explains many observations. For example, the theory of evolution explains why living things change over time. To be a theory, an idea must be supported by a lot of data.

- A **scientific law** describes what always happens in a given situation. For example, the law of gravity says that a dropped object always falls to the ground.

Answer the following question. Use your textbook and the ideas above.

4. Read each word in the box. In each sentence below, fill in one of the words.

law	hypothesis	theory

a. A scientific _____ is an idea that explains many observations.

b. A scientific _____ describes what always happens in a given situation.

Introduction to Earth Science

The Study of Earth Science
(pages 13–18)

Big Ideas of Earth Science (pages 14–15)

Key Concept: **Earth scientists use several big ideas to guide their work: the structure of the Earth system, Earth's history, and Earth in the solar system.**

- **Earth science** is the study of Earth and its place in the universe.

- Earth scientists divide Earth into four parts:
  1. The atmosphere is the mixture of gases that surrounds Earth.
  2. The lithosphere is the rocky surface of Earth.
  3. The hydrosphere is the water on Earth.
  4. The biosphere is all of the living things on Earth.

- These four parts make up the Earth system. A **system** is a group of parts that work together as a whole.

- Earth has a very long history. During that history, forces have changed Earth's surface. For example, some forces have built up mountains.

- Earth is part of the solar system. The solar system includes the sun and the planets that move around the sun.

Answer the following questions. Use your textbook and the ideas above.

1. A group of parts that work together as a whole is a(an)

   _____.

2. Is the following sentence true or false? Earth's surface has always been the same as it is today. _____

3. Draw a line from each part of Earth to its description.

Name _____ Date _____ Class _____

Part of Earth	Description
atmosphere	a. rocky surface of Earth
lithosphere	b. all of the living things on Earth
hydrosphere	c. mixture of gases surrounding Earth
biosphere	d. water on Earth

The Branches of Earth Science (pages 16–17)

Key Concept: **The branches of Earth science include geology, oceanography, meteorology, astronomy, and environmental science.**

- Geology is the study of the solid Earth. **Geologists** study the forces that have changed Earth's surface.

- Oceanography is the study of Earth's oceans. **Oceanographers** study everything about the oceans—from the salt in ocean water to valleys on the ocean floor.

- Meteorology is the study of Earth's atmosphere. **Meteorologists** study data on weather and climate.

- Astronomy is the study of the universe beyond Earth. **Astronomers** study the solar system or other parts of the universe.

- Environmental science is the study of Earth's environment and resources. **Environmental scientists** study how people affect Earth.

Answer the following questions. Use your textbook and the ideas above.

4. The kind of Earth scientist that studies how people affect Earth is a(an) _____.

5. Draw a line from each term to its meaning.

Term	Meaning
geology	**a.** study of Earth's oceans
oceanography	**b.** study of the universe beyond Earth
meteorology	**c.** study of the solid Earth
astronomy	**d.** study of Earth's atmosphere

Models in Earth Science (page 18)

Key Concept: **Earth scientists often use models to represent complex objects or processes.**

- A model car is an example of a model. Like many other kinds of models, a model car is a smaller, simpler version of a real object.

- Models are used in science. Models help scientists understand things that are complicated or that cannot be observed directly.

- An example of a model used in Earth science is a weather map. A weather map shows what is happening in Earth's atmosphere. For example, symbols on a weather map show the direction of the wind and how fast the wind is blowing.

Answer the following question. Use your textbook and the ideas above.

6. Circle the letter of the problem that an Earth scientist would probably study with a model.

a. how tornadoes form

b. how much salt is in a sample of ocean water

c. what kinds of rocks are found in a certain place

Introduction to Earth Science

The Nature of Technology
(pages 20–22)

What Is Technology? (page 20)

Key Concept: **The goal of technology is to improve the way people live.**

- **Technology** is how people change the world around them. People use technology to meet their needs or to solve problems.

- There are different areas of technology. For example, a car is an example of transportation technology. A telephone is an example of communication technology.

- Some of the other areas of technology are energy technology and manufacturing technology.

Answer the following questions. Use your textbook and the ideas above.

1. People use _____ to meet their needs or to solve problems.

2. The area of technology that you use when you ride in a car is _____ technology.

How Does Science Relate to Technology? (page 21)

Key Concept: **Science is the study of the natural world. Technology, on the other hand, changes, or modifies, the natural world to meet human needs or solve problems.**

- Science and technology are related. But science and technology are not the same thing.

Introduction to Earth Science

- The goal of science is to understand the natural world. People who study science are called scientists.

- The goal of technology is to change the natural world. People who create technology are called engineers. An **engineer** uses science and technology to solve everyday problems.

Answer the following questions. Use your textbook and the ideas on page 11 and above.

3. Someone who uses science and technology to solve

   everyday problems is a(an) _____.

4. Circle the letter of the problem that an engineer might try to solve.

   a. how the wind can be used for energy

   b. what causes the wind to blow

   c. why the wind often blows from the same direction

Technology's Impact on Society (page 22)

Key Concept: From the Stone Age thousands of years ago to the Information Age today, technology has had a large impact on society.

- A society is a group of people who live together in an area and have things in common. For example, Americans form a society.

- During the Stone Age, people used stones to make tools such as spears and shovels. Stone tools helped people hunt animals and grow crops.

- You live in the Information Age. Technology in the Information Age includes computers and cellular phones. These inventions let people share information quickly with other people around the world.

Introduction to Earth Science

Answer the following questions. Use your textbook and the ideas on page 12.

5. A group of people who live together in an area and have things in common is a(an)

_____.

6. Is the following sentence true or false? Technology has had a large impact on society only since the start of the Information Age. _____

Introduction to Earth Science

Safety in the Science Laboratory (pages 23–27)

Safety in the Lab (pages 24–26)

Key Concept: **Good preparation helps you stay safe when doing science activities in the laboratory.**

- Before you work in a science lab, you must learn how to use lab equipment. Lab equipment includes thermometers, balances, and glassware.

- You should start to get ready for a science lab on the day before the lab. Read the directions and make sure you understand them. Review safety guidelines for any equipment you will use.

- When you do the lab, follow your teacher's instructions and the textbook directions exactly. Pay attention to safety symbols and make sure you know what they mean. Take your time, and keep your work area neat.

- At the end of the lab, clean up your work area. Unplug and return any equipment to its correct place. Get rid of any waste materials as directed by your teacher.

Answer the following questions. Use your textbook and the ideas above.

1. When should you start to get ready for a science lab? Circle the letter of the correct answer.
   a. the day before the lab
   b. an hour before the lab
   c. when the lab begins

2. Is the following sentence true or false? When you do a lab, you should always work as quickly as possible.

_____

3. Each of the pictures below is a lab safety symbol. Circle the letter of the safety symbol that warns you not to touch broken glassware.

a.

b.

c.

Safety in the Field (page 26)

Key Concept: **Just as in the laboratory, good preparation helps you stay safe when doing science activities in the field.**

- The "field" is any outdoor area where you do a science activity. For example, the field could be a schoolyard or park.

- Possible safety problems in the field are dangerous weather, wild animals, and poisonous plants.

- When you work in the field, always tell an adult where you will be. Never work in the field alone.

Answer the following questions. Use your textbook and the ideas above.

4. Any outdoor area where you do a science activity is

called the _____.

5. Is the following sentence true or false? You should

never work in the field alone. _____

Introduction to Earth Science

In Case of an Accident (page 27)

Key Concept: When any accident occurs, no matter how minor, notify your teacher immediately. Then, listen to your teacher's directions and carry them out quickly.

- Tell your teacher right away if there is an accident.

- Make sure you know where emergency equipment is in your lab room. Learn how to use the emergency equipment.

- Know what to do in different kinds of accidents. For example, if you spill something on your skin, you and your teacher should pour large amounts of water on your skin.

Answer the following questions. Use your textbook and the ideas above.

6. Circle the letter of what you should do immediately if an accident occurs in the laboratory.
   a. Find emergency equipment.
   b. Ask another student what to do.
   c. Tell your teacher.

7. Is the following sentence true or false? Only the teacher needs to know where emergency equipment is in the laboratory. _____

Exploring Earth's Surface (pages 34–38)

Topography (page 35)

Key Concept: **The topography of an area includes the area's elevation, relief, and landforms.**

- **Topography** (tuh PAWG ruh fee) is the shape of the land. An area's topography may be flat, sloping, hilly, or mountainous.

- **Elevation** is a place's height above sea level. Mountains have high elevation. Valleys have low elevation.

- **Relief** is the difference in elevation between the highest points and lowest points of an area. An area with mountains and valleys has high relief.

- A **landform** is a feature of the land such as a hill or valley.

Answer the following question. Use your textbook and the ideas above.

1. Read the words in the box. In each sentence below, fill in one of the words.

relief	topography	elevation	landform

   a. A place's height above sea level is its

      _____.

   b. A feature of the land such as a valley is

      a(an) _____.

   c. The difference in elevation between the highest and lowest points of an area is the

      area's _____.

Name _____ Date _____ Class _____

Mapping Earth's Surface

Types of Landforms (pages 36–38)

Key Concept: **There are three main types of landforms: plains, mountains, and plateaus.**

- A **plain** is a landform with nearly flat or gently rolling land. A plain has low relief.

- A **mountain** is a landform with peaks and steep sides. A mountain has high elevation and high relief.

- A **mountain range** is a group of mountains in the same area. The mountains in a range formed around the same time.

- A mountain system is a group of mountain ranges in the same region. The Rocky Mountains are an example of a mountain system.

- A **plateau** is a landform with high elevation and a flat surface.

- A **landform region** is a large area where there is mainly just one type of landform. The Great Plains is a landform region. The Great Plains is an area of plains that covers several states.

Answer the following questions. Use your textbook and the ideas above.

2. Draw a line from each term to its meaning.

Term	Meaning
mountain	a. landform with nearly flat or gently rolling land
plain	b. landform with high elevation and a flat surface
plateau	c. landform with high elevation and high relief

Mapping Earth's Surface

3. Fill in the blanks in the concept map about landforms.

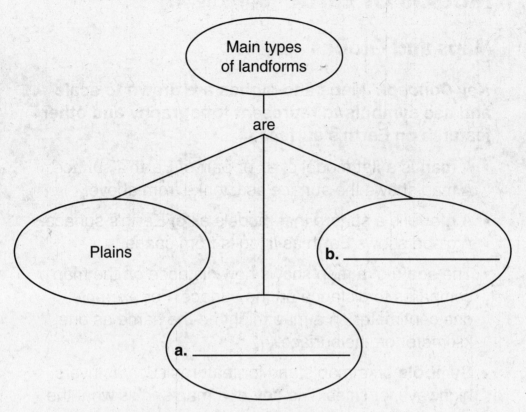

4. Fill in the blanks in the table about mountain landforms.

Mountain Landforms	
Kind of Mountain Landform	**Description**
a. _____	landform with peaks and steep sides
Mountain range	group of mountains
b. _____ _____	group of mountain ranges

Models of Earth (pages 39–47)

Maps and Globes (page 40)

Key Concept: **Maps and globes are drawn to scale and use symbols to represent topography and other features on Earth's surface.**

- A **map** is a flat model of all or part of Earth's surface. A map shows the surface as it looks from above.

- A **globe** is a sphere that models all of Earth's surface. A globe shows Earth as it looks from space.

- The **scale** of a map shows how distance on the map compares to distance on the surface. For example, one centimeter on a map might be the same as one kilometer on the surface.

- **Symbols** on a map stand for features such as rivers, highways, or cities. The **key** of a map shows what the symbols stand for.

- A compass rose or north arrow shows how directions on a map compare to directions on the surface. The top of a map usually is north.

Answer the following questions. Use your textbook and the ideas above.

1. A flat model of Earth's surface is a(an)

_____.

2. Circle the letter of each sentence that is true about globes.
   a. Globes are spheres.
   b. Globes model all of Earth's surface.
   c. Globes show Earth as it looks from space.

Mapping Earth's Surface

3. Read the words in the box. In each sentence below, fill in one of the words.

scale	compass	key	symbol

   a. A feature such as a city is shown on a map with a _____.

   b. Distance on a map is compared to distance on the surface by the map's _____.

   c. You can see how roads are shown on a map by looking at the map's _____.

An Earth Reference System (pages 41–43)

Key Concept: **Most maps and globes show a grid of lines on Earth's surface. Two of the lines that make up the grid, the equator and prime meridian, are the baselines for measuring distances on Earth's surface.**

- Earth is a sphere. Distances around a sphere are measured in **degrees** (°). The distance all the way around a sphere is 360°.

- The **equator** is an imaginary line that goes around Earth halfway between the North Pole and the South Pole.

- The equator divides Earth into two halves. The two halves are called the Northern Hemisphere and Southern Hemisphere. A **hemisphere** (HEM ih sfeer) is one half of Earth's surface.

- The **prime meridian** is an imaginary line that goes through the North Pole and the South Pole. The prime meridian passes through Greenwich, England.

Mapping Earth's Surface

- Another imaginary line through both poles lies opposite the prime meridian. That line and the prime meridian divide Earth into two halves. The two halves are called the Eastern Hemisphere and Western Hemisphere.

Answer the following question. Use your textbook and the ideas on page 21 and above.

4. Fill in the blanks in the drawing of Earth's surface.

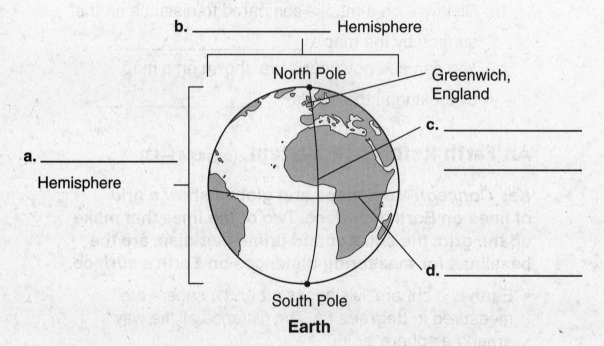

Earth

Locating Points on Earth's Surface (pages 44–45)

Key Concept: **The lines of latitude and longitude form a grid that can be used to find locations anywhere on Earth.**

- **Latitude** is distance north or south of the equator. Lines of latitude go around the globe from east to west. All lines of latitude are parallel to the equator.

- The latitude of the equator is 0°. The latitude of the North Pole is 90° North. The latitude of the South Pole is 90° South.

Name _____ Date _____ Class _____

Mapping Earth's Surface

- **Longitude** is distance east or west of the prime meridian. Lines of longitude go around the globe from north to south. All lines of longitude pass through both poles.

- The longitude of the prime meridian is 0°. Longitude goes up to 180° East and 180° West.

- You can find any place on a map or globe if you know the place's latitude and longitude.

Answer the following question. Use your textbook and the ideas on page 22 and above.

5. Use the map below to answer the following questions.

   a. What is the latitude of New Orleans,

      Louisiana? _____

   b. What is the longitude of New Orleans,

      Louisiana? _____

   c. What city on the map has latitude of 30° North and

      longitude of 120° East? _____

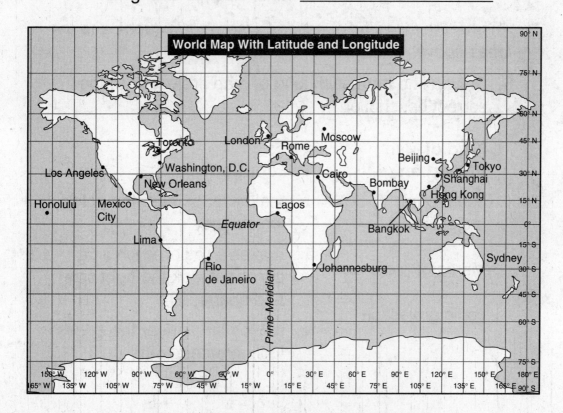

Mapping Earth's Surface

Map Projections (pages 46–47)

Key Concept: **Three common map projections are the Mercator projection, the equal-area projection, and the conic projection.**

- A **map projection** is a way to show Earth's curved surface on a flat map.

- A Mercator projection has straight lines of latitude and straight lines of longitude. The lines form a grid of rectangles. This kind of map spreads out lands near the poles, so these lands look bigger than they really are.

- An equal-area projection has straight lines of latitude and curved lines of longitude. All the lines of longitude pass through the North and South Poles. This kind of map spreads out lands near the edges of the map.

- A conic projection has curved lines of latitude and straight lines of longitude. This kind of map makes lands the right size and shape, but only for small areas of the surface.

Answer the following questions. Use your textbook and the ideas above.

6. Draw a line from each kind of map projection to the correct description.

Kind of Map Projection	Description
equal-area projection	**a.** makes lands near the poles look bigger
Mercator projection	**b.** makes a region such as a continent look the right size and shape
conic projection	**c.** makes lands near the edges look stretched out

Name _____ Date _____ Class _____

Mapping Earth's Surface

7. Label each map with the kind of projection it shows.

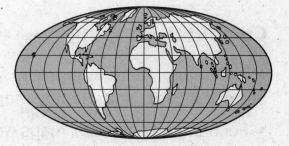

a. _____

_____

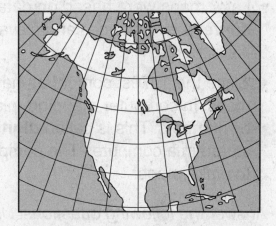

b. _____

_____

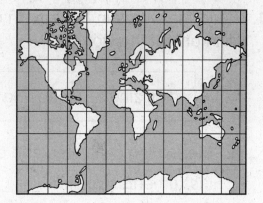

c. _____

_____

Maps and Computers (pages 49–51)

Computer Mapping (page 49)

Key Concept: **With computers, mapmakers can store, process, and display map data electronically.**

- For hundreds of years, maps were drawn by hand. Early maps were based only on what people saw.

- Later maps were based on data from surveying. In **surveying**, distances and elevations are measured with instruments.

- Since the 1970s, computers have been used to make maps. In computer mapping, places are represented by numbers. This is called **digitizing**. The numbers are stored in a computer. The computer uses the numbers to make maps.

Answer the following questions. Use your textbook and the ideas above.

1. Read the words in the box. In each sentence below, fill in one of the words.

   ┌───┐
   │ digitizing   mapping   surveying │
   └───┘

   a. Measuring distances and elevations with

      instruments is called _____.

   b. Representing places by numbers is called

      _____.

2. Is the following sentence true or false? Most maps

   today are drawn by hand. _____

Mapping Earth's Surface

Sources of Map Data (pages 50–51)

Key Concept: **Computers produce maps using data from many sources, including satellites and the Global Positioning System.**

- Satellites in space collect data about Earth's surface. The satellites send the data to computers on Earth.

- The computers use the data to make pictures. The pictures are called **satellite images**.

- Satellite images show what materials cover Earth's surface. Different materials show up as different colors in the images. For example, forests are red and water is black.

- Today, some maps are based on GPS data. GPS stands for **Global Positioning System**. GPS uses satellites to find latitude, longitude, and elevation of places on Earth's surface.

Answer the following questions. Use your textbook and the ideas above.

3. Circle the letter of each sentence that is true about satellite images.
    a. Satellite images are based on GPS data.
    b. Satellite images use symbols to show features such as forests.
    c. Satellite images show what materials cover Earth's surface.

4. Circle the letter of each kind of data that you can get from the Global Positioning System.
    a. what materials cover the surface
    b. latitude
    c. longitude

Mapping Earth's Surface

Topographic Maps (pages 54–58)

Mapping Earth's Topography (page 55)

Key Concept: **Mapmakers use contour lines to represent elevation, relief, and slope on topographic maps.**

- A **topographic** (tahp uh GRAF ik) **map** is a map that shows elevation, relief, and slope. Slope is how steep or flat the ground is.

- A topographic map shows elevation, relief, and slope with contour lines. A **contour line** connects points that have the same elevation.

- Every fifth contour line is called an **index contour**. Index contours are darker than other contour lines. Index contours also are labeled with the elevation.

- The **contour interval** is the change in elevation from one contour line to the next.

Answer the following questions. Use your textbook and the ideas above.

1. A map that shows elevation and relief is a(an)

   _____ map.

2. Draw a line from each term to its meaning.

Term	Meaning
contour interval	a. line connecting points that have the same elevation
contour line	b. darker line that is labeled with the elevation
index contour	c. change in elevation between contour lines

Mapping Earth's Surface

Reading a Topographic Map (pages 56–57)

Key Concept: **To read a topographic map, you must familiarize yourself with the map's scale and symbols and interpret the map's contour lines.**

- Topographic maps are usually large-scale maps. Large-scale maps show a close-up view of a small area.

- Like other maps, topographic maps use symbols to show features such as rivers, swamps, highways, and airports.

- A topographic map also has contour lines. You can tell the slope of an area from the contour lines. Where contour lines are close together, the ground has a steep slope. Where contour lines are far apart, the ground has a gentle slope.

- If a contour line is a closed loop without any other contour lines inside the loop, it shows a hilltop. If the closed loop has dashes inside, it shows a hollow.

Answer the following questions. Use your textbook and the ideas above.

3. Is the following sentence true or false? Topographic maps show only elevation and relief. _____

4. Label each set of contour lines to show whether it stands for a steep slope, gentle slope, hilltop, or hollow.

a. _____ b. _____ c. _____ d. _____

_____   _____

Mapping Earth's Surface

Uses of Topographic Maps (page 58)

Key Concept: **Topographic maps have many uses in science and engineering, business, government, and everyday life.**

- Remember, topographic maps show how steeply or gently the land slopes. Topographic maps also show where there are rivers, swamps, and other features.

- Topographic maps can be used to plan highways. The maps also can be used to decide where to build new houses, factories, and other buildings.

- A topographic map can even be used to plan a bicycle trip. The map shows where the trip would be flat or hilly.

Answer the following questions. Use your textbook and the ideas above.

5. Circle the letter of each use for a topographic map.
   a. planning a bike path that is not too hilly
   b. finding out where the ground is steep enough to build a ski slope
   c. learning how much rain a city gets each year

6. Is the following sentence true or false? Topographic maps would be useful for planning a new highway.

   _____

Properties of Minerals
(pages 66–74)

What Is a Mineral? (pages 66–67)

Key Concept: **A mineral is a naturally occurring, inorganic solid that has a crystal structure and a definite chemical composition.**

• A **mineral** has all five of the following characteristics.

• A mineral must be formed by natural processes. For example, a mineral might be formed by the cooling of melted materials.

• A mineral must be **inorganic**. Something that is inorganic was never part of a living thing.

• A mineral is always a solid. A mineral is not a liquid or a gas.

• The particles that make up a mineral always line up in a certain pattern that keeps repeating. The repeating pattern forms a solid called a **crystal**. A crystal has flat sides that meet at sharp edges.

• A mineral has a certain "recipe." For example, the mineral quartz is always made of oxygen and silicon, and there is always twice as much oxygen as silicon.

Answer the following questions. Use your textbook and the ideas above.

1. Circle the letter of each sentence that is true about minerals.
   a. Some minerals are gases.
   b. Some minerals come from living things.
   c. All minerals have a definite makeup.

Name _____ Date _____ Class _____

Minerals

2. Read the words in the box. In each sentence below, fill in one of the words.

| crystal | inorganic | solid | mineral | silicon |

  a. Something that was never part of a living thing is
     _____.

  b. A solid made up of particles in a repeating pattern
     is a(an) _____.

  c. A material that is not a liquid or a gas is a(an)
     _____.

  d. Quartz is an example of a(an)
     _____.

3. Fill in the blanks in the concept map about minerals.

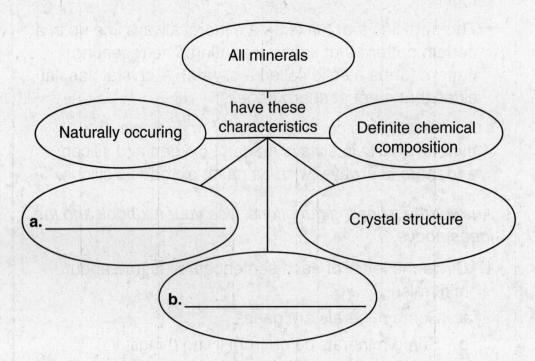

Minerals

Identifying Minerals (pages 68–74)

Key Concept: **Each mineral has characteristic properties that can be used to identify it.**

- There are almost 4,000 known minerals. You can tell minerals apart by their properties. You can observe some properties just by looking at minerals. You can observe other properties only by testing minerals.

- Color is a property that is easy to observe. Only a few minerals can be identified by color alone. Malachite is one of them. Malachite is always green, and no other mineral is exactly the same color.

- The **streak** of a mineral is the color of its powder. You can see streak by rubbing a mineral against rough tile. The streak color may not be the same as the color of the mineral itself.

- **Luster** depends on how a mineral reflects light. A mineral's luster is described by a word such as *shiny, metallic, waxy, dull,* or *greasy.*

- A mineral's density is always the same. Remember, density is the amount of mass in a given volume of a substance. Density equals mass divided by volume.

- Each mineral has a certain hardness. Hardness is measured by scratching a mineral. A mineral can be scratched by any mineral harder than itself. The softest mineral is talc. The hardest mineral is diamond.

- A mineral's crystals always have the same shape. For example, a mineral's crystals might be shaped like cubes.

- Some minerals split easily into flat pieces. These minerals have a property called **cleavage**. Mica is a mineral with cleavage.

Minerals

- Other minerals do not split easily into flat pieces. These minerals have a property called **fracture**. A mineral with fracture always breaks into pieces with a certain shape. For example, quartz always breaks into pieces shaped like seashells.

- Some minerals can be identified by special properties. For example, magnetite is magnetic. It attracts iron.

Answer the following questions. Use your textbook and the ideas on page 33 and above.

4. Read the words in the box. In each sentence below, fill in one of the words.

streak	luster	density
hardness	cleavage	fracture
crystal		

   a. If a mineral does not split easily into flat pieces, it has a property called _____.

   b. The color of a mineral's powder is its

   _____.

   c. How a mineral reflects light is its

   _____.

   d. If a mineral splits easily into flat pieces, it has a property called _____.

   e. The amount of mass in a given volume of a substance is the substance's

   _____.

   f. A property measured by scratching a mineral is

   _____.

5. Fill in the blanks to label the mineral that has cleavage and the mineral that has fracture.

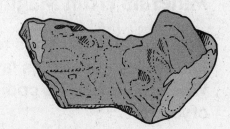

a. _____   **b.** _____

6. The table shows scratch-test results for five minerals. Circle the letter of the choice that shows the minerals in the correct order, from softest to hardest.

  a. feldspar, talc, quartz, calcite, diamond

  b. talc, calcite, feldspar, quartz, diamond

  c. talc, quartz, feldspar, diamond, calcite

Scratch-Test Results for Five Minerals				
Talc	**Diamond**	**Calcite**	**Quartz**	**Feldspar**
scratched by all	scratched by none	scratched by feldspar, quartz, diamond	scratched by diamond	scratched by quartz, diamond

How Minerals Form (pages 76–79)

Minerals From Magma and Lava (page 77)

Key Concept: **Minerals form as hot magma cools inside the crust, or as lava hardens on the surface. When these liquids cool to a solid state, they form crystals.**

- Minerals form in a process called crystallization. In **crystallization**, particles of a substance form crystals. Remember, crystals are solids that have their particles lined up in repeating patterns. Crystals have flat sides and sharp edges.

- Many minerals form when magma or lava cools. **Magma** is melted material inside Earth. **Lava** is magma that reaches Earth's surface.

- The size of the crystals that form from magma or lava depends on how fast the material cools. When the material cools slowly, there is more time for large crystals to form.

- When magma cools deep under Earth's surface, it cools very slowly. The crystals that form are very large.

- When magma cools closer to the surface, it cools faster. The crystals that form are smaller.

- When magma erupts to the surface and forms lava, it cools even faster. The crystals that form from lava are very small.

Answer the following questions. Use your textbook and the ideas above.

1. Is the following sentence true or false? Very few minerals form from magma or lava. _____

2. Circle the letter of the process in which particles of a substance line up in a repeating pattern.

  a. mineralization

  b. eruption

  c. crystallization

Minerals From Solutions (pages 77–79)

Key Concept: **When elements and compounds that are dissolved in water leave a solution, crystallization occurs.**

- Substances that form minerals may be dissolved in water. The water and dissolved substances form a solution. A **solution** is a mixture in which one substance is dissolved in another.

- Some dissolved substances form mineral crystals when they leave a solution. Dissolved substances can leave a solution in two ways.

- Dissolved substances can leave a solution when the solution evaporates, or turns into gases. This happens on Earth's surface. For example, the mineral halite formed when ancient seas evaporated.

- Dissolved substances can leave a solution when the solution cools. This happens below Earth's surface. Underground water heated by magma dissolves many substances. When the water cools, minerals come out of the solution and form crystals.

- A **vein** is a narrow band of minerals that lies between rock layers. Veins look like streaks of fudge in vanilla fudge ice cream. Veins form when solutions of hot water flow through cracks and then cool. Silver is a mineral that may form in veins.

Name _____ Date _____ Class _____

Minerals

Answer the following questions. Use your textbook and the ideas on page 37.

3. Read the words in the box. In each sentence below, fill in one of the words.

solution	silver	halite	vein

a. A narrow band of a mineral that lies between rock layers is a _____.

b. A mixture in which one substance is dissolved in another is a _____.

c. A mineral that formed when ancient seas evaporated is _____.

4. Fill in the blanks in the concept map about how minerals form from solutions.

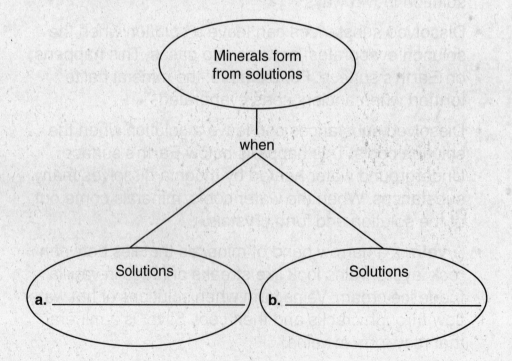

Minerals form from solutions

when

Solutions
a. _____

Solutions
b. _____

Minerals

Using Mineral Resources
(pages 80–85)

The Uses of Minerals (page 81)

Key Concept: **Minerals are the source of gemstones, metals, and a variety of materials used to make many products.**

- A **gemstone** is a hard, colorful mineral that is shiny. Gemstones are used mainly for jewelry. Examples are rubies, sapphires, and diamonds.

- Minerals such as copper, gold, and silver are called metals. Metals are usually softer than gemstones. Metals are used for wires, jewelry, tools, and buildings.

- Other useful minerals include quartz and gypsum. Quartz is used to make glass. Gypsum is used to make cement.

Answer the following questions. Use your textbook and the ideas above.

1. A hard, colorful mineral that is shiny is a(an)

   _____.

2. Circle the letter of a mineral that is might be used to make wire.
   a. gypsum
   b. ruby
   c. copper

3. Circle the letter of a mineral that is used to make glass.
   a. quartz
   b. sapphire
   c. silver

Minerals

Producing Metals From Minerals
(pages 82–85)

Key Concept: **To produce metal from a mineral, a rock containing the mineral must be located through prospecting and mined, or removed from the ground. Then the rock must be processed to extract the metal.**

- Most metals are found in rocks that also contain other substances. An **ore** is a rock that contains a metal or other useful mineral.

- A prospector is someone who looks for ore. To find ore, a prospector might look at rocks on the surface and study maps of underground rocks.

- Mining is removing ore from the ground. There are different kinds of mines. For example, in a shaft mine, miners dig tunnels to follow veins of ore.

- **Smelting** is removing metal from ore. For example, the ore hematite is smelted to remove iron. In smelting, hematite is crushed, mixed with other materials, and heated.

- After smelting, a metal may be mixed with other substances to make an alloy. An **alloy** is a solid mixture containing at least one metal. For example, iron is mixed with carbon to form the alloy steel. Steel is harder and stronger than pure iron.

Answer the following questions. Use your textbook and the ideas above.

4. Is the following sentence true or false? Most metals are found in the ground in pure form. _____

Minerals

5. Read the words in the box. In each sentence below, fill in one of the words.

ore	miner	smelting
alloy	hematite	prospector

a. A solid mixture containing at least one metal is

a(an) _____.

b. A rock containing a metal or other useful mineral is

a(an) _____.

c. The process of removing metal from ore is called

_____.

d. Someone who looks for ore is a(an)

_____.

e. Iron occurs in an ore called

_____.

6. Fill in the blank in the flowchart about producing metals.

Steps in Producing Metals

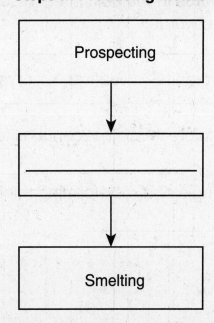

Rocks

Classifying Rocks (pages 94–97)

Mineral Composition and Color (page 95)

Key Concept: **When studying a rock sample, geologists observe the rock's mineral composition and color.**

- Rocks are mixtures of minerals and other materials. A rock may contain one or more minerals. **Granite** contains at least four minerals: feldspar, quartz, hornblende, and mica.

- About 20 minerals make up most of the rocks in Earth's crust. These 20 minerals are known as **rock-forming minerals**.

- A rock's color may help identify its minerals. For example, granite is usually light-colored because it is made of minerals that contain a lot of silica.

- To identify the minerals in most rocks, you also need to see the shape and color of the mineral crystals.

Answer the following questions. Use your textbook and the ideas above.

1. Read the words in the box. In each sentence below, fill in one of the words.

+--------------------------------------+
| granite   quartz   crystal |
+--------------------------------------+

   a. A light-colored rock that contains feldspar and other

      minerals is _____.

   b. An example of a rock-forming mineral is

      _____.

Rocks

2. Is the following sentence true or false? The color of a rock lets you identify all the minerals that the rock contains. _____

Texture (page 96)

Key Concept: **When studying a rock sample, geologists also observe the rock's texture.**

- Most rocks are made up of particles, called **grains**. Grains are particles of minerals or other rocks.

- Grains give rocks their texture. A rock's **texture** is how the rock's surface looks and feels. For example, a rock's texture could be smooth or rough. Texture is used to help identify rocks.

- The grains in rock may be big or small. Some grains are big enough to see easily. Other grains are too small to see, even with a microscope. Rocks with big grains have a rougher texture than rocks with small grains.

- The grains in rock have many different shapes. For example, some grains are smooth and rounded. Other grains are jagged.

- The grains in rock often form patterns. Some rocks have grains in flat layers like a stack of pancakes. Other rocks have grains in bands of different colors.

Answer the following questions. Use your textbook and the ideas above.

3. Draw a line from each term to its meaning.

Term	Meaning
grains	**a.** how a rock's surface looks and feels
texture	**b.** the particles that make up rocks

Rocks

4. Read the words in the box. In each sentence below, fill in one of the words.

   | grains   bands   texture |

   a. Rocks are made up of particles called

   _____.

   b. If you say the surface of a rock feels smooth, you

   are describing the rock's _____.

5. Fill in the blanks in the concept map about grains in rock.

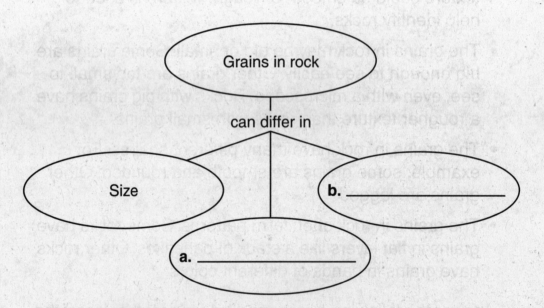

6. Circle the letter of each choice that describes a grain pattern in rock. '
   a. Grains are stacked in flat layers.
   b. Grains are large with jagged edges.
   c. Grains are in bands of different colors.

Rocks

How Rocks Form (page 97)

Key Concept: **Geologists classify rocks into three major groups: igneous rock, sedimentary rock, and metamorphic rock.**

- Rocks are classified into the three major groups based on how they form.

- **Igneous** (IG nee us) **rock** forms when magma or lava cools.

- **Sedimentary** (sed uh MEN tur ee) **rock** forms when particles are pressed and stuck together. Sedimentary rock slowly builds up in layers. Newer layers cover up older layers.

- **Metamorphic** (met uh MAWR fik) **rock** forms when heat and pressure change any kind of rock. Metamorphic rock forms below Earth's surface.

Answer the following question. Use your textbook and the ideas above.

7. Label each diagram with the kind of rock that could form.

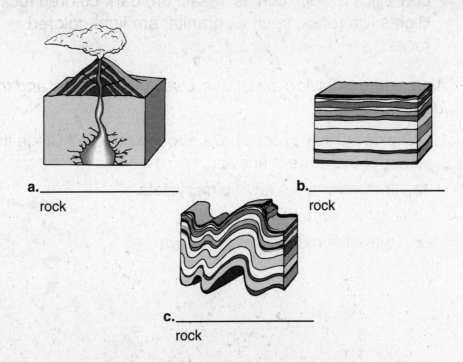

a._____
rock

b._____
rock

c._____
rock

Igneous Rocks (pages 98–101)

Classifying Igneous Rocks (pages 98–100)

Key Concept: **Igneous rocks are classified according to their origin, texture, and mineral composition.**

- Igneous rock is rock that forms from magma or lava. Igneous rock may form on or below Earth's surface. Where igneous rock forms is its origin.

- **Extrusive rock** is igneous rock that forms on Earth's surface, when lava cools. Lava cools quickly, forming small crystals. As a result, extrusive rock has a smooth texture. The most common extrusive rock is basalt.

- **Intrusive rock** is igneous rock that forms below Earth's surface, when magma cools. Magma cools slowly, forming big crystals. As a result, intrusive rock has a rough texture. The most common intrusive rock is granite.

- Igneous rocks differ in how much silica they contain. **Silica** is a material formed from oxygen and silicon. Low-silica rocks, such as basalt, are dark-colored rocks. High-silica rocks, such as granite, are light-colored rocks.

Answer the following questions. Use your textbook and the ideas above.

1. Why do intrusive rocks have a rough texture? Circle the letter of the correct answer.

   a. Intrusive rocks have big crystals.

   b. Intrusive rocks form quickly.

   c. Intrusive rocks form from lava.

2. Label each circle in the Venn diagram with the kind of igneous rock it describes.

a. _____   b. _____

   Rock   **Rock**

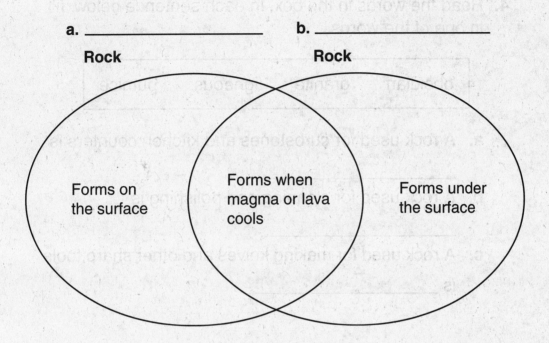

Forms on the surface

Forms when magma or lava cools

Forms under the surface

3. If an igneous rock is light-colored it probably contains a lot of _____.

Uses of Igneous Rocks (page 101)

Key Concept: **People throughout history have used igneous rock for tools and building materials.**

- Igneous rocks have several uses. Examples of useful igneous rocks are granite, pumice, and obsidian.

- Granite is very hard and dense. Granite has long been used for buildings and bridges. Today, granite is also used for curbstones and kitchen counters.

- Pumice is very rough. Pumice is used for cleaning and polishing.

- Obsidian is sharp and smooth like glass. Obsidian was used by ancient native Americans to make knives and other sharp tools.

Name _____ Date _____ Class _____

Rocks

Answer the following question. Use your textbook and the ideas on page 47.

4. Read the words in the box. In each sentence below, fill in one of the words.

┌───┐
│ obsidian   granite   igneous   pumice   │
└───┘

   a. A rock used for curbstones and kitchen counters is

      _____.

   b. A rock used for cleaning and polishing is

      _____.

   c. A rock used for making knives and other sharp tools

      is _____.

Sedimentary Rocks

(pages 102–106)

From Sediment to Rock (pages 102–103)

Key Concept: **Most sedimentary rocks are formed through a series of processes: erosion, deposition, compaction, and cementation.**

- **Sediment** is the particles that make up sedimentary rock. Sediment may include pieces of rock, shell, or bone.

- Most sediment comes from erosion. In **erosion**, moving water, wind, or ice loosens and carries away pieces of rock.

- When the moving water, wind, or ice slows down, it drops the sediment. This is called **deposition**.

- Layers of sediment build up over millions of years. Newer layers press down on older layers. This squeezes the sediment together. The squeezing is called **compaction**.

- Water seeps between sediment particles. Dissolved minerals in the water form crystals. The crystals "glue" the sediment particles together. This is called **cementation**.

Answer the following questions. Use your textbook and the ideas above.

1. Circle the letter of the process that loosens and carries away pieces of rock.

   a. compaction

   b. erosion

   c. deposition

2. Fill in the blanks in the flowchart showing the series of processes that forms sedimentary rocks.

Process That Form Sedimentary Rocks

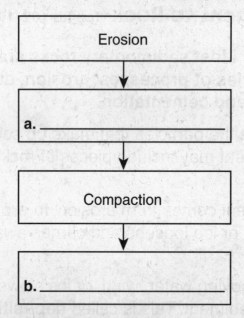

Erosion

a. _____

Compaction

b. _____

Types of Sedimentary Rock (pages 104–105)

Key Concept: **There are three major groups of sedimentary rocks: clastic rocks, organic rocks, and chemical rocks.**

- Sedimentary rocks are classified by the kind of sediments they are made of.

- **Clastic rock** is made of rock particles. The particles can be tiny or huge. Sandstone is clastic rock. Sandstone is made of particles of sand.

- **Organic rock** is made of the remains of plants and animals. "Organic" means alive or once living. Limestone is organic rock. Limestone is made of bones and shells.

- **Chemical rock** is made of dissolved minerals that came out of solution and formed crystals. Rock salt is chemical rock. Rock salt forms when a solution evaporates and leaves behind crystals of halite.

Name _____ Date _____ Class _____

Rocks

Answer the following questions. Use your textbook and the ideas on page 50.

3. Fill in the blanks in the table about kinds of sedimentary rock.

Kinds of Sedimentary Rock	
Kind of Rock	**Kind of Sediment It Contains**
Clastic rock	rock particles
a. _____ _____	remains of plants and animals
b. _____ _____	mineral crystals from solutions

4. Read the words in the box. In each sentence below, fill in one of the words.

sandstone	limestone	halite

a. The kind of sedimentary rock that forms from bones and shells is _____.

b. The kind of sedimentary rock that forms from particles of sand is _____.

Name _____ Date _____ Class _____

Rocks

Uses of Sedimentary Rocks (page 106)

Key Concept: **People have used sedimentary rocks throughout history for many different purposes, including building materials and tools.**

- Flint is a sedimentary rock that was used to make arrowheads for thousands of years. Flint forms when tiny particles of silica settle out of water.

- Sandstone and limestone have been used for the outside walls of buildings for thousands of years. Both rocks are soft enough to cut into blocks.

Answer the following questions. Use your textbook and the ideas above.

5. Read the words in the box. In each sentence below, fill in one of the words.

silica	limestone	flint

   a. A rock that was used to make arrowheads is

   _____.

   b. A rock used to make building blocks is

   _____.

6. Why is sandstone useful for the outside walls of buildings? Circle the letter of the correct answer.
   a. Sandstone is soft enough to cut into blocks.
   b. Sandstone is the hardest kind of rock on Earth.
   c. Sandstone forms on Earth's surface, so it is easy to find.

Rocks From Reefs (pages 107–109)

Coral Reefs (page 108)

Key Concept: **When coral animals die, their skeletons remain. More corals build on top of them, gradually forming a coral reef.**

- Coral animals are tiny. They live in the oceans. Coral animals live together in huge groups.

- As coral animals die, their skeletons pile up and grow together. Over time, the skeletons form a **coral reef**. A coral reef may grow to be hundreds of kilometers long.

- Coral animals can live only in warm, shallow water. So coral reefs are found only in tropical oceans near coasts. In the United States, there are coral reefs only off the coasts of southern Florida and Hawaii.

Answer the following questions. Use your textbook and the ideas above.

1. The skeletons of coral animals pile up and grow

   together and form a(an) _____.

2. Circle the letter of each sentence that is true about coral reefs.

   a. Coral reefs are made of animal skeletons.

   b. You can find coral reefs off the coast of every island and continent in the world.

   c. The biggest coral reefs are a few meters long.

Rocks

Limestone From Coral Reefs (page 109)

Key Concept: **Limestone deposits that began as coral reefs provide evidence of how Earth's surface has changed. These deposits also provide evidence of past environments.**

• A coral reef is a kind of limestone. Remember, limestone is a sedimentary rock. Limestone from coral reefs has been forming in Earth's oceans for more than 400 million years.

• Limestone from ancient coral reefs has been found in midwestern states, such as Illinois and Indiana. The limestone is now far above sea level. The limestone shows that warm seas once covered North America.

Answer the following questions. Use your textbook and the ideas above.

3. Circle the letter of each sentence that is true about coral reefs.

　　a. Coral reefs are a kind of limestone.

　　b. Coral reefs last for just a few thousand years.

　　c. Limestone from some coral reefs is now far above sea level.

4. Is the following sentence true or false? Limestone from coral reefs has been found in Indiana because coral animals used to live on land. _____

Metamorphic Rocks (pages 110–112)

Types of Metamorphic Rocks
(pages 110–111)

Key Concept: **Heat and pressure deep beneath Earth's surface can change any rock into metamorphic rock. Geologists classify metamorphic rocks according to the arrangement of the grains that make up the rocks.**

- When a rock becomes a metamorphic rock, the pattern of its grains can change. Metamorphic rocks are classified by their grain patterns.

- **Foliated** rocks are metamorphic rocks with their grains lined up in layers. Foliated rocks split into flat pieces. Slate is a foliated rock.

- Nonfoliated rocks are metamorphic rocks with their grains scattered at random. Nonfoliated rocks do not split into flat pieces. Marble is a nonfoliated rock.

Answer the following questions. Use your textbook and the ideas above.

1. Label each circle in the Venn diagram with the type of metamorphic rock it describes.

a. _____   b. _____

     Rock   **Rock**

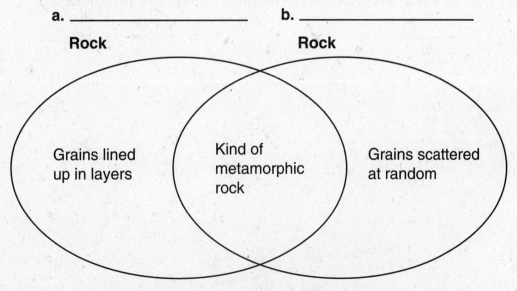

Grains lined up in layers   Kind of metamorphic rock   Grains scattered at random

Rocks

2. Metamorphic rocks are classified by their

_____ patterns.

Uses of Metamorphic Rock (page 112)

Key Concept: **Certain metamorphic rocks are important materials for building and sculpture.**

- Marble and slate are two of the most useful metamorphic rocks.

- Marble can be cut, carved, and polished. Marble is used for buildings and statues.

- Slate splits easily into flat pieces. Slate is used for floors, roofs, and chalkboards.

Answer the following questions. Use your textbook and the ideas above.

3. Circle the letter of each sentence that is true about marble.
    a. Marble is a kind of sedimentary rock.
    b. Marble is used for buildings.
    c. Marble can be carved.

4. Is the following sentence true or false? Slate is good for chalkboards because it splits easily into flat pieces.

_____

The Rock Cycle (pages 114–116)

A Cycle of Many Pathways (pages 114–116)

***Key Concept:* Forces deep inside Earth and at the surface produce a slow cycle that builds, destroys, and changes the rocks in the crust.**

- The **rock cycle** is a series of processes that slowly change rocks from one kind to another. There are many ways rocks go through the rock cycle. Here is one way rocks go through the rock cycle:

- Igneous rock on the surface is turned into sediment by erosion. The sediment is deposited and slowly becomes sedimentary rock.

- The sedimentary rock is buried by more sediment. Heat and pressure slowly change the sedimentary rock into metamorphic rock.

- The metamorphic rock is forced into the mantle. The metamorphic rock melts to form magma. The magma erupts and cools to form igneous rock again.

Answer the following questions. Use your textbook and the ideas above.

1. Read the words in the box. In each sentence below, fill in one of the words.

sedimentary	igneous	metamorphic

   a. A rock that melts to form magma will next become a(an) _____ rock.

   b. A rock that is being heated and pressed is on its way to becoming a(an) _____ rock.

Name _____ Date _____ Class _____

Rocks

2. The diagram shows the rock cycle. Fill in each blank in the diagram with the kind of rock that forms.

Rock Cycle

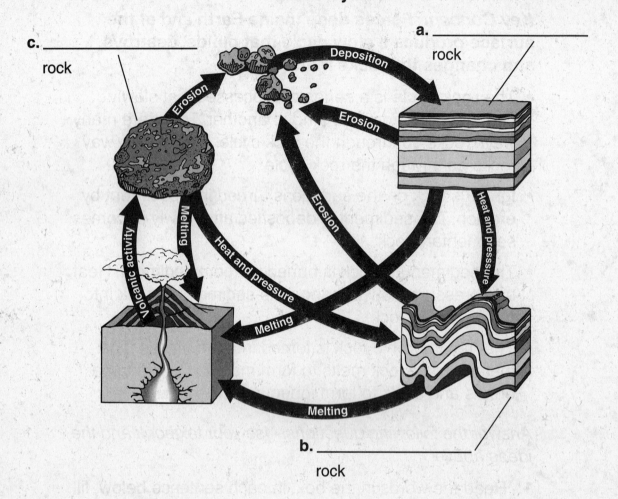

c. _____
rock

a. _____
rock

b. _____
rock

Earth's Interior (pages 124–131)

Exploring Inside Earth (pages 125–126)

Key Concept: Geologists have used two main types of evidence to learn about Earth's interior: direct evidence from rock samples and indirect evidence from seismic waves.

- Scientists cannot travel inside Earth to explore it. So scientists must learn about Earth's interior, or inside, in other ways.

- Scientists use drills to get rock samples from inside Earth. The rock samples help scientists learn what conditions were like inside Earth when the rocks formed.

- Scientists study how seismic waves travel through Earth. **Seismic** (SYZ mik) **waves** are waves made by earthquakes. Seismic waves show that Earth is made up of layers like an onion.

Answer the following questions. Use your textbook and the ideas above.

1. Circle the letter of a way that scientists can learn about Earth's interior.

    a. travel inside Earth and explore it directly

    b. study rock samples from inside Earth

    c. peel away Earth's layers like an onion

2. Is the following sentence true or false? Earth is made up of layers. _____

Plate Tectonics

A Journey to the Center of Earth (page 127)

Key Concept: **The three main layers of Earth are the crust, the mantle, and the core. These layers vary greatly in size, composition, temperature, and pressure.**

- Earth has three main layers. The crust is the outside layer. The mantle is the middle layer. The core is the inside layer.

- Temperature increases from the crust to the core. It is very hot inside Earth. One reason it is so hot is that some substances inside Earth give off energy.

- Pressure also increases from the crust to the core. **Pressure** is caused by a force pressing on an area. There is great pressure inside Earth because of all the rock pressing down from above.

Answer the following questions. Use your textbook and the ideas above.

3. Fill in the blanks in the diagram about Earth's layers.

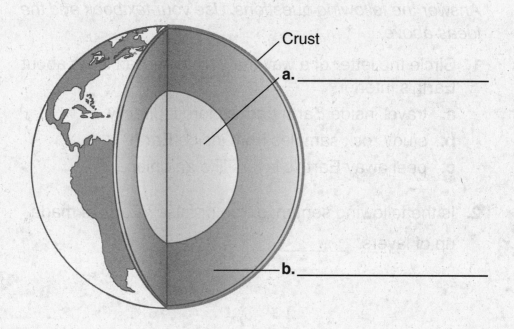

Crust

a. _____

b. _____

4. Is the following sentence true or false? Earth's temperature decreases from the crust to the core.

_____

5. The layer of Earth that is under the greatest pressure is the _____.

The Crust (page 128)

Key Concept: **The crust is a layer of solid rock that includes both dry land and the ocean floor.**

- The **crust** is a layer of rock that forms Earth's outer skin. The crust is Earth's thinnest layer. It is only 5 to 70 kilometers thick.

- The crust that makes up the ocean floors is called oceanic crust. Oceanic crust is made mostly of a rock called **basalt** (buh SAWLT).

- The crust that makes up the continents is called continental crust. Continental crust is made mostly of a rock called **granite**.

- Continental crust is thicker than oceanic crust.

Answer the following questions. Use your textbook and the ideas above.

6. Earth's outside layer is the _____.

7. Fill in the blanks in the table about Earth's crust.

Earth's Crust	
Part of Crust	**Kind of Rock It Contains**
Oceanic crust	**a.** _____
b. _____	granite

Plate Tectonics

8. Is the following sentence true or false? Oceanic crust is thicker than continental crust. _____

The Mantle (page 129)

Key Concept: **Earth's mantle is made up of rock that is very hot, but solid. Scientists divide the mantle into layers based on the physical characteristics of those layers. Overall, the mantle is nearly 3,000 kilometers thick.**

- The **mantle** is the layer below the crust. The mantle is Earth's thickest layer. The mantle has three layers.

- The top layer of the mantle, along with the crust, is the **lithosphere** (LITH uh sfeer). The top layer of the mantle is hard rock.

- The middle layer of the mantle is the **asthenosphere** (as THEN uh sfeer). The middle layer is soft rock, like hot road tar.

- The bottom layer of the mantle is called the lower mantle. It is also hard rock.

Answer the following questions. Use your textbook and the ideas above.

9. Circle the letter of each sentence that is true about the mantle.

    a. The mantle is the layer below the crust.

    b. The mantle is Earth's thinnest layer.

    c. The lower mantle is made of hard rock.

10. Read the words in the box. In each sentence below, fill in one of the words.

| lithosphere | crust | asthenosphere |

  a. The top layer of the mantle is part of the

  _____.

  b. The layer of the mantle that is made of soft rock is

  the _____.

The Core (pages 130–131)

Key Concept: **The core is made mostly of the metals iron and nickel. It consists of two parts—a liquid outer core and a solid inner core.**

- The core is Earth's inside layer. The core has two layers: the outer core and the inner core.

- The **outer core** is made of liquid metal. The liquid metal flows in currents. The currents make Earth act like a giant magnet, with north and south poles that attract iron.

- The **inner core** is made of solid metal. The inner core is solid because it is under so much pressure.

Answer the following questions. Use your textbook and the ideas above.

11. Circle the letter of each sentence that is true about Earth's core.

  a. The core is made mostly of iron and nickel.

  b. The core is Earth's inside layer.

  c. The core is a giant magnet.

Name _____ Date _____ Class _____

Plate Tectonics

12. Fill in the blanks in the concept map about Earth's core.

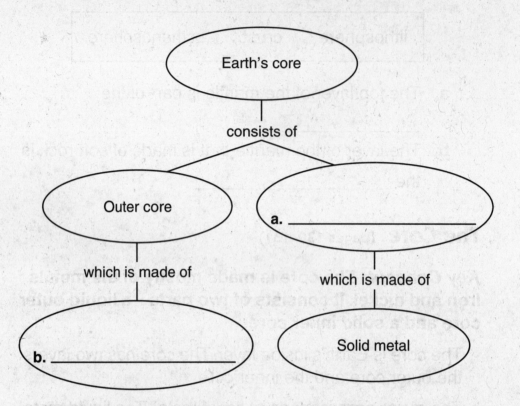

Earth's core

consists of

Outer core

a. _____

which is made of

b. _____

which is made of

Solid metal

13. Is the following sentence true or false? Earth acts like a giant magnet because of currents in the outer core.

_____

© Pearson Education, Inc., publishing as Pearson Prentice Hall. All rights reserved.

64

Convection and the Mantle
(pages 132–135)

Types of Heat Transfer (pages 133–134)

Key Concept: **There are three types of heat transfer: radiation, conduction, and convection.**

- When an object heats up, particles in the object have more energy and move faster. This energy can travel, or transfer, from a warmer object to a cooler object.

- **Radiation** is the transfer of energy through space. For example, sunlight travels through space by radiation and warms Earth's surface. Radiation also explains why your hands get warm when you hold them near a fire.

- **Conduction** is the transfer of heat between objects that are touching. If you touch a hot pot, heat travels from the pot to your hand by conduction.

- **Convection** is the transfer of heat by the movement of particles in fluids such as water. Moving particles transfer heat throughout the fluid.

Answer the following questions. Use your textbook and the ideas above.

1. The kind of heat transfer that warms Earth's surface on a sunny day is _____.

2. Circle the letter an example of conduction.
   a. A sidewalk gets hot on a sunny day.
   b. A pot gets hot on a stove.
   c. A bench gets hot near a campfire.

3. The transfer of heat by the movement of particles in fluids is _____.

Plate Tectonics

Convection Currents (page 134)

Key Concept: **Heating and cooling of a fluid, changes in the fluid's density, and the force of gravity combine to set convection currents in motion.**

- Remember, convection is the transfer of heat by the movement of particles in fluids. This movement of particles is called a **convection current**.

- A convection current starts when there are differences in temperature and density in a fluid. **Density** is the amount of mass in a given volume of a substance. A high-density substance feels heavy for its size.

- Suppose you put a pot of soup on a stove. The soup at the bottom of the pot gets warm first. Because it is warmer, the soup at the bottom is less dense than the cooler soup above it. So the warmer soup rises. At the same time, the cooler, denser soup sinks to the bottom of the pot.

- The cooler soup now at the bottom gets warmer, and the process repeats. A constant flow of particles begins. Warmer soup keeps rising, and cooler soup keeps sinking. This movement of particles transfers heat throughout the soup.

Answer the following questions. Use your textbook and the ideas above.

4. Circle the set of arrows that shows how a convection current flows through the liquid in the pot.

5. Is the following sentence true or false? A convection current starts when there are differences in temperature and volume in a fluid. _____

Convection Currents in Earth (page 135)

Key Concept: **Heat from the core and the mantle itself causes convection currents in the mantle.**

- The heat inside Earth causes convection currents in the mantle and outer core.

- Convection currents inside Earth are like convection currents in a pot of soup. Hot materials at the bottom rise to the top. Cooler materials at the top sink to the bottom.

- Convection currents in the mantle move very slowly. This is because the mantle is made of solid rock.

- Remember, Earth is like a giant magnet because of currents in the outer core. Those currents are convection currents.

Answer the following questions. Use your textbook and the ideas above.

6. The layers of Earth that have convection currents are the mantle and _____.

7. Circle the letter of the sentence that correctly describes how convection currents move inside Earth.
   a. Hot materials rise, while cooler materials sink.
   b. Hot materials sink, while cooler materials rise.
   c. Hot materials move up or down, while cooler materials move sideways.

Plate Tectonics

Drifting Continents (pages 136–140)

Continental Drift (pages 137–139)

Key Concept: **Alfred Wegener's hypothesis was that all the continents were once joined together in a single landmass and have since drifted apart. Wegener gathered evidence from different scientific fields to support his ideas about continental drift. He studied land features, fossils, and evidence of climate change.**

- Some continents are shaped like puzzle pieces. For example, the west side of Africa and the east side of South America look like matching puzzle pieces.

- Scientist Alfred Wegener (VAY guh nur) tried to explain why continents are shaped this way.

- Wegener thought that Earth had one big continent about 300 million years ago. The big continent broke into smaller pieces and formed smaller continents. The continents slowly drifted apart. Wegener called this **continental drift**.

- Evidence shows that continental drift really happened. Mountain ranges in Africa and South America line up as if they were once part of the same mountain range. Other evidence shows that continents once had different climates. This could happen if continents had drifted.

Answer the following questions. Use your textbook and the ideas above.

1. Wegener called the slow movement of continents

_____.

Name _____ Date _____ Class _____

Plate Tectonics

2. Circle the letter of the drawing that shows how Wegener thought South America and Africa were once joined as part of a single, giant continent.

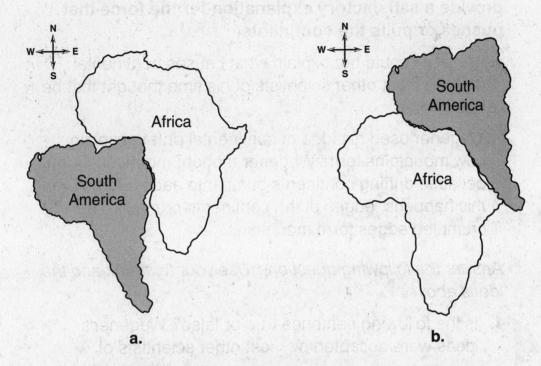

a.

b.

3. Circle the letter of evidence that supports Wegener's idea of continental drift.

   a. Mountain ranges on different continents line up.

   b. Evidence shows that climates have not changed.

   c. Old maps show that Earth had a single, giant continent about 3,000 years ago.

Wegener's Hypothesis Rejected (page 140)

Key Concept: Unfortunately, Wegener could not provide a satisfactory explanation for the force that pushes or pulls the continents.

- Wegener could not explain what causes continental drift. So most other scientists of his time thought that he was wrong.

- Wegener used his idea of continental drift to explain how mountains form. Wegener thought mountains form because drifting continents bump into each other. When this happens, edges of the continents crumple. The crumpled edges form mountains.

Answer the following questions. Use your textbook and the ideas above.

4. Is the following sentence true or false? Wegener's ideas were accepted by most other scientists of

   his time. _____

5. Circle the letter of the sentence that describes how Wegener thought mountains form.
   a. Earth slowly cools and shrinks.
   b. Continents drift apart.
   c. Continents bump into each other.

Plate Tectonics

Sea-Floor Spreading
(pages 141–147)

Mid-Ocean Ridges (page 142)

Key Concept: **Mid-ocean ridges lie beneath Earth's oceans.**

- Since the mid-1900s, scientists have used sonar to study the ocean floor. **Sonar** is a device that bounces sound waves off underwater objects. The longer it takes the sound waves to bounce back, the farther away the objects are.

- Using sonar, scientists found long mountain ranges on the ocean floors. Scientists call the mountain ranges **mid-ocean ridges**. Mid-ocean ridges run through the middle of all oceans.

- In a few places, mid-ocean ridges poke above the surface and form islands. Iceland is the top of a mid-ocean ridge in the North Atlantic Ocean.

Answer the following questions. Use your textbook and the ideas above.

1. Is the following sentence true or false? Scientists use sound waves to study the ocean floor. _____

2. Circle the letter of each sentence that is true about mid-ocean ridges.
   a. Mid-ocean ridges are mountain ranges on the ocean floor.
   b. Mid-ocean ridges sometimes form islands.
   c. Mid-ocean ridges are found only in the Atlantic Ocean.

Plate Tectonics

What Is Sea-Floor Spreading? (page 143)

Key Concept: **In sea-floor spreading, the sea floor spreads apart along both sides of a mid-ocean ridge as new crust is added. As a result, the ocean floors move like conveyor belts, carrying the continents along with them.**

- **Sea-floor spreading** is a process that slowly adds new rock to the ocean floors. Scientist Harry Hess came up with the idea of sea-floor spreading in 1960.

- Here is how sea-floor spreading works. In the center of a mid-ocean ridge, melted rock pushes up through cracks in the ocean floor. The melted rock pushes older, solid rock away from both sides of the ridge. The melted rock cools and forms new solid rock at the center of the ridge.

- This process keeps repeating. Slowly, the ocean floor is pushed farther and farther away from both sides of the mid-ocean ridge. At the same time, new rock keeps adding to the ocean floor in the center of the ridge.

Answer the following questions. Use your textbook and the ideas above.

3. The process that slowly adds new rock to the ocean

   floors is called _____.

4. Circle the letter of each sentence that is true about sea-floor spreading.

   a. Harry Hess came up with the idea of sea-floor spreading.

   b. Sea-floor spreading happens at mid-ocean ridges.

   c. In sea-floor spreading, the ocean floor is pushed aside by hard rock from the core.

5. The diagram shows sea-floor spreading. Circle the letter of the two arrows that show the directions in which the sea floor is spreading.

   a. A and B   **b.** A and C   **c.** B and C

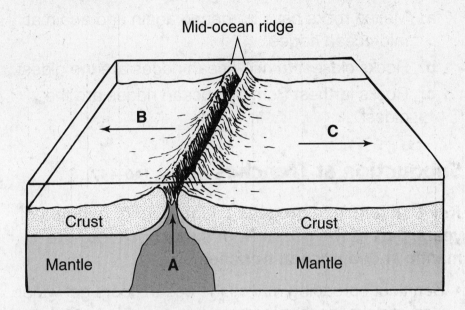

Evidence for Sea-Floor Spreading (pages 144–145)

***Key Concept:* Several types of evidence supported Hess's theory of sea-floor spreading: eruptions of molten material, magnetic stripes in the rock of the ocean floor, and the ages of the rocks themselves.**

- In the 1960s, scientists tried to find evidence for sea-floor spreading.

- Scientists used a submarine to get rocks from a mid-ocean ridge. The rocks showed that melted rock had hardened again and again along the ridge.

- Scientists used a drill to get rocks from below the ocean floor. Rocks closest to a mid-ocean ridge were the newest. Rocks farthest from a mid-ocean ridge were the oldest.

- From evidence such as this, scientists knew that sea-floor spreading really happens.

Name _____ Date _____ Class _____

Plate Tectonics

Answer the following question. Use your textbook and the ideas on page 73.

6. Circle the letter of each choice that correctly describes evidence for sea-floor spreading.

   a. Melted rocks have hardened again and again at mid-ocean ridges.

   b. Rocks closest to mid-ocean ridges are the oldest.

   c. Rocks farthest from mid-ocean ridges are the oldest.

Subduction at Trenches (pages 146–147)

Key Concept: **In a process taking tens of millions of years, part of the ocean floor sinks back into the mantle at deep-ocean trenches.**

- Sea-floor spreading makes the ocean floors get wider. New rock keeps forming at mid-ocean ridges. Old rock keeps getting pushed farther and farther away from both sides of the ridges.

- After millions of years, old rock reaches underwater canyons, called **deep-ocean trenches**. At a deep-ocean trench, the rocky crust of the ocean floor bends downward and sinks into the mantle. This process is called **subduction** (sub DUK shun).

- Sea-floor spreading and subduction work together. They keep the ocean floors moving like conveyor belts in an airport. As new rock is added to the ocean floors, old rock disappears. Overall, the size of the ocean floors does not change very much.

Answer the following questions. Use your textbook and the ideas above.

7. The process in which ocean floors sink into the mantle is called _____.

Plate Tectonics

8. Fill in the blanks in the table about changes in the ocean floors.

How the Ocean Floors Change		
Process	**Happens at**	**Makes Ocean Floor**
Sea-floor spreading	mid-ocean ridges	bigger
Subduction	a. _____ _____	b. _____

9. Is the following sentence true or false? Overall, the size of the ocean floor does not change very much.

_____

The Theory of Plate Tectonics (pages 150–154)

How Plates Move (page 151)

Key Concept: **The theory of plate tectonics explains the formation, movement, and subduction of Earth's plates.**

- Earth's surface is broken into many jagged pieces. The surface is like the shell of a hard-boiled egg that has been dropped. The pieces of Earth's surface are called **plates**. Plates carry continents, ocean floors, or both.

- The theory of **plate tectonics** (tek TAHN iks) says that Earth's plates move because of convection currents in the mantle. Currents in the mantle carry plates on Earth's surface, like currents in water carry boats on a river.

- Plates can meet in three different ways. Plates may pull apart, push together, or slide past each other. Wherever plates meet, you usually find volcanoes, mountain ranges, or deep-ocean trenches.

Answer the following questions. Use your textbook and the ideas above.

1. Jagged pieces of Earth's surface are called

   _____.

2. Is the following sentence true or false? Earth's plates carry only the continents. _____

Plate Tectonics

3. Circle the letter of the sentence that states the theory of plate tectonics.

    a. Earth's plates cannot move because they are made of solid rock.

    b. Earth's plates move because of convection currents in the mantle.

    c. Earth's moving plates cause convection currents in the mantle.

Plate Boundaries (pages 152–154)

Key Concept: **There are three kinds of plate boundaries: divergent boundaries, convergent boundaries, and transform boundaries. A different type of plate movement occurs along each type of boundary.**

- A plate boundary is where two plates meet. Faults form along plate boundaries. A **fault** is a break in Earth's crust where blocks of rock have slipped past each other.

- Where two plates move apart, the boundary is called a **divergent** (dy VUR junt) **boundary**. A divergent boundary between two oceanic plates forms a mid-ocean ridge. A divergent boundary between two continental plates forms a deep valley called a **rift valley**.

- Where two plates push together, the boundary is called a **convergent** (kun VUR junt) **boundary**. A convergent boundary between two oceanic plates forms a deep-ocean trench. A convergent boundary between two continental plates forms a mountain range.

- Where two plates slide past each other in opposite directions, the plate boundary is called a **transform boundary**. At a transform boundary, earthquakes may occur.

Name _____ Date _____ Class _____

Plate Tectonics

Answer the following questions. Use your textbook and the ideas on page 77.

4. Read the words in the box. In each sentence below, fill in one of the words.

> fault   boundary   rift

   a. The edges of two plates meet at a plate

   _____.

   b. A break in Earth's crust where blocks of rock have slipped past each other is a

   _____.

5. Fill in the blanks in the table about plate boundaries.

Plate Boundaries		
Type of Plate Boundary	**How Plates Move**	**What Forms or Happens**
Divergent boundary	plates move apart	mid-ocean ridges or rift valleys
Convergent boundary	a. _____ _____ _____	deep-ocean trenches or mountain ranges
b. _____ _____	plates slide past each other	earthquakes

Earthquakes

Forces in Earth's Crust
(pages 162–168)

Types of Stress (page 163)

Key Concept: **Tension, compression, and shearing work over millions of years to change the shape and volume of rock.**

- When Earth's plates move, rocks are pushed and pulled. The pushes and pulls are called **stress**.

- Stress adds energy to rocks. Rocks keep storing the energy until they cannot stand any more stress. Then the rocks break or change shape.

- **Tension** is stress that pulls and stretches rocks. Tension makes rocks thinner in the middle. Tension happens when two plates move apart.

- **Compression** is stress that squeezes rocks. Compression makes rocks fold or break. Compression happens when two plates push together.

- **Shearing** is stress that pushes rocks in opposite directions. Shearing makes rocks break, slip apart, or change shape. Shearing happens when two plates slip past each other in opposite directions.

Answer the following questions. Use your textbook and the ideas above.

1. Circle the letter of the choice that describes how stress affects rocks.
   a. Stress adds energy to rocks.
   b. Stress uses up the energy in rocks.
   c. Stress squeezes energy out of rocks.

Name _____ Date _____ Class _____

Earthquakes

2. Read the words in the box. In each sentence below, fill in one of the words.

shearing	compression	stress
folding	tension	

a. Pushes and pulls on rocks are called

_____.

b. Stress that makes rocks fold is called

_____.

c. Stress that stretches rocks is called

_____.

d. Stress that makes rocks slip apart or change

shape is called _____.

3. Fill in the blanks to label the kinds of stress shown.

Before stress   **Kinds of stress**   **After stress**

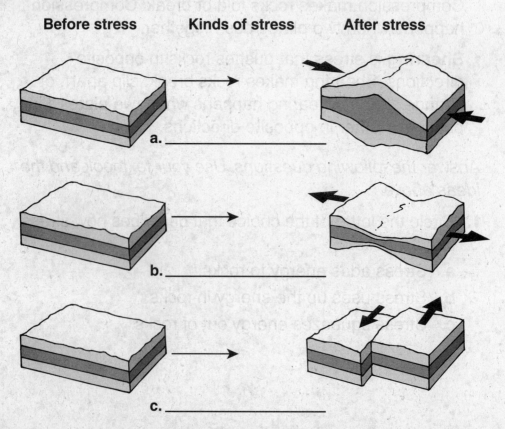

a. _____

b. _____

c. _____

Kinds of Faults (pages 164–165)

Key Concept: **Most faults occur along plate boundaries, where the forces of plate motion push or pull the crust so much that the crust breaks. There are three main types of faults: normal faults, reverse faults, and strike-slip faults.**

- A fault is a break in Earth's crust where rocks are under stress.

- In many faults, the fault line is slanted. So the block of rock on one side of the fault is above the block of rock on the other side of the fault. The top block is called the **hanging wall**. The bottom block is called the **footwall**.

- There are three different types of faults: normal faults, reverse faults, and strike-slip faults. Each type is caused by a different kind of stress on rocks.

- A **normal fault** happens when tension pulls rocks apart. In a normal fault, the hanging wall slips down and becomes lower than the footwall.

- A **reverse fault** happens when compression pushes rocks together. In a reverse fault, the hanging wall slides up and becomes higher than the footwall.

- A **strike-slip fault** happens when shearing pushes rocks in opposite directions. In a strike-slip fault, two blocks of rock move past each other, but neither block moves up or down.

Answer the following questions. Use your textbook and the ideas above.

4. Circle the letter of the choice that explains what causes a fault.

   a. Stress increases on rocks until they move.

   b. Energy slowly drains away from rocks.

   c. Rocks heat up and melt.

Earthquakes

5. Fill in the blanks in the table about faults and stresses.

Faults and Stresses	
Kind of Fault	**Type of Stress That Causes Fault**
Normal fault	a. _____
b. _____ _____	compression
c. _____ _____	shearing

6. Fill in the blanks to label the kind of fault shown in each diagram.

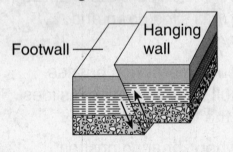

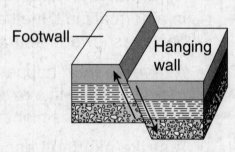

a. _____

b. _____

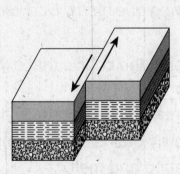

c. _____

Earthquakes

Changing Earth's Surface (pages 166–168)

Key Concept: **Over millions of years, the forces of plate movement can change a flat plain into landforms such as anticlines and synclines, folded mountains, fault-block mountains, and plateaus.**

- Stresses in Earth's crust cause the surface to change. Different stresses cause different changes.

- Compression causes folding. Folding is like a rug getting wrinkled up when it is pushed across the floor.

- Folds that bend upward into ridges are called **anticlines**. Folds that bend downward into valleys are called **synclines**.

- Tension causes stretching. When crust stretches, many normal faults form.

- Sometimes a block of rock moves upward between two normal faults. The block forms a mountain called a fault-block mountain.

- Stresses in the crust can also form plateaus. A **plateau** is a large area of flat land that has been lifted up above sea level.

Answer the following questions. Use your textbook and the ideas above.

7. Circle the letter of the sentence that describes how a fault-block mountain forms.

　　a. A block of rock moves upward between two normal faults.

　　b. The crust becomes wrinkled like a rug.

　　c. Rocks are pushed together by compression.

8. Is the following sentence true or false? A plateau forms when flat land is pushed up above the surrounding

　　land. _____

Earthquakes

9. Circle the letter of the stress that causes Earth's
   surface to look like the surface in the diagram below.
   a. tension
   b. compression
   c. shearing

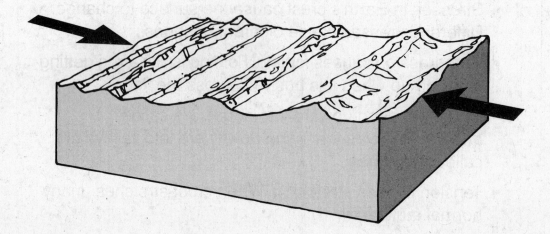

Earthquakes and Seismic Waves (pages 169–175)

Types of Seismic Waves (pages 170–171)

Key Concept: **Seismic waves carry energy from an earthquake away from the focus, through Earth's interior, and across the surface.**

- An **earthquake** is the shaking that results when rocks move inside Earth. An earthquake is caused by stress along a fault. Stress increases until the rocks break and release stored energy.

- The place where rocks break and cause an earthquake is called the **focus** (FOH kus). The point on the surface directly above the focus is called the **epicenter** (EP uh sen tur).

- Earthquakes cause waves, called seismic waves, to travel through Earth. Seismic waves carry the energy released by the rocks. There are three kinds of seismic waves: P waves, S waves, and surface waves.

- **P waves** move rocks back and forth, like a wave passing through a spring toy when you push in the coils. P waves are the fastest seismic waves.

- **S waves** move rocks up and down, like a wave passing through a rope when you flick it. S waves travel more slowly than P waves but do more damage.

- **Surface waves** are combined P and S waves that travel along Earth's surface. Surface waves are the slowest seismic waves. They also do a lot of damage.

Answer the following questions. Use your textbook and the ideas above.

1. When the ground shakes because rocks have moved inside Earth, it is called a(an) _____.

Earthquakes

2. Label the circles in the Venn diagram to show which circle describes P waves and which circle describes S waves.

a. _____   b. _____

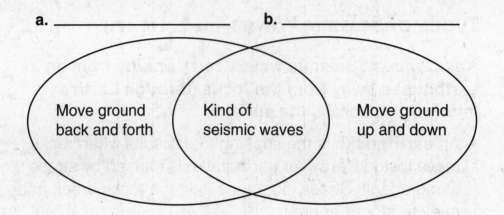

Move ground
back and forth

Kind of
seismic waves

Move ground
up and down

3. Circle the letter of the kind of seismic waves that are the slowest.

   a. P waves

   b. S waves

   c. surface waves

Measuring Earthquakes (pages 172–174)

***Key Concept:* Three commonly used methods of measuring earthquakes are the Mercalli scale, the Richter scale, and the moment magnitude scale.**

- The **Mercalli scale** is based on the amount of damage an earthquake does. For example, a weak earthquake only rattles dishes. A strong earthquake can destroy buildings.

- The **Richter scale** is based on the size of the seismic waves. A stronger earthquake makes bigger seismic waves. An instrument called a **seismograph** measures the size of seismic waves.

- The **moment magnitude scale** is based on the amount of energy an earthquake releases. The amount of energy is based on many things, including the size of the seismic waves.

Earthquakes

Answer the following questions. Use your textbook and the ideas on page 86.

4. Fill in the blanks in the table about ways to measure earthquake strength.

Ways to Measure Earthquake Strength	
Method	**How It Measures Earthquake Strength**
Mercalli scale	amount of damage done
Richter scale	a. _____ _____
b. _____ _____	amount of energy released

5. An instrument that measures the size of seismic waves is a(an) _____.

6. Which way of measuring earthquake strength is based on the kind of information shown in the drawing?

_____

Earthquakes

Locating the Epicenter (pages 174–175)

Key Concept: Geologists use seismic waves to locate an earthquake's epicenter.

- The epicenter is the point on the surface that lies directly above an earthquake's focus. Scientists use P waves and S waves to find an earthquake's epicenter.

- P waves travel faster than S waves. So P waves arrive at a seismograph sooner than S waves. The longer it takes S waves to reach the seismograph after P waves have arrived, the farther away the epicenter is.

- To find the exact location of the epicenter, you need seismographs in three different places. You can draw a circle around each seismograph to show how far the epicenter is from that seismograph. The point where all three circles cross is the epicenter.

Answer the following questions. Use your textbook and the ideas above.

7. Suppose it takes a long time for S waves to reach a seismograph after P waves have arrived. What does that tell you about the earthquake? Circle the letter of the correct answer.

   a. The earthquake was strong.

   b. The earthquake was close to the surface.

   c. The earthquake was far away.

8. Is the following sentence true or false? One seismograph can tell you exactly where the epicenter

   of an earthquake is. _____

9. The map shows three different seismographs in the United States. Each circle shows the distance from a seismograph to the epicenter of an earthquake. Where is the epicenter? Circle the letter of the correct answer.

   a. A

   b. B

   c. C

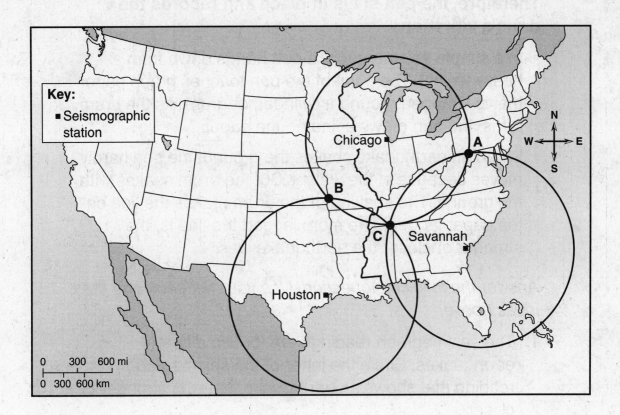

Monitoring Earthquakes (pages 178–183)

The Seismograph (page 179)

Key Concept: **Seismic waves cause the seismograph's drum to vibrate. But the suspended weight with the pen attached moves very little. Therefore, the pen stays in place and records the drum's vibrations.**

- In a simple seismograph, a pen hangs down from a heavy weight. The point of the pen touches graph paper that is wrapped around a cylinder, or drum. As the drum turns, the pen draws a line on the paper.

- When an earthquake shakes the ground, the pen hardly moves because of the weight. But the drum shakes with the ground. The shaking of the drum makes the line on the paper jagged. The more jagged the line is, the stronger or closer the earthquake was.

Answer the following question. Use your textbook and the ideas above.

1. The seismograph readings are for two different earthquakes. Circle the letter of the seismograph reading that shows an earthquake that was stronger or closer.

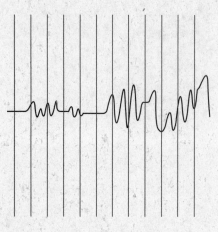
a.

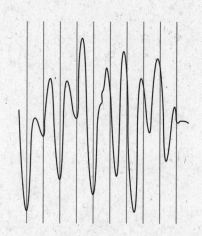
b.

Earthquakes

Instruments That Monitor Faults (pages 180–181)

Key Concept: **To monitor faults, geologists have developed instruments to measure changes in elevation, tilting of the land surface, and ground movements along faults.**

- Ground movements near a fault are a clue that an earthquake might happen. So scientists measure ground movements near faults. They use tiltmeters, creep meters, and GPS satellites.

- Tiltmeters show how much the ground is tilting, or tipping. A tiltmeter works like a carpenter's level. When the ground tilts, water inside a glass bulb shows how much tilting there is.

- Creep meters show how far the sides of a fault have moved in opposite directions. A creep meter uses a wire stretched across the fault. The wire gets longer when the two sides move apart.

- Scientists put markers along both sides of a fault. GPS satellites detect tiny movements of the markers in any direction.

Answer the following questions. Use your textbook and the ideas above.

2. Why do scientists measure ground movements near faults? Circle the letter of the correct answer.

   a. Ground movements are a clue that an earthquake may happen.

   b. Ground movements show that an earthquake is over.

   c. Ground movements show that rocks are no longer under stress.

3. Fill in the blanks in the concept map about instruments that measure ground movements.

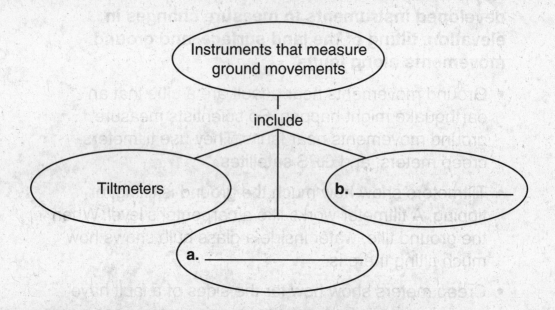

Using Seismographic Data (pages 182–183)

Key Concept: **Seismographs and fault-monitoring devices provide data used to map faults and detect changes along faults. Geologists are also trying to use these data to develop a method of predicting earthquakes.**

- When seismic waves reach a fault, they bounce off it, like a ball bouncing off a wall. Seismographs record the waves that bounce back. Scientists can use the seismographic data to find the fault.

- Seismographic data can also be used to learn how easily rocks move at a fault. At faults where rocks do not move easily, stress builds up, and big earthquakes are likely.

- Even with data from many sources, scientists cannot predict exactly where or when an earthquake will happen.

Earthquakes

Answer the following questions. Use your textbook and the ideas on page 92.

4. Circle the letter that shows what happens to seismic waves when they reach a fault.

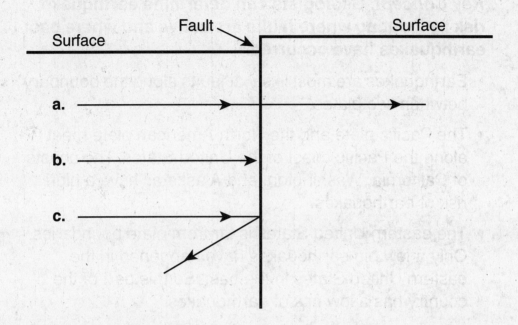

5. Circle the letter of the choice that describes where big earthquakes are likely to happen.

    a. at faults where rocks move easily

    b. at faults where rocks do not move easily

    c. at rocks where there are no faults

6. Is the following sentence true or false? Scientists can now predict exactly where and when earthquakes will happen. _____

Earthquakes

Earthquake Safety (pages 186–191)

Earthquake Risk (page 187)

Key Concept: **Geologists can determine earthquake risk by locating where faults are active and where past earthquakes have occurred.**

- Earthquakes are most likely at faults along the boundary between two plates.

- The Pacific plate and the North American plate meet along the Pacific coast of the United States. The coasts of California, Washington, and Alaska all have a high risk of earthquakes.

- The eastern United States is far from plate boundaries. Only a few big earthquakes have happened in the eastern United States in the past. So this part of the country has a low risk of earthquakes.

Answer the following questions. Use your textbook and the ideas above.

1. Is the following sentence true or false? Earthquakes are most likely to happen far from plate boundaries.

   _____

2. Circle the letter of each sentence that is true about earthquake risk in the United States.

   a. The risk of earthquakes is high along the Pacific coast.

   b. There is no risk of earthquakes in the East.

   c. Alaska has a high risk of earthquakes.

Earthquakes

How Earthquakes Cause Damage

(pages 188–189)

Key Concept: Causes of earthquake damage include shaking, liquefaction, aftershocks, and tsunamis.

- When an earthquake happens, seismic waves cause the ground to shake. The shaking can destroy buildings and break gas and water pipes.

- Sometimes the shaking turns soft soil into mud. This is called **liquefaction** (lik wih FAK shun). Liquefaction can make buildings sink.

- Smaller earthquakes, called **aftershocks**, can follow a big earthquake. Aftershocks add to the damage done by the big earthquake.

- An earthquake on the ocean floor can cause a huge ocean wave, called a **tsunami** (tsoo NAH mee). Tsunamis can cause a great deal of damage along coasts.

Answer the following question. Use your textbook and the ideas above.

3. Read the words in the box. In each sentence below, fill in one of the words.

aftershock	tsunami	liquefaction	shaking

   a. When an earthquake causes soft soil to turn to

      mud, it is called _____.

   b. A smaller earthquake that follows a big earthquake

      is called a(an) _____.

   c. A huge ocean wave caused by an earthquake is

      a(an) _____.

Earthquakes

Steps to Earthquake Safety (page 189)

Key Concept: **The best way to protect yourself in an earthquake is to drop, cover, and hold.**

- If you are indoors when an earthquake hits, you should drop down under a sturdy table or desk. Then, you should cover your head and neck with your arms and hold onto the table or desk.

- If you are outdoors when an earthquake hits, you should move to an open area such as a playground. You should sit on the ground so you will not be thrown to the ground when the earthquake shakes.

- After an earthquake, you may have no electricity or running water for a while. Stores and roads may also be closed.

- If you live where earthquakes are likely, you should have an earthquake kit. The kit should contain canned food, water, and other emergency supplies.

Answer the following questions. Use your textbook and the ideas above.

4. Is the following sentence true or false? The best place to be if you are indoors when an earthquake hits is

   under a sturdy table or desk. _____

5. Circle the letter of the safest place to be if you are outdoors when an earthquake hits.
   a. beside a tall building
   b. under a bridge
   c. in the middle of an open field

Earthquakes

Designing Safer Buildings (pages 190–191)

Key Concept: **To reduce earthquake damage, new buildings must be made stronger and more flexible. Older buildings may be modified to withstand stronger quakes.**

- The main danger in earthquakes is falling buildings and objects. To reduce this danger, plywood can be added to walls to make buildings stronger. Tall furniture can also be attached to walls.

- Another danger in earthquakes is liquefaction. To reduce this danger, buildings can be attached to solid rock below the soil. This keeps the buildings from sinking if the soil turns to mud.

- When gas and water pipes break, it may cause fires and flooding. To reduce this danger, pipes can be changed so they bend instead of break when the ground shakes.

Answer the following questions. Use your textbook and the ideas above.

6. Is the following sentence true or false? The main danger in earthquakes is falling buildings and objects.

_____

7. Circle the letter of a way to reduce earthquake damage.
   a. add plywood to the walls of buildings
   b. change pipes so they do not bend
   c. attach buildings to soil instead of rock

Volcanoes and Plate Tectonics (pages 200–203)

Volcanoes and Plate Boundaries

(pages 201–202)

Key Concept: Volcanic belts form along the boundaries of Earth's plates.

- A **volcano** is a weak spot in the crust where melted material comes to the surface. The melted material is called **magma.** Magma rises to the surface because it is less dense than solid rock.

- Most volcanoes happen at plate boundaries. Remember, plate boundaries are where two plates pull apart or push together.

- Where plates pull apart, magma rises and pours out of cracks in the crust.

- Where plates push together, the denser plate sinks into the mantle. Some of the sinking plate melts and forms magma. The magma rises and pours out of cracks.

- Once magma reaches the surface, it is called **lava**. As lava cools, it forms solid rock.

- Lava can build up to form mountains. When the mountains are on the ocean floor, islands form if the mountains poke above the water's surface.

Answer the following questions. Use your textbook and the ideas above.

1. A weak spot in the crust where melted material comes to the surface is a(an) _____.

Name _____ Date _____ Class _____

2. Read the words in the box. In each sentence below, fill in one of the words.

rock	lava	magma	mantle

a. Melted material beneath the surface inside a

volcano is called _____.

b. Once melted material reaches the surface, it is

called _____.

c. When lava cools to a solid, it forms

_____.

3. The diagram shows how some volcanoes form. During subduction, Plate A sinks beneath Plate B and melts, forming _____.

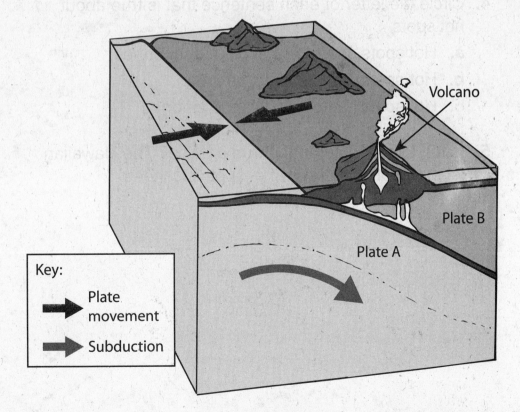

Volcano

Plate B

Plate A

Key:

➡ Plate movement

⇨ Subduction

Volcanoes

Hot Spot Volcanoes (page 203)

Key Concept: **A volcano forms above a hot spot when magma erupts through the crust and reaches the surface.**

- A **hot spot** is a place where material rises from deep in the mantle. The material forms magma.

- If the magma breaks through the crust, a volcano forms. Hot spot volcanoes on the ocean floor can become islands. This how the Hawaiian Islands formed.

- Some hot spots are under the middle of plates, far from plate boundaries. For example, there is a hot spot under the North American plate at Yellowstone National Park in Wyoming.

Answer the following questions. Use your textbook and the ideas above.

4. Circle the letter of each sentence that is true about hot spots.
    a. Hot spots occur only at plate boundaries.
    b. Hot spots can cause volcanoes.
    c. Hot spots can cause islands to form.

5. Is the following sentence true or false? The Hawaiian Islands were formed by hot spot volcanoes.

    _____

Volcanoes

Properties of Magma
(pages 205–208)

Physical and Chemical Properties
(pages 205–206)

Key Concept: Each substance has a particular set of physical and chemical properties. These properties can be used to identify a substance or to predict how it will behave.

- Like other substances, magma has a certain set of properties, or traits. Properties can be physical or chemical.

- **Physical properties** are traits that can be observed without changing what a substance is made of. Examples of physical properties are hardness and color.

- **Chemical properties** are traits that can be observed only by changing what a substance is made of. An example of a chemical property is being able to burn. Another example is being able to combine with other substances.

Answer the following questions. Use your textbook and the ideas above.

1. Circle the letter of an example of a physical property.
   a. being able to burn
   b. being able to combine with other substances
   c. hardness

2. Is the following sentence true or false? You can observe a chemical property without changing what a substance is made of. _____

3. Fill in the blanks in the concept map about properties of substances.

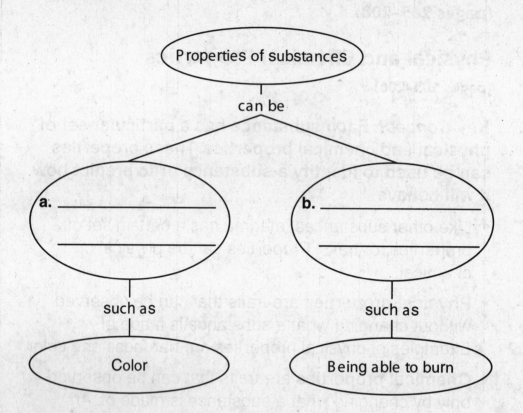

What Is Viscosity? (page 206)

Key Concept: **Because liquids differ in viscosity, some liquids flow more easily than others.**

- **Viscosity** (vis KAHS uh tee) is a physical property of liquids. How well a liquid flows depends on its viscosity.

- A liquid with high viscosity is thick. It flows slowly. An example of a liquid with high viscosity is honey.

- A liquid with low viscosity is thin. It flows quickly. An example of a liquid with low viscosity is water.

Answer the following question. Use your textbook and the ideas above.

4. Is the following sentence true or false? Honey has

higher viscosity than water. _____

Name _____ Date _____ Class _____

Volcanoes

Viscosity of Magma (pages 207–208)

Key Concept: **The viscosity of magma depends upon its silica content and temperature.**

- **Silica** is a common substance in Earth's crust. Magma contains silica. Magma that contains more silica has higher viscosity.

- High-silica magma produces high-viscosity lava. This lava flows slowly. High-silica lava or magma cools to form rocks such as granite.

- Low-silica magma produces low-viscosity lava. This lava flows quickly. Low-silica lava cools to form rocks such as basalt.

- Hotter magma has lower viscosity than cooler magma.

- Very hot magma produces lava called **pahoehoe** (pah HOH ee hoh ee). Pahoehoe has low viscosity. It flows quickly. It hardens into a rippled surface.

- Cooler magma produces lava called **aa** (AH ah). Aa has high viscosity. It flows slowly. It hardens into rough chunks.

Answer the following questions. Use your textbook and the ideas above.

5. Is the following sentence true or false? High-silica magma has high viscosity. _____

6. Fill in the blanks in the table about kinds of lava.

Kinds of Lava		
Kind of Lava	**Temperature**	**Viscosity**
Pahoehoe	hotter	**a.** _____
b. _____	cooler	higher

Volcanoes

Volcanic Eruptions (pages 209–216)

Magma Reaches Earth's Surface
(pages 210–211)

Key Concept: **When a volcano erupts, the force of the expanding gases pushes magma from the magma chamber through the pipe until it flows or explodes out of the vent.**

- A volcano has a pocket of magma below the surface, called a **magma chamber**. A long tube, called a **pipe**, connects the magma chamber to the surface.

- At the top of a pipe is an opening called a **vent**. Magma leaves the volcano through the vent and becomes lava. The area covered by lava as it pours out of a vent is called a **lava flow**.

- As magma nears the surface, pressure on the magma falls. Dissolved gases in magma start to form bubbles. The bubbles take up more space than the dissolved gases. The bubbles force magma out of the vent, like the bubbles that force warm pop out of a bottle.

Answer the following questions. Use your textbook and the ideas above.

1. Read the words in the box. In each sentence below, fill in one of the words.

pipe	vent	chamber

   a. Magma leaves a volcano through a

   _____.

   b. Magma flows from a magma chamber to the

   surface through a _____.

Volcanoes

2. Circle the letter of the choice that explains why a volcano erupts.

   a. Dissolved gases in magma form bubbles, forcing the magma out of a vent.

   b. Magma gets warmer and less dense as it nears the surface, causing the magma to flow out of a pipe.

   c. Pressure on magma increases as it nears the surface, forcing the magma into a magma chamber.

3. Read the words in the box. Use the words to fill in the blanks in the diagram of a volcano.

Magma chamber	Pipe	Lava flow	Vent

a. _____

b. _____

c. _____

d. _____

Volcanoes

Kinds of Volcanic Eruptions (pages 212–214)

Key Concept: Geologists classify volcanic eruptions as quiet or explosive.

- When magma pours out of a volcano, it is called a volcanic eruption. An eruption can happen slowly and quietly. Or an eruption can happen all at once with an explosion. How a volcano erupts depends on the magma.

- A volcano erupts quietly if the magma is low in silica and flows easily. The lava may flow for many kilometers before it starts to harden into rock.

- A volcano erupts with an explosion if the magma is high in silica and does not flow easily. Magma builds up in the pipe until it explodes out of the vent. The lava cools quickly. The hard lava pieces range in size from ashes and cinders to very large chunks called bombs.

- Both kinds of eruptions can do damage. A quiet eruption can cover a large area with a layer of lava. An explosive eruption can start fires and bury towns in ash.

Answer the following questions. Use your textbook and the ideas above.

4. What explains whether a volcano has a quiet or explosive eruption? Circle the letter of the correct answer.

   a. how much space there is in the magma chamber

   b. how much magma there is in the pipe

   c. how much silica there is in the magma

5. Is the following sentence true or false? Only explosive eruptions do damage. _____

Volcanoes

6. Label each circle in the Venn diagram with the kind of eruption it describes.

a. _____   b. _____

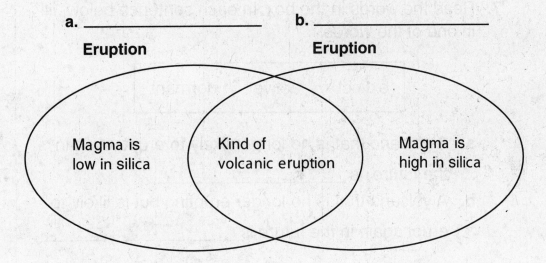

Stages of Volcanic Activity (pages 215–216)

Key Concept: **Geologists often use the terms** *active,* *dormant,* **or** *extinct* **to describe a volcano's stage of activity.**

* A volcano is active when it is erupting or showing signs that it will erupt soon.

* A volcano is **dormant** when it is no longer erupting but is likely to erupt again in the future. A dormant volcano may not erupt for thousands of years. But it can become active at any time.

* A volcano is **extinct** when it is no longer likely to erupt, even in the future.

* Scientists try to predict when a volcano will erupt. They watch for signs that magma is moving upward. Scientists often can predict when a volcano will erupt. But they cannot predict what kind of eruption or how strong an eruption it will be.

Name _____ Date _____ Class _____

Volcanoes

Answer the following questions. Use your textbook and the ideas on page 107.

7. Read the words in the box. In each sentence below, fill in one of the words.

> extinct   active   dormant

a. A volcano that is no longer likely to erupt, even in the future, is _____.

b. A volcano that is no longer erupting but is likely to erupt again in the future is _____.

8. How do scientists try to predict volcanoes? Circle the letter of the correct answer.

a. by measuring the amount of silica in magma

b. by measuring the size of the magma chamber

c. by watching for signs that magma is moving upward

9. Is the following sentence true or false? Scientists sometimes can predict when a volcano is about to erupt. _____

Volcanoes

Volcanic Landforms
(pages 217–223)

Landforms From Lava and Ash
(pages 218–220)

Key Concept: Volcanic eruptions create landforms made of lava, ash, and other materials. These landforms include shield volcanoes, cinder cone volcanoes, composite volcanoes, and lava plateaus.

• A **shield volcano** is a gently sloping mountain. It forms when a volcano erupts quietly. Thin layers of lava build up slowly over a large area around the vent.

• A **cinder cone** is a steep, cone-shaped hill or small mountain. It forms when a volcano erupts explosively. Ashes, cinders, and bombs pile up around the vent.

• A **composite volcano** is a tall, cone-shaped mountain. It forms when a volcano erupts quietly and then explosively, over and over again. Layers of lava are followed by layers of ash, cinders, and bombs.

• Sometimes lava forms a plateau instead of a mountain. A lava plateau is a high, level area. It forms when thin lava flows out of many long cracks.

• If a magma chamber empties, a volcano can collapse. This leaves a huge hole called a **caldera** (kal DAIR uh). A caldera may fill with water and form a lake.

Answer the following questions. Use your textbook and the ideas above.

1. If a volcano collapses, it leaves a huge hole called a(an) _____.

Volcanoes

2. Fill in the blank beside each drawing with the kind of volcano the drawing shows.

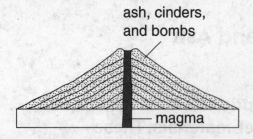

ash, cinders, and bombs

magma

a. _____

_____

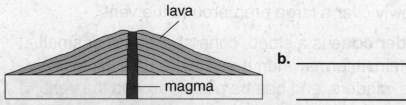

lava

magma

b. _____

_____

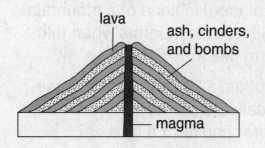

lava

ash, cinders, and bombs

magma

c. _____

_____

3. Circle the letter of the choice that describes how a lava plateau forms.

a. Thick lava erupts from a central vent.

b. Thin lava flows out of many long cracks.

c. Thick lava erupts from a caldera.

Volcanoes

Landforms From Magma (pages 221-222)

Key Concept: **Features formed by magma include volcanic necks, dikes, and sills, as well as batholiths and dome mountains.**

- A **volcanic neck** forms when magma hardens in the pipe of a volcano. Softer rock around the pipe wears away, leaving just the neck standing. A volcanic neck looks like a giant tooth stuck in the ground.

- A **dike** forms when magma hardens across rock layers. A dike is a vertical, or up-and-down, layer of hardened magma.

- A **sill** forms when magma hardens between rock layers. A sill is a horizontal, or sideways, layer of hardened magma.

- A **batholith** (BATH uh lith) forms when a large amount of magma hardens inside the crust. A batholith is a large rock mass. It may become part of a mountain range.

- A dome mountain forms when a batholith or smaller chunk of hardened magma is pushed up to the surface. The hardened magma forces the layers of rock above it to bend upward into a dome shape.

Answer the following questions. Use your textbook and the ideas above.

4. A volcanic neck forms when magma hardens in a

volcano's _____.

5. Circle the letter of each sentence that is true about batholiths.

   a. Batholiths form on the surface.

   b. Batholiths are large masses of rock.

   c. Batholiths may form dome mountains.

6. Fill in the blanks to label the dike and the sill.

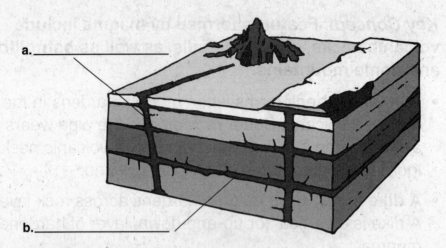

a. _____

b. _____

Geothermal Activity (pages 222–223)

Key Concept: **Hot springs and geysers are types of geothermal activity that are often found in areas of present or past volcanic activity.**

- Magma below the surface can heat underground water. The heating of underground water by magma is called **geothermal activity**. Geothermal activity is common where there are volcanoes.

- A hot spring forms when water heated by magma rises to the surface and collects in a natural pool.

- A **geyser** (GY zur) forms when hot water and steam are trapped underground in a narrow crack. Pressure builds up until the hot water and steam erupt from the ground. This happens over and over again. Old Faithful is a geyser in Yellowstone National Park. It erupts about once an hour.

- Hot water from underground can be piped into homes to heat them. This is how many people in Iceland heat their homes.

- Steam from underground can be piped into electric power plants. In the power plants, the heat energy in the steam is turned into electric energy.

Name _____ Date _____ Class _____

Volcanoes

Answer the following questions. Use your textbook and the ideas on page 112.

7. In geothermal activity, what heats underground water? Circle the letter of the correct answer.

    a. lava

    b. steam

    c. magma

8. What kind of geothermal activity is shown in the picture below? _____

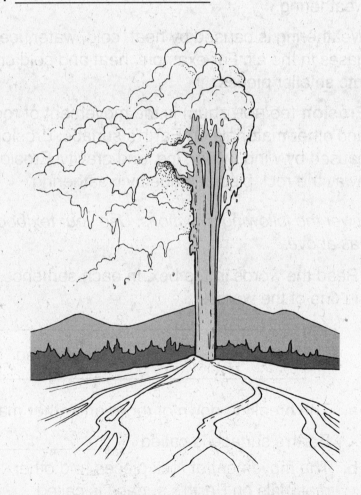

9. Is the following sentence true or false? Underground water and steam can be used for energy. _____

Weathering and Soil Formation

Rocks and Weathering (pages 238–245)

Weathering and Erosion (page 239)

Key Concept: **Weathering and erosion work together continuously to wear down and carry away the rocks at Earth's surface.**

- **Weathering** is the breaking down of rocks and other materials at Earth's surface. There are two kinds of weathering: mechanical weathering and chemical weathering.

- Weathering is caused by heat, cold, water, ice, and gases in the air. For example, heat and cold crack rocks into smaller pieces.

- **Erosion** (ee ROH zhun) is the movement of rock pieces and other materials on Earth's surface. Erosion is caused by wind, water, ice, and gravity. Erosion carries away the rock pieces made by weathering.

Answer the following questions. Use your textbook and the ideas above.

1. Read the words in the box. In each sentence below, fill in one of the words.

erosion	gravity	weathering

   a. The breaking down of rocks and other materials at Earth's surface is called _____.

   b. The movement of rock pieces and other materials on Earth's surface is called

   _____.

2. Fill in the blank in the concept map about kinds of weathering.

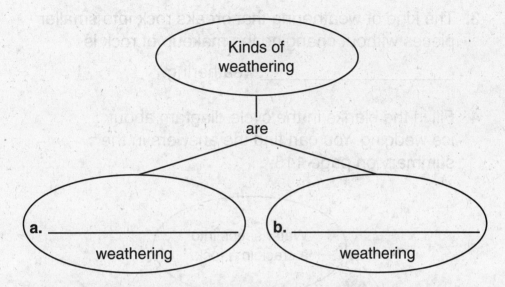

Mechanical Weathering (pages 240–241)

Key Concept: **The causes of mechanical weathering include freezing and thawing, release of pressure, plant growth, actions of animals, and abrasion.**

- In **mechanical weathering**, rock is broken into smaller pieces. But the makeup of rock does not change.

- Freezing and thawing cause **ice wedging**.

- In ice wedging, water seeps into a crack in a rock. The water freezes. Ice needs more space than water, so the ice pushes the crack apart. The ice melts. Water seeps into the deeper crack. This process keeps repeating until the rock breaks apart.

- Plant roots can grow into cracks and break apart rocks. Animals that dig in the ground can also break apart rocks.

- Rock particles can be carried by water, ice, wind, or gravity. The particles scrape rock like sandpaper scrapes wood. This scraping is called **abrasion** (uh BRAY shun).

Name _____ Date _____ Class _____

Weathering and Soil Formation

Answer the following questions. Use your textbook and the ideas on page 115.

3. The kind of weathering that breaks rock into smaller pieces without changing the makeup of rock is

   _____ weathering.

4. Fill in the blanks in the cycle diagram about ice wedging. You can find the answers in the summary on page 115.

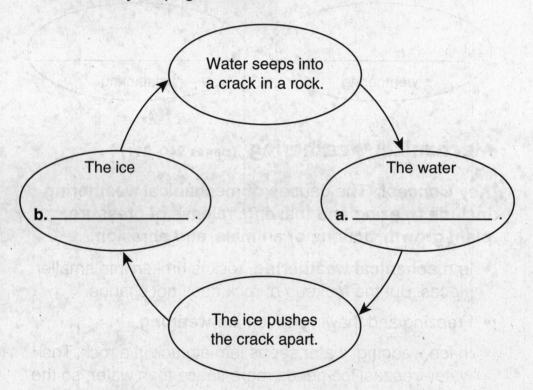

Water seeps into a crack in a rock.

The ice
b. _____ .

The water
a. _____ .

The ice pushes the crack apart.

5. Circle the letter of each example of mechanical weathering.
   a. Moles dig tunnels in the ground.
   b. Wind blows sand against a rock.
   c. Plant roots grow into a crack in a rock.

Weathering and Soil Formation

Chemical Weathering (pages 242–243)

Key Concept: **The causes of chemical weathering include the action of water, oxygen, carbon dioxide, living organisms, and acid rain.**

- In **chemical weathering**, the makeup of rock changes.

- Chemical weathering makes holes or soft spots in rock. This makes it easier for mechanical weathering to break rocks into smaller pieces.

- Water slowly dissolves rock.

- Some rocks contain iron. Oxygen turns iron to rust. When iron in rocks turns to rust, the rocks get soft.

- Carbon dioxide in air mixes with rainwater to make a weak acid. The acid easily dissolves some rocks.

- Plant roots also make weak acids. The acids slowly dissolve rocks around the roots.

- Acid rain is rain that contains acids because of air pollution. Acid rain quickly dissolves rocks.

Answer the following questions. Use your textbook and the ideas above.

6. Fill in the blanks in the concept map about chemical weathering.

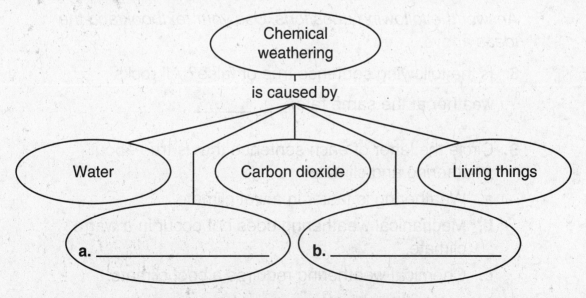

Weathering and Soil Formation

7. How does chemical weathering help mechanical weathering? Circle the letter of each correct answer.

   a. by breaking rocks into smaller pieces

   b. by making holes in rocks

   c. by making rocks softer

Rate of Weathering (pages 244–245)

Key Concept: **The most important factors that determine the rate at which weathering occurs are the type of rock and the climate.**

- The rate of weathering is how fast a rock weathers. Some kinds of rock weather faster than others.

- Certain minerals dissolve easily in water. Rocks made of these minerals weather quickly. Some rocks are full of tiny holes that water can enter. These rocks also weather quickly.

- Rocks weather more quickly in some climates than in other climates. Climate is an area's average weather.

- Both mechanical and chemical weathering are faster in a wet climate than in a dry climate. Mechanical weathering is faster in a cool climate. Chemical weathering is faster in a warm climate.

Answer the following questions. Use your textbook and the ideas above.

8. Is the following sentence true or false? All rocks weather at the same rate. _____

9. Circle the letter of each sentence that is true about weathering and climate.

   a. Weathering is faster in a wet climate.

   b. Mechanical weathering does not occur in a warm climate.

   c. Chemical weathering requires a cool climate.

How Soil Forms (pages 248–254)

What Is Soil? (pages 248–249)

Key Concept: **Soil is a mixture of rock particles, minerals, decayed organic material, water, and air.**

- **Soil** is the material on Earth's surface in which plants can grow. Soil contains pieces of rock and other materials.

- Most pieces of rock in soil come from the weathering of bedrock. **Bedrock** is a solid layer of rock under the soil.

- Pieces of rock in soil can be small or large. Plants grow best in soils that have rock pieces of different sizes.

- When dead plants and animals decay, or break down, they form **humus** (HYOO mus). Humus mixes with rock pieces to form soil.

- Humus in soil helps plants grow. Humus makes tiny spaces in soil for air and water that plants need. Humus also contains substances called minerals that plants need.

Answer the following questions. Use your textbook and the ideas above.

1. Read the words in the box. In each sentence below, fill in one of the words.

humus	bedrock	water	soil

   a. The material on Earth's surface in which

   plants can grow is _____.

   b. The material that forms when plants and

   animals decay is _____.

   c. Most pieces of rock in soil come from

   weathering of _____.

2. Why is humus good for plants? Circle the letter of each correct answer.

    a. Humus makes spaces in soil for air and water.

    b. Humus contains minerals that plants need.

    c. Humus makes bedrock weather faster.

The Process of Soil Formation (page 250)

Key Concept: Soil forms as rock is broken down by weathering and mixes with other materials on the surface. Soil is constantly being formed wherever bedrock is exposed.

- Soil forms in layers called horizons. A **soil horizon** is a layer of soil that is different from the soil above it or below it.

- The top layer of soil is the A horizon, or topsoil. **Topsoil** is a mixture of humus and tiny rock pieces.

- Below the A horizon is the B horizon, or subsoil. **Subsoil** is made up mostly of rock pieces.

- The bottom layer of soil is the C horizon. The C horizon contains only partly weathered rock pieces.

- The C horizon forms first, as bedrock weathers. The A horizon forms next, as humus is added to rock pieces on the surface. The B horizon forms last, as smaller pieces of rock wash down from the A horizon.

Answer the following questions. Use your textbook and the ideas above.

3. Circle the letter of the correct order in which soil horizons form.

    a. A→B→C

    b. C→B→A

    c. C→A→B

4. Label the soil horizons in the diagram. Use the letters A, B, and C.

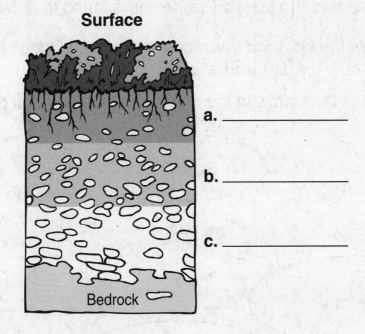

Surface

a. _____

b. _____

c. _____

Bedrock

5. Draw a line from each term to its meaning.

Term	Meaning
topsoil	**a.** soil that contains pieces of rock and humus
subsoil	**b.** soil that contains rock pieces and clay

Soil Types (page 251)

Key Concept: **Scientists classify the different types of soil into major groups based on climate, plants, and soil composition.**

- Climate affects the kind of soil in an area. For example, in a rainy climate, humus may be washed out of the soil.

- Different kinds of plants grow in different kinds of soil. For example, prairie plants such as grasses grow in a different kind of soil than forest plants such as trees.

- Soil composition is the makeup of soil. For example, the composition of soil can be rocky or sandy.

Name _____ Date _____ Class _____

Weathering and Soil Formation

- In the United States, forest soil covers most of the eastern states. Desert soil and mountain soil cover most of the western states. Prairie soil is found in between.

Answer the following questions. Use your textbook and the ideas on page 121 and above.

6. Fill in the blanks in the concept map about soil types.

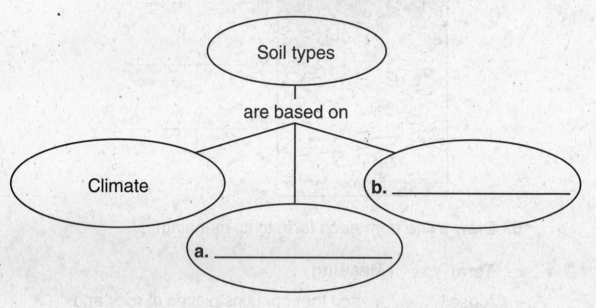

7. Label the map with the kind of soil found in each area. Use the following soil types: Forest soil, Mountain soil, Prairie soil, and Desert soil. One area has more than one kind of soil.

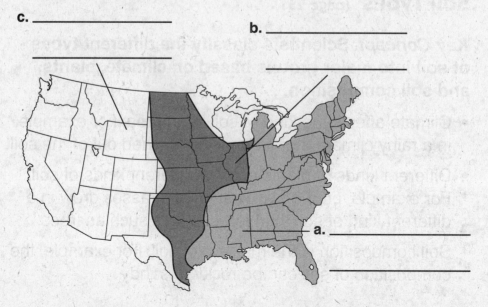

Living Organisms in Soil (pages 252–254)

Key Concept: **Some soil organisms make humus, the material that makes soil fertile. Other soil organisms mix the soil and make spaces in it for air and water.**

- Living things in soil break down dead plants and animals. This process makes humus. The process is called decomposition.

- Living things that break down dead organisms are called **decomposers**. Bacteria and mushrooms are examples of decomposers.

- Earthworms and burrowing animals such as moles mix humus and air into soil.

Answer the following questions. Use your textbook and the ideas above.

8. Draw a line from each term to its meaning.

Term	Meaning
decomposer	**a.** process in which humus forms
decomposition	**b.** living thing that turns dead plants and animals into humus

9. What do earthworms and burrowing animals do to soil? Circle the letter of each correct answer.

   a. break down, or decompose, dead plants and animals

   b. mix humus into soil

   c. mix air into soil

Weathering and Soil Formation

Soil Conservation (pages 256–259)

The Value of Soil (page 257)

Key Concept: **Soil is one of Earth's most valuable natural resources because everything that lives on land, including humans, depends directly or indirectly on soil.**

- A **natural resource** is anything in the environment that humans use.

- Plants depend directly on soil to live and grow. Humans and other animals depend on plants for food. So, humans and other animals depend indirectly on soil.

- Soil that is good for growing plants is valuable because there is not very much of it. Less than one eighth of the soil on Earth is good for farming.

Answer the following questions. Use your textbook and the ideas above.

1. Anything in the environment that humans use is

   called a(an) _____.

2. Circle the letter of each sentence that is true about the value of soil.

   a. Only plants depend on soil.

   b. Less than one eighth of Earth's soil is good for farming.

   c. Soil is not a natural resource.

3. Is the following sentence true or false? People do not

   depend on soil for anything. _____

Weathering and Soil Formation

Soil Damage and Loss (pages 257–258)

Key Concept: **The value of soil is reduced when soil loses its fertility and when topsoil is lost due to erosion.**

- Soil fertility is a measure of how good soil is for plants. A soil with high fertility has everything plants need to grow and stay healthy.

- Soil can lose its fertility if farmers grow just one kind of plant year after year.

- When soil is bare, water and wind can carry the soil away. Plants protect soil from erosion. For example, plant roots help hold soil together.

- States such as Oklahoma used to be covered with grass. Then farmers plowed up the grass to plant crops. In the 1930s, dry weather killed the crops and turned the bare soil to dust. Wind blew away the dust.

- The area was called the **Dust Bowl**. The Dust Bowl taught people to take better care of the soil.

Answer the following questions. Use your textbook and the ideas above.

4. Circle the letter of each way that soil can become less valuable.
   a. Soil can lose its fertility.
   b. Soil can be lost because of erosion.
   c. Soil can be covered with plants.

5. Circle the letter of each sentence that is true about the Dust Bowl.
   a. The Dust Bowl included Oklahoma.
   b. In the Dust Bowl, water washed away the soil.
   c. The Dust Bowl taught people to take better care of the soil.

Weathering and Soil Formation

Soil Conservation (page 259)

Key Concept: Soil can be conserved through contour plowing, conservation plowing, and crop rotation.

- **Soil conservation** means using soil in ways that save it. Soil conservation keeps soil fertile and prevents soil erosion.

- In **contour plowing**, farmers plow fields along curves of slopes instead of straight up and down slopes. This keeps soil from washing away in heavy rains.

- In **conservation plowing**, farmers leave dead weeds and stalks in the fields. The dead plants hold soil in place. The plants also turn into humus, which makes soil more fertile.

- In **crop rotation**, farmers grow different kinds of plants in their fields each year. Crop rotation keeps soil from losing its fertility.

Answer the following questions. Use your textbook and the ideas above.

6. Using soil in ways that save it is called

_____.

7. Draw a line from each method of soil conservation to its description.

Method	Description
contour plowing	a. leaving dead plants in fields
crop rotation	b. plowing fields along curves of slopes
conservation plowing	c. growing different kinds of plants in a field each year

Name _____ Date _____ Class _____

Changing Earth's Surface
(pages 266–269)

Wearing Down and Building Up (pages 266–267)

Key Concept: **Weathering, erosion, and deposition act together in a cycle that wears down and builds up Earth's surface.**

- **Erosion** is the movement of pieces of rock and other materials on Earth's surface. Erosion can be caused by gravity, running water, glaciers, waves, or wind.

- **Sediment** is the material moved by erosion. Sediment is made up of pieces of rock or soil or remains of living things.

- Most sediment comes from weathering. Remember, weathering is the breaking down of rock and other materials at Earth's surface.

- **Deposition** happens when sediment is dropped. Dropped sediment can build up over time and make new landforms.

Answer the following questions. Use your textbook and the ideas above.

1. Draw a line from each term to its meaning.

Term	Meaning
weathering	**a.** the material moved by erosion
erosion	**b.** the movement of pieces of rock and other materials on Earth's surface
sediment	**c.** the dropping of sediment
deposition	**d.** the breaking down of rock and other materials at Earth's surface

2. Circle the letter of each choice that is a cause of erosion.

   a. gravity

   b. running water

   c. weathering

Mass Movement (pages 267–269)

Key Concept: **The different types of mass movement include landslides, mudflows, slump, and creep.**

- **Mass movement** is any process that moves sediment downhill. Mass movement is caused by gravity. **Gravity** is the force that pulls everything toward Earth's center.

- Landslides happen when rocks and soil quickly slide down a steep slope.

- Mudflows happen when rocks and mud quickly slide down a steep slope.

- Slump happens when a mass of rocks and soil suddenly slides down a steep slope. Slump is different than a landslide. The material in slump moves down the slope in one large mass.

- Creep happens when rocks and soil move very slowly down a hill. Creep can happen even on gentle slopes.

Answer the following questions. Use your textbook and the ideas above.

3. Any process that moves sediment downhill is called

   _____.

4. Circle the letter of the cause of mass movement.

   a. rain

   b. wind

   c. gravity

Name _____ Date _____ Class _____

Erosion and Deposition

5. Fill in the blanks in the concept map about kinds
   of mass movement.

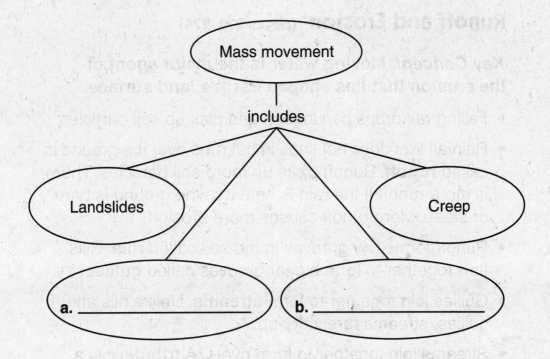

Mass movement

includes

Landslides   Creep

a. _____   b. _____

Erosion and Deposition

Water Erosion (pages 272–281)

Runoff and Erosion (pages 273–274)

Key Concept: **Moving water is the major agent of the erosion that has shaped Earth's land surface.**

* Falling raindrops can loosen and pick up soil particles.

* Rainfall that does not soak in but runs over the ground is called **runoff**. Runoff picks up more soil particles. There is more runoff if the rain is heavy or the ground is bare or steep. More runoff causes more erosion.

* Runoff forms tiny grooves in the soil called **rills**. Rills flow together to form bigger grooves called **gullies**.

* Gullies join together to form **streams**. Unlike rills and gullies, streams rarely dry up.

* Streams join together to form rivers. A **tributary** is a stream or river that flows into a bigger river.

Answer the following questions. Use your textbook and the ideas above.

1. Fill in the blanks in the flowchart showing how runoff flows into rivers.

From Runoff to Rivers

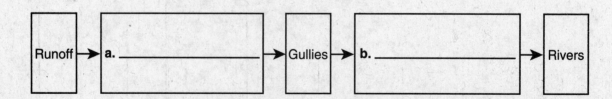

Runoff → a. _____ → Gullies → b. _____ → Rivers

2. A stream or river that flows into a bigger river is called a(an) _____.

Erosion and Deposition

Erosion by Rivers (pages 275–276)

Key Concept: **Through erosion, a river creates valleys, waterfalls, flood plains, meanders, and oxbow lakes.**

- A river on a steep slope flows quickly. The fast-moving water wears away a deep, V-shaped valley.

- A river may flow from hard rock to soft rock. The soft rock wears away faster than the hard rock. This causes a sharp drop in the riverbed, which forms a waterfall.

- A river on a gentle slope spreads out and flows slowly. The slow-moving water slowly wears away a wide, flat-bottomed valley. The valley is called a **flood plain**.

- A **meander** is a big bend in a river. A meander forms in a flood plain. It starts as a small curve and gets bigger.

- An **oxbow lake** is a meander that has been cut off from a river. An oxbow lake is curved like a meander.

Answer the following questions. Use your textbook and the ideas above.

3. Fill in the blanks in the drawing. Use the following terms: Waterfall, Meander, and Oxbow lake.

b. _____

a. _____

c. _____

Name _____ Date _____ Class _____

Erosion and Deposition

4. Is the following sentence true or false? A river forms a flood plain when it flows over a steep slope.

_____

Deposits by Rivers (pages 276–279)

Key Concept: **Deposition creates landforms such as alluvial fans and deltas. It can also add soil to a river's flood plain.**

- Rivers slow down when they leave mountains, flow into lakes or oceans, or flood their banks. When rivers slow down, they drop the sediment they are carrying. The dropped sediment is called a deposit.

- An **alluvial fan** is a deposit that forms where a river leaves a mountain range.

- A **delta** is a deposit that forms where a river flows into a lake or an ocean.

- When a river floods, it drops sediment on its flood plain. This may happen year after year. This explains why flood plain soil is usually thick and fertile.

Answer the following questions. Use your textbook and the ideas above.

5. Fill in the blanks in the table about deposits by rivers.

Deposits by Rivers	
Kind of Deposit	**Where It Forms**
a. _____ _____	where a river leaves a mountain range
b. _____	where a river flows into a lake or an ocean

Erosion and Deposition

6. Circle the letter of the sentence that explains why a flood plain usually has thick, fertile soil.

   a. A river slows down and drops sediment when it floods its banks.

   b. A river flows faster when it flows over its flood plain.

   c. A river never flows over its flood plain, so flood plain soil is not washed away.

Groundwater Erosion (pages 280–281)

Key Concept: **Groundwater can cause erosion through a process of chemical weathering.**

- When it rains, some water sinks into the ground. Underground water is called **groundwater**.

- Groundwater mixes with carbon dioxide in soil and becomes a weak acid. Groundwater can dissolve limestone and make holes in the rock. Big holes in limestone are called caves.

- Groundwater often drips from the roof of a cave. Dissolved substances can come out of the dripping water and form deposits that look like icicles.

- When one of these deposits hangs down from the roof of a cave, it is called a **stalactite** (stuh LAK tyt).

- When one of these deposits sticks up from the floor of a cave, it is called a **stalagmite** (stuh LAG myt).

- If the roof of a cave wears away, the land over it may sink in and make a hole in the ground. The hole is called a sinkhole.

Answer the following questions. Use your textbook and the ideas above.

7. Underground water is called _____.

Erosion and Deposition

8. Draw a line from each term to its meaning.

Term	**Meaning**
stalagmite	**a.** deposit that hangs down from the roof of a cave
stalactite	**b.** deposit that sticks up from the floor of a cave

9. When the roof of a cave wears away and the ground sinks in, it forms a(an) _____.

Erosion and Deposition

The Force of Moving Water (pages 286–290)

Work and Energy (page 286)

Key Concept: **As gravity pulls water down a slope, the water's potential energy changes to kinetic energy that can do work.**

- Moving water has energy. An object has **energy** if it can do work. Moving water can run machines.

- Two kinds of energy are potential energy and kinetic energy.

- **Potential energy** is stored energy. This kind of energy is waiting to be used. Water behind a dam has potential energy.

- **Kinetic energy** is the energy of moving objects. Water moving over a dam has kinetic energy.

Answer the following questions. Use your textbook and the ideas above.

1. An object that can do work has

   _____.

2. Fill in the blanks in the table about kinds of energy.

Kinds of Energy	
Kind of Energy	**Description**
a. _____ energy	stored energy
b. _____ energy	energy of moving objects

Erosion and Deposition

How Water Erodes (page 287)

Key Concept: **Most sediment washes or falls into a river as a result of mass movement and runoff. Other sediment erodes from the bottom or sides of the river.**

- A river erodes Earth's surface by picking up and moving sediment. Sediment can get into a river in different ways.

- A landslide can dump sediment into a river. Runoff can wash sediment into a river. A river can also get sediment by abrasion.

- In **abrasion**, sediment in the water scrapes against the bottom and sides of the river. Bits of rock are chipped away to form new sediment.

- Sediment **load** is the amount of sediment a river carries.

- Sediment moves downstream with the water. Bigger pieces of sediment roll or bounce along the bottom. Smaller pieces are lifted and carried by the water.

Answer the following question. Use your textbook and the ideas above.

3. Read the words in the box. In each sentence below, fill in one of the words.

load	abrasion	runoff	sediment

a. A river erodes the surface by picking up and moving _____.

b. How much sediment a river carries is its sediment _____.

c. The scraping of the bottom and sides of a river by sediment is called _____.

Erosion and Deposition

Erosion and Sediment Load (pages 288–290)

Key Concept: A river's slope, volume of flow, and the shape of its streambed all affect how fast the river flows and how much sediment it can erode.

- How much erosion a river can cause depends mainly on how much sediment the river can carry. The amount of sediment a river can carry depends on how fast the water moves and how much water there is.

- Fast-moving water can carry more sediment than slow-moving water. Fast-moving water can also carry bigger pieces of sediment.

- A big river with a lot of water can carry more sediment than a small river. A big river can also carry bigger pieces of sediment.

- Big rocks in a streambed can make water rough. Rough water wears away the streambed faster than smooth water.

- Where a river curves, water moves faster along the outside of the curve. The faster water wears away the outside bank. The water moves slower on the inside of the curve. The slower water drops sediment along the inside bank. In this way, the curve keeps getting bigger.

Answer the following questions. Use your textbook and the ideas above.

4. How much erosion a river can cause depends mainly on how much _____ the river can carry.

5. Circle the letter of each sentence that is true about erosion by rivers.

   a. A fast river causes more erosion than a slow river.

   b. A small river causes more erosion than a big river.

   c. A river with rough water causes more erosion than a river with smooth water.

Erosion and Deposition

Glaciers (pages 291–295)

How Glaciers Form and Move (pages 292–293)

Key Concept: **There are two kinds of glaciers— continental glaciers and valley glaciers. Glaciers can form only in an area where more snow falls than melts. Once the depth of snow and ice reaches more than 30 to 40 meters, gravity begins to pull the glacier downhill.**

- A **glacier** is a huge chunk of ice that moves over the land. A glacier forms when snow and ice build up year after year.

- A **continental glacier** covers all or most of a continent. This kind of glacier moves very slowly in all directions.

- At times, continental glaciers have covered much of Earth's surface. These times are called **ice ages**.

- A **valley glacier** is a long, narrow glacier in a mountain valley. A valley glacier moves only down the valley. A valley glacier can move faster than a continental glacier.

Answer the following questions. Use your textbook and the ideas above.

1. A huge chunk of ice that moves over the land is

    a(an) _____.

2. Fill in the blanks in the Venn diagram about glaciers.

a. _____   b. _____
Glacier   **Glacier**

Long and narrow

Forms when snow and ice build up

Very wide

Moves faster

Moves slower

Erosion and Deposition

How Glaciers Shape the Land
(pages 293–295)

Key Concept: **The two processes by which glaciers erode the land are plucking and abrasion.**

- As a glacier moves, it erodes the land under it.

- The weight of a glacier can break off pieces of rock. The rock pieces stick to the glacier and become sediment. This process is called **plucking**.

- As the glacier moves, the sediment on the bottom scrapes the land. The scraping is called abrasion.

- Abrasion can make valleys wider. Abrasion can also scrape away mountainsides. This leaves a sharp mountain peak called a horn.

Answer the following questions. Use your textbook and the ideas above.

3. Draw a line from each term to its meaning.

Term	Meaning
plucking	**a.** process in which sediment scrapes the land
abrasion	**b.** process in which rocks are picked up by glaciers

4. Is the following sentence true or false? Glaciers can make valleys wider and scrape away mountain sides.

_____

Key Concept: **When a glacier melts, it deposits the sediment it eroded from the land, creating various landforms.**

- Wherever a glacier melts, it drops its sediment. Sediment dropped by a glacier is called **till**. Till makes many different landforms.

Erosion and Deposition

- A **moraine** is a ridge or mound that forms where till is dropped along the edge of a glacier.

- Sometimes a glacier drops a big chunk of ice instead of rock or soil. When the ice melts, it leaves a low spot in the ground called a **kettle**.

Answer the following questions. Use your textbook and the ideas on page 139 and above.

5. The sediment dropped by a glacier is called

   _____.

6. Fill in the blanks in the table about landforms from glaciers.

Landforms from Glaciers	
Landform	**Description**
Horn	sharp mountain peak formed by abrasion
a. _____	low spot in the ground formed by a big chunk of ice
b. _____	ridge or mound formed by till at the edge of a glacier

Name _____ Date _____ Class _____

Erosion and Deposition

Waves (pages 296–300)

How Waves Form (page 296)

Key Concept: **The energy in waves comes from wind that blows across the water's surface.**

- When ocean wind touches ocean water, energy passes from the wind to the water. This energy causes waves. The waves carry the energy across the ocean.

- Where the ocean is deep, waves affect only the surface of the water.

- Close to shore, the water is shallow. There, waves drag on the bottom and crash against the shore.

Answer the following questions. Use your textbook and the ideas above.

1. Circle the letter of each sentence that is true about ocean waves.

   a. Ocean waves cause ocean winds.

   b. Ocean waves carry energy across the ocean.

   c. Ocean waves affect only the surface of deep water.

2. How do ocean waves change close to shore? Circle the letter of the correct answer.

   a. The waves move higher in the water.

   b. The waves drag on the bottom.

   c. The waves affect only the water's surface.

Name _____ Date _____ Class _____

Erosion and Deposition

Erosion by Waves (pages 297–298)

Key Concept: **Waves shape the coast through erosion by breaking down rock and transporting sand and other sediment.**

• Waves are the major cause of erosion along coasts. When waves hit the shore, the force of the water can crack rocks. Over time, the rocks break into smaller pieces and wash away.

• Close to shore, waves pick up sediment from the bottom. When the waves hit rocks on shore, the sediment wears away the rocks by abrasion.

• Some rock on shore may be harder than the rock around it. The harder rock wears away slower and forms a headland. A **headland** is part of a shore that sticks out into the ocean.

• Waves can wear away the bottoms of cliffs along the shore. Waves can also wear away holes in cliffs and form caves.

Answer the following question. Use your textbook and the ideas above.

3. Read the words in the box. In each sentence below, fill in one of the words.

```
    cliff     abrasion     headland     waves
```

   a. A part of a shore that sticks out into the

      ocean is called a(an) _____.

   b. The major cause of erosion along coasts is

      _____.

   c. Waves that carry sediment cause

      _____.

Erosion and Deposition

Deposits by Waves (pages 299–300)

Key Concept: **Waves shape a coast when they deposit sediment, forming coastal features such as beaches, spits, and barrier beaches.**

• When waves slow down at a coast, they drop sediment. The sediment can build up to make different landforms.

• A **beach** is an area of sediment at the edge of the water. The sediment on a beach is usually sand.

• If waves hit a beach at an angle, they can carry sand down the beach. This is called **longshore drift**.

• If a headland stops longshore drift, the sand piles up and forms a spit. A **spit** is a beach that sticks out into the water like a finger.

• Sometimes waves drop sand in a long ridge parallel to shore. The ridge of sand is called a sandbar. If the sand builds up above the surface of the water, it forms a long, narrow island parallel to the shore. This kind of island is called a barrier beach.

Answer the following question. Use your textbook and the ideas above.

4. Draw a line from each term to its meaning.

Term	Meaning
barrier beach	**a.** beach that sticks out into the water like a finger
spit	**b.** long ridge of sand parallel to the shore
longshore drift	**c.** movement of sand down a beach by waves
sandbar	**d.** long, narrow island parallel to the shore

Name _____ Date _____ Class _____

Wind (pages 301–303)

How Wind Causes Erosion (pages 301–302)

Key Concept: **Wind causes erosion by deflation and abrasion.**

- Deflation is the main way that wind causes erosion. **Deflation** is the process by which wind picks up sediment from the surface. The stronger the wind, the bigger the pieces of sediment the wind can pick up.

- Wind may carry away all the sediment in a desert and leave behind only rocks. The rocky surface that is left is called desert pavement.

- Sediment carried by wind causes abrasion. The blowing sediment scrubs and polishes rock.

Answer the following questions. Use your textbook and the ideas above.

1. The process by which wind picks up sediment from

   the surface is called _____.

2. Fill in the blanks in the concept map about how wind causes erosion.

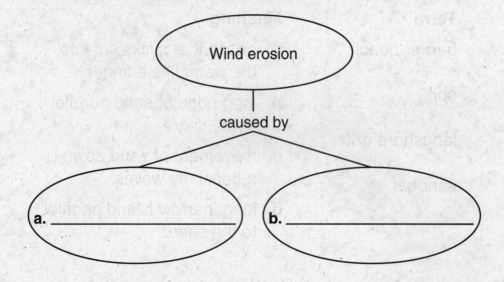

Erosion and Deposition

Wind Deposition (page 303)

Key Concept: **Wind erosion and deposition may form sand dunes and loess deposits.**

- Wind drops the sediment it is carrying when a wall or other barrier slows the wind. The sediment may form sand dunes or loess deposits.

- **Sand dunes** are ridges or mounds that form when the wind drops sand. Sand dunes can be small or large. Wind may slowly move sand dunes across the ground.

- **Loess** (LES) is tiny pieces of sediment that are dropped by the wind. Loess helps make soil fertile. There are big loess deposits in states such as Nebraska and Iowa.

Answer the following questions. Use your textbook and the ideas above.

3. Is the following sentence true or false? Wind drops the sediment it is carrying when the wind slows down. _____

4. Fill in the blanks in the Venn diagram to show which circle describes a sand dune and which circle describes a loess deposit.

a. _____   b. _____

_____   _____

Forms if sediment is sand

Forms when wind drops sediment

Forms if sediment is tiny pieces

A Trip Through Geologic Time

Fossils (pages 310–316)

How a Fossil Forms (pages 310–313)

Key Concept: **Most fossils form when living things die and are buried by sediments. The sediments slowly harden into rock and preserve the shapes of the organisms.**

- **Fossils** are remains of organisms that died long ago. An organism is any kind living thing.

- Fossils are usually found in **sedimentary rock**. This kind of rock forms when sediment builds up over time.

- Sedimentary rock usually forms in shallow water. So most organisms that turn into fossils once lived in or near shallow water.

- Suppose an animal dies and sinks into shallow water. Sediment slowly covers the dead animal and turns to rock. Part of the animal may also turn to rock and become a fossil.

Answer the following questions. Use your textbook and the ideas above.

1. Remains of organisms that died long ago are called

   _____.

2. Circle the letter of each sentence that is true about how most fossils form.

   a. Most fossils form when water washes away sediment from dead organisms.

   b. Most fossils form from organisms that once lived in or near shallow water.

   c. Most fossils form when dead organisms are buried by sediment.

A Trip Through Geologic Time

Key Concept: Fossils found in rock include molds and casts, petrified fossils, carbon films, and trace fossils. Other fossils form when the remains of organisms are preserved in substances such as tar, amber, or ice.

- A **mold** is a hollow area in a rock in the shape of an organism. A mold forms when sediment buries a hard part of a dead organism. The hard part later breaks down and leaves a mold.

- A **cast** is a copy of an organism in rock. A cast forms when sediment fills a mold and turns to rock.

- **Petrified fossils** are dead organisms that have turned to stone. Water soaks into dead organisms. Minerals in the water harden and turn into stone.

- All organisms contain carbon. When a dead organism breaks down in rock, it may leave behind a thin **carbon film** on the rock. The film is like a picture of the organism.

- **Trace fossils** show how ancient organisms behaved. Trace fossils include fossil footprints and burrows.

- Sometimes organisms are trapped in something sticky that keeps them from breaking down. For example, insects may be trapped in tree sap. The sap hardens around the insect and forms a clear solid called amber.

Answer the following question. Use your textbook and the ideas above.

3. Draw a line from each kind of fossil to its description.

Kind of Fossil	Description
carbon film	**a.** hollow area in rock in the shape of an organism
mold	
	b. solid copy of an organism in rock
trace fossil	**c.** organism that has turned to stone
petrified fossil	**d.** thin layer of carbon on rock
cast	**e.** preserved trace such as a footprint

A Trip Through Geologic Time

Change Over Time (pages 314–316)

Key Concept: **The fossil record provides evidence about the history of life and past environments on Earth. The fossil record also shows that different groups of organisms have changed over time.**

- Scientists collect fossils from all over the world. All the fossils together make up the fossil record. The fossil record shows what past life forms were like.

- The fossil record also shows what past environments were like. For example, fossils of swamp creatures have been found in areas that are now dry. The fossils show that the areas used to be much wetter.

- The fossil record shows that organisms have changed slowly over time. For example, the fossil record shows that elephants used to have shorter trunks.

- This change in elephants is an example of evolution. **Evolution** is gradual change in living things that happens over a long period of time.

- The fossil record shows that all kinds of organisms have changed. The fossil record also shows that many kinds of organisms have died out, or gone **extinct**.

Answer the following questions. Use your textbook and the ideas above.

4. All the fossils that scientists have found make up

   the _____.

5. What have scientists learned from the fossil record? Circle the letter of each correct choice.
   a. what past environments were like
   b. what past life forms were like
   c. how organisms have changed over time

The Relative Age of Rocks

(pages 317–321)

The Position of Rock Layers (page 318)

Key Concept: **According to the law of superposition, in horizontal sedimentary rock layers the oldest layer is at the bottom. Each higher layer is younger than the layers below it.**

- To understand how life has changed, scientists must know how old fossils are. Scientists can tell how old fossils are from the rocks where the fossils are found.

- Remember, fossils are found in sedimentary rocks. This kind of rock forms when sediment builds up over time.

- In sedimentary rock, lower rock layers are older than upper rock layers. So fossils found in lower rock layers are older than fossils found in upper rock layers.

Answer the following question. Use your textbook and the ideas above.

1. Use the diagram below to answer the questions.

   a. Which rock layer is youngest? _____

   b. Which rock layer is oldest? _____

   c. Which fossil is older? _____

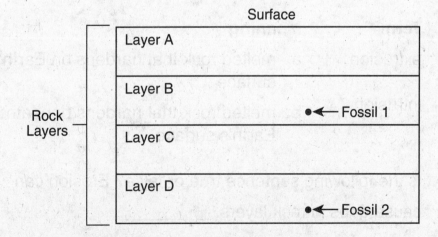

Determining Relative Age (pages 319–320)

Key Concept: To determine relative age, geologists also study extrusions and intrusions of igneous rock, faults, and gaps in the geologic record.

- Sedimentary rock layers do not always line up neatly. Positions of rock layers may change after the rocks form. This can happen in different ways.

- Melted rock can harden and form new rock on top or inside of sedimentary rock. New rock that forms on top of sedimentary rock is called an **extrusion**. New rock that forms inside of sedimentary rock is called an **intrusion**.

- At a fault, rock layers may move so they no longer line up. A **fault** is a break in rock where rocks can move.

- New rock layers can be worn away by erosion before they are covered by sediment. This makes a time gap in the rock layers. Younger rock layers are directly on top of very old rock layers.

Answer the following questions. Use your textbook and the ideas above.

2. A break in rock where rocks can move is a(an)

    _____.

3. Draw a line from each term to its meaning.

Term	Meaning
extrusion	a. melted rock that hardens on Earth's surface
intrusion	b. melted rock that hardens beneath Earth's surface

4. Is the following sentence true or false? Erosion can cause gaps in rock layers. _____

A Trip Through Geologic Time

Using Fossils to Date Rocks (pages 320-321)

Key Concept: Index fossils are useful because they tell the relative ages of the rock layers in which they occur.

- The rock layers in different places can be hard to match up. It can be hard to tell which layers are older and which layers are younger.

- Index fossils help scientists match rock layers in different places. An **index fossil** is a fossil of an organism that lived over a wide area and existed for just a short period of time.

- Two rock layers in different places that contain the same index fossil are about the same age.

Answer the following question. Use your textbook and the ideas above.

5. The diagram below shows rock layers and fossils from two different places, A and B. Use the diagram to answer the questions.

   a. Which fossil could be an index fossil? _____

   b. Use this index fossil to find the rock layer in place B

      that matches rock layer 2 in place A. _____

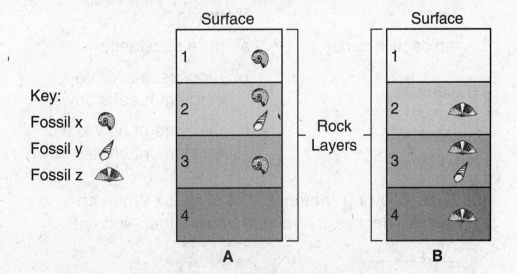

A Trip Through Geologic Time

Radioactive Dating (pages 323–326)

Radioactive Decay (page 324)

***Key Concept:* During radioactive decay, the atoms of one element break down to form atoms of another element.**

- Everything is made up of one or more pure substances. These pure substances are called **elements**.

- Some elements break down, or decay. When an element decays, it changes into another kind of element. The process is called **radioactive decay**.

- Elements that decay are called radioactive elements. Potassium-40 is an example. Potassium-40 decays into argon-40.

- How fast an element decays is given by its half-life. The **half-life** is the time it takes for half of a sample of an element to decay. For example, the half-life of potassium-40 is 1.3 billion years.

Answer the following questions. Use your textbook and the ideas above.

1. Draw a line from each term to its meaning.

Term	Meaning
radioactive decay	**a.** pure substance
element	**b.** process in which an element breaks down
half-life	**c.** measure of how fast an element breaks down

2. Is the following sentence true or false? When an element decays, it changes into another element.

_____

A Trip Through Geologic Time

Determining Absolute Ages (pages 325–326)

Key Concept: **Geologists use radioactive dating to determine the absolute ages of rocks.**

- Scientists test rocks to measure how much radioactive decay has happened. The more decay that has happened, the older the rocks is.

- This method of dating rocks is called radioactive dating. Using this method, scientists can give rocks a rough age in years. When age is given in years, it is called absolute age.

- Suppose that half of the potassium-40 in a rock has decayed to argon-40. The half-life of potassium-40 is 1.3 billion years, so the rock is about 1.3 billion years old.

- Radioactive dating works well for igneous rocks. But this kind of dating does not work well for sedimentary rocks. This is because sedimentary rocks are made of rock particles of different ages.

Answer the following questions. Use your textbook and the ideas above.

3. The method of dating rocks that gives rock a rough

   age in years is called _____.

4. Circle the letter of each sentence that is true about radioactive dating.
   a. Radioactive dating is based on how much radioactive decay has happened.
   b. Radioactive dating gives rocks an absolute age.
   c. Radioactive dating works well for sedimentary rock.

A Trip Through Geologic Time

5. The half-life of carbon-14 is 5,730 years. If half of the carbon-14 in a sample has decayed, how old is the sample? Circle the letter of the correct answer.

   a. 2,865 years old

   b. 5,730 years old

   c. 11,460 years old

The Geologic Time Scale
(pages 327–329)

The Geologic Time Scale (pages 327–328)

Key Concept: Because the time span of Earth's past is so great, geologists use the geologic time scale to show Earth's history.

- Earth has a very long history. Years and centuries are not very helpful for such a long history. So scientists use the geologic time scale for Earth's history.

- The **geologic time scale** is a record of how Earth and its life forms have changed through time. For example, the scale shows when life first appeared on Earth.

- In the geologic time scale, time is divided into bigger blocks than years or centuries. The scale begins when Earth formed 4.6 billion years ago and goes to the present.

Answer the following questions. Use your textbook and the ideas above.

1. The record of how Earth and its life forms have

   changed through time is the _____.

2. When does the geologic time scale begin? Circle the letter of the correct answer.
   a. 4 billion years ago
   b. 4.6 billion years ago
   c. 544 million years ago

3. Is the following sentence true or false? The geologic time scale divides time into years and centuries.

   _____

A Trip Through Geologic Time

Divisions of Geologic Time (page 329)

Key Concept: **After Precambrian Time, the basic units of the geologic time scale are eras and periods.**

- The geologic time scale begins with a very long block of time called **Precambrian** (pree KAM bree un) **Time**. Precambrian Time goes from 4.6 billion to 544 million years ago. It covers most of Earth's history.

- The rest of the geologic time scale is divided into three major blocks of time called **eras**. The eras are the Paleozoic, Mesozoic, and Cenozoic eras.

- Each era is divided into shorter blocks of time called **periods**. For example, the Paleozoic Era is divided into six periods.

Answer the following questions. Use your textbook and the ideas above.

4. Fill in the blanks in the diagram of the geologic time scale.

Geologic Time Scale

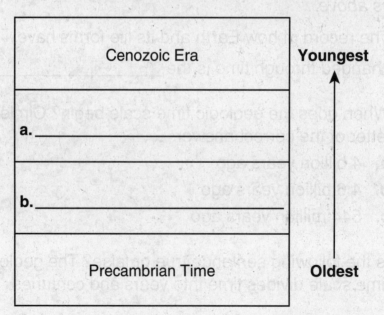

A Trip Through Geologic Time

5. Which part of the geologic time scale is the longest?
   Circle the letter of the correct answer.

   a. Precambrian Time

   b. Paleozoic Era

   c. Cenozoic Era

6. Is the following sentence true or false? Each era of the geologic time scale is part of a longer block of time called a period. _____

A Trip Through Geologic Time

Early Earth (pages 330–333)

The Planet Forms (pages 330–331)

Key Concept: **Scientists hypothesize that Earth formed at the same time as the other planets and the sun, roughly 4.6 billion years ago.**

- Rocks from the moon are known to be 4.6 billion years old. Scientists think that Earth and the moon are the same age. So Earth must also be 4.6 billion years old.

- Scientists think that Earth began as a ball of dust, rock, and ice in space. Gravity pulled these materials together, and Earth got bigger.

- As Earth got bigger, its gravity got stronger. Earth's gravity pulled more rocks toward Earth. The rocks hit Earth and gave the planet energy.

- Energy from the rocks made Earth so hot that it melted. But the surface layers later lost heat to space and got hard again.

Answer the following question. Use your textbook and the ideas above.

1. Fill in the blanks in the flowchart about how Earth formed.

How Earth Formed

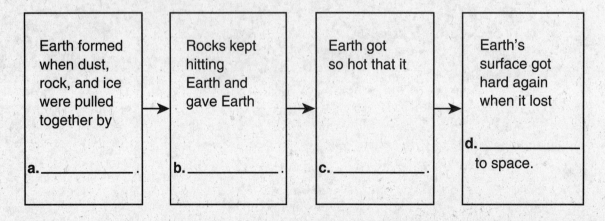

Earth formed when dust, rock, and ice were pulled together by

a. _____ .

Rocks kept hitting Earth and gave Earth

b. _____ .

Earth got so hot that it

c. _____ .

Earth's surface got hard again when it lost

d. _____

to space.

A Trip Through Geologic Time

Earth's Surface Forms (page 332)

Key Concept: **During the first several hundred million years of Precambrian Time, an atmosphere, oceans, and continents began to form.**

- Earth slowly developed an atmosphere. This early atmosphere was made up mostly of the gases carbon dioxide, nitrogen, and water vapor.

- At first, Earth's surface was too hot for liquid water. All the water was in the form of water vapor.

- As Earth's surface cooled, liquid water formed. The water fell as rain.

- Rain slowly wore away Earth's rocky surface. Rain also collected on the surface and formed oceans.

- Continents slowly formed on Earth's surface. The continents began to move over the surface. As the continents moved, new continents formed and old continents disappeared.

Answer the following questions. Use your textbook and the ideas above.

2. Earth's early atmosphere was made up mostly of

   carbon dioxide, nitrogen, and _____.

3. Why was there no liquid water on early Earth? Circle the letter of the correct answer.
   a. The surface was too hot for liquid water.
   b. The planet was too dry for water to form.
   c. Earth did not yet have an atmosphere.

4. Is the following sentence true or false? Once the continents formed, they never changed.

   _____

A Trip Through Geologic Time

Life Develops (page 333)

Key Concept: **Scientists have found fossils of single-celled organisms in rocks that formed about 3.5 billion years ago. These earliest life forms were probably similar to present-day bacteria.**

- The earliest forms of life on Earth lived in water. These early life forms were tiny and very simple. They slowly evolved into other forms of life.

- About 2.5 billion years ago, many organisms began using energy from the sun to make food. This way of making food is called photosynthesis.

- Oxygen is given off during photosynthesis. The oxygen collected in Earth's early atmosphere.

- Some of the oxygen turned to ozone. Ozone protects Earth's surface from the sun's rays. With ozone to protect them, organisms could live on land for the first time.

Answer the following questions. Use your textbook and the ideas above.

5. Is the following sentence true or false? There have been organisms living on land for 3.5 billion years.

   _____

6. How did photosynthesis change Earth? Circle the letter of the correct answer.
   a. Photosynthesis allowed organisms to live in the water.
   b. Photosynthesis added oxygen to Earth's early atmosphere.
   c. Photosynthesis destroyed ozone in Earth's atmosphere.

Eras of Earth's History (pages 334–345)

The Paleozoic Era (pages 335–341)

Key Concept: At the beginning of the Paleozoic Era, a great number of different kinds of organisms evolved.

- The Paleozoic (pay lee uh ZOH ik) Era is the first era after Precambrian Time. This era lasted from 544 million to 245 million years ago. The era has six periods.

- The Cambrian Period is the first period of the Paleozoic Era. In the Cambrian Period, shallow seas covered most of Earth. All organisms lived in water.

- During the Cambrian Period, there was an "explosion" of new life forms. For example, for the first time many organisms had parts such as shells.

- All animals in the Cambrian Period were invertebrates. An **invertebrate** does not have a backbone.

Answer the following question. Use your textbook and the ideas above.

1. Fill in the blanks in the concept map about life forms in the Cambrian Period.

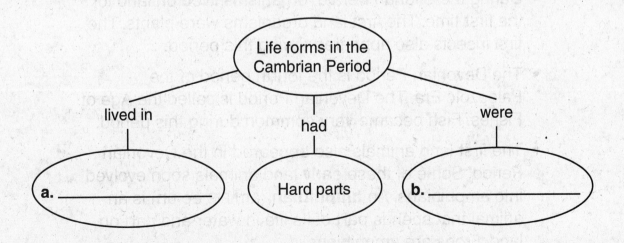

Key Concept: During the Ordovician Period, jawless fishes evolved. Jawless fishes were the first vertebrates.

- The Ordovician (awr duh VISH ee un) Period is the second period of the Paleozoic Era. In this period, shallow seas still covered most of Earth.

- During the Ordovician Period, the first vertebrates appeared. A **vertebrate** is an animal with a backbone. The earliest vertebrates were jawless fishes.

Answer the following questions. Use your textbook and the ideas above.

2. A major new kind of life that appeared during the Ordovician Period was _____.

3. Is the following sentence true or false? The earliest vertebrates were insects. _____

Key Concept: During the Silurian Period, plants started living on land. During the Devonian Period, animals began to invade the land.

- The Silurian (sih LOOR ee un) Period is the third period of the Paleozoic Era.

- During the Silurian Period, organisms lived on land for the first time. The first land organisms were plants. The first insects also appeared during this period.

- The Devonian Period is the fourth period of the Paleozoic Era. The Devonian Period is called the Age of Fishes. Fish became very common during this period.

- The first land animals also appeared in the Devonian Period. Some of these early land animals soon evolved into amphibians. An **amphibian** (am FIB ee un) is an animal that spends part of its life in water and part on land. Frogs are amphibians.

Name _____ Date _____ Class _____

A Trip Through Geologic Time

Answer the following question. Use your textbook and the ideas on page 162.

4. Fill in the blanks in the table about events in the middle Paleozoic Era.

Events in the Middle Paleozoic Era	
Period	**Event**
a. _____	first land plants appeared
b. _____	first land animals appeared

Key Concept: During the rest of the Paleozoic Era, life expanded over Earth's continents.

- The Carboniferous Period is the fifth period of the Paleozoic Era. During this period, the climate was warm and wet. There were huge, swampy forests.

- The first reptiles appeared during the Carboniferous Period. **Reptiles** have scaly skin and lay eggs with tough, leathery shells. Lizards are reptiles.

- The first insects with wings also appeared during the Carboniferous Period.

Answer the following questions. Use your textbook and the ideas above.

5. Is the following sentence true or false? Climates were cold and dry during the Carboniferous Period.

   _____

6. Which kinds of life appeared for the first time during the Carboniferous Period? Circle the letter of each correct choice.

   a. insects with wings   **b.** amphibians   **c.** reptiles

Name _____ Date _____ Class _____

A Trip Through Geologic Time

Key Concept: During the Permian Period, about 260 million years ago, many organisms went extinct. This mass extinction affected both plants and animals, on land and in the seas. During the Permian Period, Earth's continents moved together to form a great landmass, or supercontinent, called Pangaea.

- The last period of the Paleozoic Era is the Permian Period. Reptiles were the main land animals in this period.

- During the Permian Period, many kinds of organisms died out. When many kinds of organisms die out at the same time, it is called a **mass extinction**.

- Scientists are not sure what caused this mass extinction. But a change in climate was probably one cause.

- During the Permian Period, all of the continents moved together, so there was just one huge continent. Scientists call this huge continent Pangaea (pan JEE uh).

- As Pangaea formed, there were major changes in climate. Areas that had been warm and wet became cold and dry. Many organisms could not live in the new climate. These organisms went extinct.

Answer the following questions. Use your textbook and the ideas above.

7. What do scientists think caused the mass extinction in the Permian Period? Circle the letter of the correct answer.

    a. Many organisms could not live in the new climate.

    b. Humans appeared and killed many animals.

    c. The land was becoming too crowded.

A Trip Through Geologic Time

8. Read the words in the box. In each sentence below, fill in one of the words. The sentences are about the map. The map shows what scientists think Earth looked like 260 million years ago.

Permian	climate	extinction	Pangaea

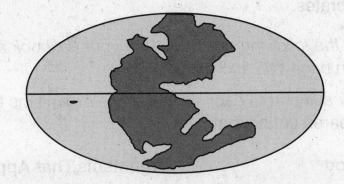

a. The name of the single, huge continent shown on the map is _____.

b. This huge continent formed during the _____ Period.

c. As this continent formed, there were major changes in _____.

Mesozoic Era (pages 342–343)

Key Concept: **Reptiles were so successful during the Mesozoic Era that this time is often called the Age of Reptiles.**

- The Mesozoic (mez uh ZOH ik) Era is the second era of the geologic time scale. This era lasted from 245 million to 66 million years ago. The era has three periods.

- The first period of the Mesozoic Era is the Triassic (try AS ik) Period. During this period, the first dinosaurs and mammals appeared. Dinosaurs were reptiles. **Mammals** are warm-blooded vertebrates that feed their young milk.

A Trip Through Geologic Time

- The second period of the Mesozoic Era is the Jurassic (joo RAS ik) Period. During this period, dinosaurs became the main kind of land animals. The first birds also appeared in this period.

- The third period of the Mesozoic Era is the Cretaceous (krih TAY shus) Period. During this period, plants with flowers appeared. Reptiles were still the main vertebrates.

Answer the following question. Use your textbook and the ideas on page 165 and above.

9. Draw a line from each period to the organisms that appeared during that period.

Period	**Organisms That Appeared**
Triassic Period	**a.** plants with flowers
Jurassic Period	**b.** birds
Cretaceous Period	**c.** dinosaurs and mammals

Key Concept: **At the close of the Cretaceous Period, about 65 million years ago, another mass extinction occurred. Scientists hypothesize that this mass extinction occurred when an object from space struck Earth.**

- A second mass extinction happened at the end of the Mesozoic Era. Most scientists think that this mass extinction was caused by a chunk of space rock, called an asteroid.

- Scientists think the asteroid crashed into Earth. The crash caused dust and clouds that blocked out sunlight for years. Without sunlight, many organisms died out, including all of the dinosaurs.

- Some scientists think that an asteroid crash was not the only cause of this mass extinction. They think that ashes from many volcanoes were another cause.

A Trip Through Geologic Time

Answer the following question. Use your textbook and the ideas on page 166.

10. Circle the letter of each sentence that is true about the mass extinction at the end of the Mesozoic Era.

    a. Most scientists think that an asteroid caused it.

    b. Organisms went extinct because of floods.

    c. Mammals went extinct then.

The Cenozoic Era (pages 344–345)

Key Concept: **The extinction of dinosaurs created an opportunity for mammals. During the Cenozoic Era, mammals evolved to live in many different environments—on land, in water, and even in the air.**

- The Cenozoic (sen uh ZOH ik) Era is the third era of the geologic time scale. This era began 66 million years ago and goes to the present. The era is often called the Age of Mammals. The era has two periods.

- The first period of the Cenozoic Era is the Tertiary Period. This period lasted until 1.8 million years ago.

- During the Tertiary Period, climates were mild. Many new kinds of mammals appeared. Some were very large.

Answer the following questions. Use your textbook and the ideas above.

11. The third era of the geologic time scale is the

_____.

12. Why were so many mammals able to evolve in the Cenozoic Era? Circle the letter of the correct answer.

    a. Dinosaurs showed mammals how to survive.

    b. Dinosaurs had gone extinct.

    c. Mammals hunted dinosaurs for food.

A Trip Through Geologic Time

Key Concept: Earth's climate cooled, causing a series of ice ages during the Quaternary Period.

- The second period of the Cenozoic Era is the Quaternary Period. This period began 1.8 million years ago. We are still in the Quaternary Period.

- During this period, the climate got colder. At times, glaciers covered much of the land. These times are called ice ages.

- Mammals, flowering plants, and insects were the main life forms in the Quaternary Period.

- Modern humans appeared late in the Quaternary Period, around 100,000 years ago.

Answer the following questions. Use your textbook and the ideas above.

13. Which period of the Cenozoic Era are we still in?

    a. Tertiary Period

    b. Quaternary Period

    c. Modern Period

14. Fill in the blanks in the concept map about the main life forms in the Quaternary Period.

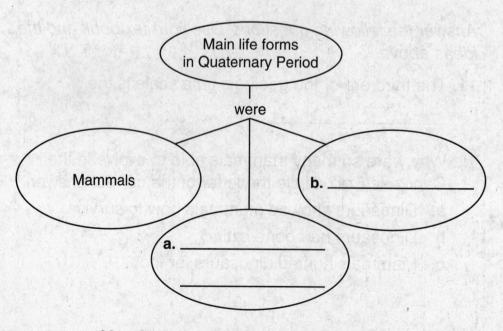

Fossil Fuels (pages 354–360)

Energy Transformation and Fuels
(pages 354–355)

Key Concept: When fuels are burned, the chemical energy that is released can be used to generate another form of energy, such as heat, light, motion, or electricity.

- A **fuel** is a substance that provides energy as a result of a chemical change. A fuel might provide energy in the form of heat, light, motion, or electricity.

- An **energy transformation** is a change from one form of energy to another. An energy transformation is also called an energy conversion. Changing chemical energy into heat is an example of an energy transformation.

- Fuels contain stored energy. The stored energy in fuels can be released by combustion. **Combustion** is the burning of a substance. The release of energy from fuels is used to make other forms of energy.

- When gasoline burns in a car engine, some of the chemical energy in the gasoline is converted into heat. The heat is converted into mechanical energy. The mechanical energy moves the car.

- Burning fuel in an electric power plant produces heat. The heat is used to boil water to make steam. The steam turns a turbine. The turbine turns magnets inside a generator. The turning magnets produce an electric current. Each of the steps in this process involves an energy transformation.

Name _____ Date _____ Class _____

Energy Resources

Answer the following questions. Use your textbook and the ideas on page 169.

1. Read each word in the box. In each sentence below, fill in the correct word or words.

energy transformation combustion electricity fuel

a. The burning of a substance is called

_____.

b. A change from one form of energy to another is

called a(an) _____.

c. A substance that provides energy as a result of a

chemical change is a(an) _____.

2. Read each word in the box. Then use the words to complete the flowchart about energy transformations in a car engine.

chemical   car   mechanical   gasoline   heat

a. _____ burns in a car engine.

↓

b. Chemical energy in the gasoline is changed into

_____.

↓

c. Heat is then changed into _____ energy.

↓

d. Mechanical energy moves the _____.

Energy Resources

What Are Fossil Fuels? (pages 356–359)

Key Concept: The three major fossil fuels are coal, oil, and natural gas.

- **Fossil fuels** are formed from the remains of organisms. Fossil fuels such as coal, oil, and natural gas are rich in energy.

- Fossil fuels are made of hydrocarbons. **Hydrocarbons** are chemicals that contain carbon and hydrogen atoms.

- Coal is a solid fossil fuel. Coal is formed from plant remains that have been buried for millions of years. Coal is the fuel used in many electrical power plants.

- Oil is a thick, black, liquid fossil fuel. Oil forms from the remains of ocean organisms. When oil is pumped from the ground, it is called crude oil. **Petroleum** is another name for oil. **Petrochemicals** are chemical compounds made from oil.

- Natural gas is a mixture of gases, including a gas called methane. Natural gas forms from the remains of ocean organisms.

Answer the following questions. Use your textbook and the ideas above.

3. Draw a line from each term to its meaning.

Term	Meaning
fossil fuels	**a.** another name for oil
hydrocarbons	**b.** fuel substances formed from the remains of organisms
petroleum	**c.** chemical compounds made from oil
petrochemicals	**d.** chemicals that contain carbon and hydrogen atoms

Energy Resources

4. Circle the letter of each substance that is a fossil fuel.
   a. hydrogen
   b. natural gas
   c. coal

Fuel Supply and Demand (page 360)

Key Concept: **Since fossil fuels take hundreds of years to form, they are considered nonrenewable resources.**

- Fossil fuels are nonrenewable resources. They are nonrenewable because they take so long to form.

- Earth's oil took 500 million years to form. People have already used one fourth of this oil.

- The United States uses about one third of all oil produced in the world.

- The United States has only 3 percent of Earth's oil supply. As a result, the United States has to buy oil from other countries.

Answer the following questions. Use your textbook and the ideas above.

5. Is the following sentence true or false? Fossil fuels are renewable resources. _____

6. Circle the letter of the reason why the United States needs to buy oil from other countries.
   a. The United States has most of Earth's oil supply.
   b. The United States does not use much of Earth's oil supply.
   c. The United States has only 3 percent of Earth's oil supply.

Renewable Sources of Energy

(pages 361–367)

Harnessing the Sun's Energy (pages 362–363)

Key Concept: The sun constantly gives off energy in the forms of light and heat.

- Energy from the sun is called **solar energy**.

- Solar energy does not cause pollution. It will not run out for billions of years. But solar energy is available only when the sun is shining.

- In a solar energy plant, rows of mirrors focus sunlight on a tank of water. The heat in solar energy boils the water. The boiling water is used to make electricity.

- A solar cell can change solar energy into electricity.

- Passive solar heating happens when sunlight simply heats a material. For example, a parked car heats up on a sunny day because of passive solar heating.

- Active solar heating includes using pumps and fans to move the sun's heat around a building.

Answer the following questions. Use your textbook and the ideas above.

1. Circle the letter of what energy from the sun is called.
   a. solar plants
   b. solar energy
   c. solar cells

2. A solar cell can change solar energy into

   _____.

Energy Resources

Hydroelectric Power (page 364)

Key Concept: **Water is a renewable source of energy.**

- Flowing water provides a source of energy.

- Electricity produced by flowing water is called **hydroelectric power**.

- To produce hydroelectric power, river water is sent through tunnels at the bottom of a dam. The flowing water turns turbines. The turbines are connected to generators. The generators produce electricity.

- Hydroelectric power is the most widely used source of renewable energy.

Answer the following questions. Use your textbook and the ideas above.

3. Electricity produced by flowing water is called

   _____ power.

4. Read the words in the box. Then use the words to complete the flowchart about making hydroelectric power.

turbines   water   electricity   generators

a. River _____ is sent through tunnels at the bottom of a dam.

↓

b. The flowing water turns _____ .

↓

c. The turbines are connected to _____ .

↓

d. The generators produce _____ .

Energy Resources

Capturing the Wind (pages 364–365)

***Key Concept:* Wind is a renewable source of energy.**

- Wind is air moving from one place to another.

- Wind energy is caused by solar energy. The sun heats Earth's surface unevenly. This uneven heating causes different areas of the atmosphere to have different temperatures. Different temperatures in different areas cause winds.

- On a wind farm, wind turns many windmills. Together, the windmills produce large amounts of electric power.

- Wind is the fastest-growing energy source in the world. An advantage of wind is that wind energy does not cause pollution. But few places have winds that blow enough to provide the energy a place needs.

Answer the following questions. Use your textbook and the ideas above.

5. Is the following sentence true or false? Wind energy is caused by solar energy. _____

6. Circle the letter of an advantage of using wind energy to produce power.
   a. Wind energy does not cause pollution.
   b. Most places have enough winds to provide all needed energy.
   c. Wind energy is a nonrenewable source of energy.

Biomass Fuels (page 365)

***Key Concept:* Biomass fuels are a renewable source of energy.**

- Fuels made from living things are called **biomass fuels**. Biomass fuels include wood, leaves, food wastes, and animal wastes.

- Biomass fuels can be burned for heat. For example, a wood stove burns wood for heat.

- Biomass materials can be made into other fuels. For example, alcohol can be made from corn, sugar cane, or other crops. The alcohol can be added to gasoline. The mixture of alcohol and gasoline is called **gasohol**.

- Bacteria produce methane gas when they decompose waste in landfills. The methane gas is used as fuel.

Answer the following questions. Use your textbook and the ideas above.

7. Read each word in the box. In each sentence below, fill in the correct word or words.

┌───┐
│   methane gas   biomass fuels   gasohol   │
└───┘

   a. The mixture of alcohol and gasoline is called

      _____.

   b. Fuels made from living things are called

      _____.

8. Circle the letter of each example of a biomass fuel.

   a. wood

   b. animal wastes

   c. coal

Energy Resources

Tapping Earth's Energy (page 366)

Key Concept: **Geothermal energy is a renewable source of energy.**

- Heat from Earth's interior is called **geothermal energy**.

- Liquid rock beneath Earth's surface is called magma. In some places, magma is close to Earth's surface. The magma heats underground water. The heated underground water can be used to produce electricity in a power plant. This is a use of geothermal energy.

- Iceland and New Zealand are places where magma is close to the Earth's surface. In Iceland, geothermal energy heats most homes.

- In most places, deep wells need to be drilled to get to geothermal energy.

Answer the following questions. Use your textbook and the ideas above.

9. Heat from inside Earth is called

_____ energy.

10. Circle the letter of the reason why geothermal energy can be used so much in Iceland.

 a. Deep wells have been drilled in Iceland.

 b. Magma is close to Earth's surface in Iceland.

 c. Iceland has no underground water.

Name _____ Date _____ Class _____

The Promise of Hydrogen Power (page 367)

Key Concept: **Hydrogen is a renewable source of energy.**

- Hydrogen gas can be used as a fuel. There are two main advantages of using hydrogen gas as a fuel: hydrogen gas burns cleanly, and burning hydrogen gas causes no pollution.

- Most hydrogen on Earth is combined with oxygen in water. Making pure hydrogen takes more energy than burning the hydrogen would produce.

- Scientists think that hydrogen may be an important fuel in the future. Hydrogen may be used to produce electricity. Hydrogen also may be used to fuel cars.

Answer the following questions. Use your textbook and the ideas above.

11. Circle the letter of each advantage of using hydrogen gas as a fuel.

   a. Hydrogen gas burns easily.

   b. Making pure hydrogen takes very little energy.

   c. Burning hydrogen gas causes no pollution.

12. Is the following sentence true or false? In the future, hydrogen may be an important fuel. _____

Energy Resources

Nuclear Energy (pages 370–374)

Nuclear Fission (pages 370–371)

Key Concept: When a neutron hits a U-235 nucleus, the nucleus splits apart into two smaller nuclei and two or more neutrons.

- The center part of an atom is called the **nucleus** (plural *nuclei*). The nucleus contains protons and neutrons.

- Reactions that involve the nuclei of atoms are called nuclear reactions. There are two types of nuclear reactions: nuclear fission and nuclear fusion.

- **Nuclear fission** is the splitting of an atom's nucleus. The nucleus is split into two smaller nuclei. The fuel for nuclear fission is a large atom with a nucleus that is not stable. An atom of uranium-235 (U-235) is such a fuel.

- In nuclear fission, a neutron is shot at high speed at a U-235 atom. The U-235 nucleus splits apart. The result is two smaller nuclei and two or more neutrons. Also, some of the mass of the U-235 nucleus is changed into energy.

- The release of energy during nuclear fission could cause a huge explosion. If the release of energy is controlled, though, the energy can be used to make electricity.

Answer the following questions. Use your textbook and the ideas above.

1. Circle the letter of the sentence that describes nuclear fission.
   a. It is the splitting of an atom's nucleus.
   b. It is the combining of two or more nuclei.
   c. It is the splitting of one atom from another.

Energy Resources

2. Complete the concept map about the major types of nuclear reactions.

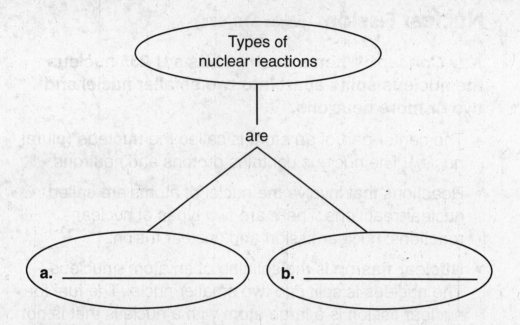

3. Is the following sentence true or false? Nuclear fission can be used to make electricity. _____

Nuclear Power Plants (pages 372–373)

Key Concept: **In a nuclear power plant, the heat released from fission reactions is used to change water into steam. The steam then turns the blades of a turbine to generate electricity.**

*   Controlled nuclear fission reactions take place in nuclear power plants.

*   Nuclear fission occurs in the part of the nuclear power plant called the **reactor vessel**.

*   A liquid is pumped through the reactor vessel. This liquid picks up heat from the nuclear reaction. The liquid is then used to boil water to make steam. The steam runs a generator that makes electricity.

Energy Resources

- A reactor vessel contains U-235 in **fuel rods**. If the fuel rods get too hot, there is danger of a meltdown. A **meltdown** is a dangerous condition in which fuel rods melt. A meltdown can cause explosions that can kill people.

- A disadvantage of nuclear power is that the waste materials from nuclear fission are dangerous to people for many thousands of years.

Answer the following questions. Use your textbook and the ideas on page 180 and above.

4. Draw a line from each term to its meaning.

Term	Meaning
reactor vessel	**a.** U-235 in the form of rods
fuel rods	**b.** the part of the nuclear power plant where fission occurs
meltdown	**c.** a dangerous condition in which fuel rods melt

5. Circle the letter of a disadvantage of using nuclear power.

   a. The steam produced by nuclear fission cannot run generators.

   b. The electricity produced in a nuclear power plant cannot leave the power plant.

   c. The waste materials from nuclear fission are dangerous for many thousands of years.

Name _____ Date _____ Class _____

The Quest to Control Fusion (page 374)

Key Concept: In nuclear fusion, two hydrogen nuclei combine to create a helium nucleus, which has slightly less mass than the two hydrogen nuclei. The lost mass is converted to energy.

- A second type of nuclear reaction is called nuclear fusion. **Nuclear fusion** is when two nuclei are combined to produce a single larger nucleus.

- In nuclear fusion, two hydrogen nuclei are combined. One result is a helium nucleus. In the nuclear fusion reaction, some mass is changed into energy.

- A nuclear fusion reaction produces more energy than a nuclear fission reaction.

- Constructing a reactor where nuclear fusion could take place is not possible at this time. The reaction requires too much pressure and too high of a temperature.

Answer the following questions. Use your textbook and the ideas above.

6. Circle the letter of the sentence that describes nuclear fusion
   a. It is the splitting of an atom's nucleus.
   b. It is the combining of two atomic nuclei.
   c. It is the splitting of one atom from another.

7. Is the following sentence true or false? Constructing a reactor where nuclear fusion could take place is very easy to do. _____

Energy Conservation (pages 375–378)

Energy Efficiency (pages 376–377)

Key Concept: **One way to preserve our current energy resources is to increase the efficiency of our energy use.**

- Fossil fuels may someday be used up. Most people think that it makes sense to use fuels wisely now.

- **Efficiency** is how much energy is used to perform work compared to how much energy is lost in the process. When an energy resource is used, some energy is lost to the surroundings. This energy is usually lost as heat.

- Insulation is one way to increase the efficiency of heating and cooling systems. For example, insulation can increase the efficiency of a home furnace. **Insulation** is a layer of a material that prevents the loss of heat from inside a building. Insulation prevents loss of heat by trapping air.

- Fluorescent light bulbs are more efficient than common light bulbs, which are called incandescent light bulbs.

Answer the following questions. Use your textbook and the ideas above.

1. A layer of a material that prevents the loss of heat from inside a building is called _____.

2. How much energy is used to perform work compared to how much energy is lost in the process is called

   _____.

3. Is the following sentence true or false? Some energy is lost to the surroundings when an energy resource is used. _____

Name _____ Date _____ Class _____

Energy Resources

4. Circle the letter of each sentence that is true about insulation.

    a. Insulation decreases the efficiency of heating and cooling systems.

    b. Insulation prevents loss of heat from a building by trapping air.

    c. Insulation can increase the efficiency of a home furnace.

Energy Conservation (page 378)

Key Concept: **Another way to preserve our current energy resources is to conserve energy whenever possible.**

- **Energy conservation** means to reduce the amount of energy used.

- You can reduce your energy use by changing your habits. For example, you can walk or ride a bike to a store rather than riding in a car.

Answer the following questions. Use your textbook and the ideas above.

5. Energy _____ means to reduce the amount of energy used.

6. Circle the letter of each way you could reduce your energy use.

    a. walking to the store

    b. riding in a car to the store

    c. riding a bike to the store.

Name _____ Date _____ Class _____

Fresh Water

Water on Earth (pages 392–395)

The Water Cycle (pages 392–393)

Key Concept: In the water cycle, water moves from
bodies of water, land, and living things on Earth's
surface to the atmosphere and back to Earth's
surface.

- The **water cycle** is how water moves from Earth's
  surface to the atmosphere and back again. The water
  cycle never stops. It has no beginning or end.

- The sun is the source of energy for the water cycle.

- Water evaporates from Earth's surface. Water is always
  evaporating from oceans and lakes. Water is given off by
  plants as water vapor.

- When water vapor in the air cools, it condenses. The
  result of this condensation is clouds.

- From clouds, water falls back to Earth as precipitation.
  Precipitation is water that falls to Earth as rain, snow,
  hail, or sleet.

- If the precipitation falls on land, it may soak into the soil.
  Or, it may run off into rivers and lakes.

*Answer the following questions. Use your textbook and the
ideas above.*

1. The process by which water moves from Earth's
   surface to the atmosphere and back again is the

   _____.

2. Water that falls to Earth as rain, snow, hail, or

   sleet is called _____.

Fresh Water

3. Circle the letter of each sentence that is true about the water cycle.

    a. The water cycle begins with the formation of clouds.

    b. When water condenses in the air, it forms clouds.

    c. The sun is the energy source for the water cycle.

Distribution of Earth's Water (pages 394–395)

Key Concept: **Most of Earth's water—roughly 97 percent—is salt water found in oceans. Only 3 percent is fresh water.**

- Earth's oceans include the Atlantic Ocean, the Pacific Ocean, and the Indian Ocean. Together, the oceans cover a larger area than all the land on Earth combined.

- Oceans hold most of Earth's water. The water in oceans is salt water.

- About three quarters of Earth's fresh water is in huge ice masses near the North and South poles. There are also floating chunks of ice called icebergs.

- Rivers and lakes also contain fresh water.

- About a quarter of Earth's fresh water is groundwater. **Groundwater** fills the cracks and spaces in underground soil and rock.

Answer the following questions. Use your textbook and the ideas above.

4. Circle the letter of each sentence that is true about the distribution of Earth's water.

    a. About a quarter of Earth's fresh water is groundwater.

    b. Rivers and lakes contain salt water.

    c. The oceans cover a larger area than all the land on Earth combined.

Name _____ Date _____ Class _____

Fresh Water

5. The circle graph below shows the distribution of Earth's water. Circle the letter of the part of Earth's water that is only 3 percent of all Earth's water.

   a. salt water

   b. fresh water

   c. groundwater

Distribution of Water on Earth

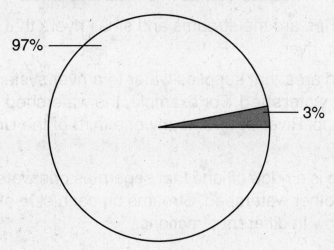

97% ————

———— 3%

6. The water that fills the cracks and spaces in underground soil and rock is called

   _____.

Surface Water (pages 396–403)

River Systems (pages 396–397)

Key Concept: **A river and all its tributaries together make up a river system.**

- Fresh water on Earth may be moving, as in streams and rivers. Or, it may be still, as in ponds and lakes.

- **Tributaries** are the streams and small rivers that flow into a big river.

- The land area that supplies water to a river system is called a **watershed**. For example, the watershed of the Mississippi River covers nearly one third of the United States.

- A **divide** is a ridge of land that separates one watershed from another watershed. Streams on each side of a divide flow in different directions.

Answer the following questions. Use your textbook and the ideas above.

1. A river and all its tributaries together make up a(an)

   _____.

2. Draw a line from each term to its meaning.

Term	Meaning
tributary	a. the land area that supplies water to a river system
watershed	b. a ridge of land that separates one watershed from another
divide	c. a stream or small river that flows into a big river

Name _____ Date _____ Class _____

Fresh Water

3. The map above shows part of a river system. Circle the letter of each river that is a tributary.

   a. Missouri River

   b. Mississippi River

   c. Ohio River

Ponds (pages 398–399)

Key Concept: **Ponds are smaller and shallower than lakes. Sunlight usually reaches to the bottom of all parts of a pond.**

- Ponds are bodies of fresh water. They contain still water, which is also called standing water.

- Ponds form when water collects in hollows and low-lying areas of land. Some ponds dry up in the summer.

- Ponds get their water from rain, from melting snow, and from runoff. Some ponds get their water from rivers or from groundwater.

- Many different kinds of organisms live in ponds. Plants grow throughout a pond.

Fresh Water

Answer the following question. Use your textbook and the ideas on page 189.

4. Circle the letter of each sentence that is true about ponds.

    a. Ponds are bodies of fresh water.

    b. Ponds contain running water.

    c. Plants grow throughout a pond.

Lakes (page 400)

Key Concept: **Lakes are generally deeper and bigger than ponds. In addition, sunlight does not reach the bottom in a deep lake, as it does in a pond.**

- No plants and few other living things can live at the bottom of a lake. The bottom of a lake may be made up of sand, pebbles, or rock.

- Lakes may form when water collects in low areas of land. Some lakes form in other ways. For example, the Great Lakes formed when huge glaciers made hollow places in the land and then melted.

- People can make a lake by building a dam across a river. A **reservoir** is a lake that stores water for human use.

Answer the following questions. Use your textbook and the ideas above.

5. Circle the letter of each sentence that is true about lakes.

    a. People can make a lake by building a dam across a river.

    b. Lakes are generally deeper and bigger than ponds.

    c. All lakes form when water collects in low areas of land.

6. A lake that stores water for human use is a(an)

_____.

Fresh Water

Wetlands (pages 401–403)

Key Concept: **The three common types of freshwater wetlands are marshes, swamps, and bogs.**

- A **wetland** is a land area that is covered with water during at least part of the year.

- Marshes are grassy areas covered by shallow water or a stream.

- Swamps have trees and shrubs growing in the water. Swamps are common in warm, wet climates.

- Bogs have acidic water. Bogs are common in cooler areas.

- The Everglades is a large wetland in southern Florida. In the Everglades, a wide, shallow stream of water flows over the land.

- The Everglades is home to many kinds of wildlife, including many rare or endangered animals.

- Human activities have been bad for the Everglades. For example, farming has added harmful chemicals to the water. Scientists are trying to preserve the Everglades and its wildlife.

Answer the following questions. Use your textbook and the ideas above.

7. A land area that is covered with shallow water during at least part of the year is a(an) _____.

8. Circle the letter of each sentence that is true about wetlands.
   a. Bogs are common in warmer areas.
   b. There is only one common type of freshwater wetland.
   c. Some wetlands are covered with water all year round.

Fresh Water

9. The picture above shows one type of wetland. Circle the letter of the type of wetland shown in the picture.

    a. marsh

    b. swamp

    c. bog

10. Is the following sentence true or false? Many rare or endangered animals live in the Everglades.

_____

Key Concept: **Because of their sheltered waters and rich supply of nutrients, wetlands provide habitats for many living things. Wetlands act as natural water filters. They also help control floods by absorbing extra runoff from heavy rains.**

• Many organisms live in wetlands. The water in wetlands is shallow. The water also contains natural fertilizers from plants and animals.

Fresh Water

- Water moves slowly through a wetland, so waste materials settle to the ground. Other waste materials are taken in by plants. In these ways, wetlands filter water.

- Wetlands act like giant sponges. Wetlands store rainwater until it slowly evaporates or drains away. In this way, wetlands help control floods.

Answer the following questions. Use your textbook and the ideas on page 192 and above.

11. Circle the letter of each sentence that is true about wetlands.

    a. Wetlands act like natural water filters.

    b. Wetlands act like giant sponges.

    c. Wetlands provide homes for many living things.

12. Is the following sentence true or false? Wetlands help control floods by storing rainwater. _____

Fresh Water

Water Underground (pages 404–409)

How Water Moves Underground
(pages 404–405)

Key Concept: **Water underground trickles down between particles of soil and through cracks and spaces in layers of rock.**

- Rock and soil have spaces between their particles. The spaces between particles of rock or soil are called pores.

- When the pores of a material are connected, water can pass through easily. A material that water can pass easily through is called a **permeable** material. Sand and gravel are permeable materials.

- Some materials have few or no pores or cracks. A material that water cannot pass through easily is called an **impermeable** material. Clay and granite are impermeable materials.

- When water reaches an impermeable layer underground, the water is trapped. The water then fills up permeable rock or soil above. An area of permeable rock or soil that is totally filled with water is called the **saturated zone**. The top of the saturated zone is called the **water table**.

- Soil and rocks above the water table also contain water. The layer of rocks and soil above the water table is called the **unsaturated zone**.

Answer the following questions. Use your textbook and the ideas above.

1. Is the following sentence true or false? When the pores of a material are connected, water can pass through easily. _____

2. Draw a line from each term to its meaning.

Term	Meaning
permeable material	**a.** the top of the saturated zone
	b. the layer of rocks and soil above the water table
impermeable material	**c.** a material that water can pass through easily
water table	**d.** an area of permeable rock or soil that is totally filled with water
saturated zone	
unsaturated zone	**e.** a material that water cannot pass through easily

3. The picture below shows the different materials that form layers underground. Circle the letter that points to the water table.

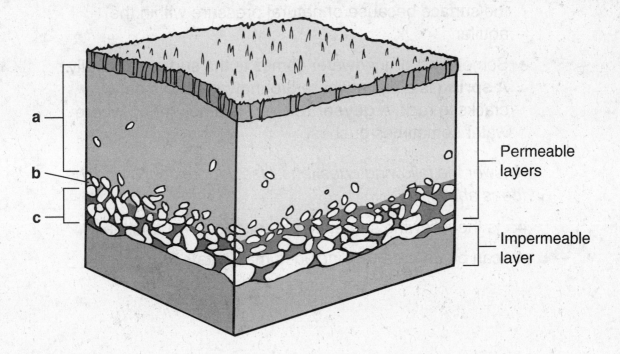

a

b

c

Permeable layers

Impermeable layer

Fresh Water

Bringing Up Groundwater (pages 406–409)

Key Concept: **People can obtain groundwater from an aquifer by drilling a well below the water table.**

- The water table in an area might be a few meters underground. In other areas it might be deep underground.

- An **aquifer** is an underground layer of rock or pieces of rock that holds water. An aquifer can be a small underground area, or it can be an area that includes many states.

- Since ancient times, people have brought groundwater to the surface by digging a well. A well must reach into the saturated zone.

- Most wells are dug with well-digging equipment. Pumps bring the groundwater to the surface.

- Sometimes, water underground is under great pressure. An **artesian** (ahr TEEZH un) **well** is where water rises to the surface because of natural pressure within the aquifer.

- Sometimes, groundwater comes to the surface naturally. A **spring** is a place where groundwater flows out of cracks in rock. A **geyser** (GY zur) is a hot spring where water sometimes gushes.

Answer the following questions. Use your textbook and the ideas above.

4. Is the following sentence true or false? An aquifer

   can be an area that includes many states. _____

Fresh Water

5. Read each word in the box. In each sentence below, fill in the correct word or words.

artesian well	wetland	aquifer

a. An underground layer of rock or pieces of rock that holds water is a(an) _____.

b. A well in which water rises to the surface because of natural pressure within the aquifer is a(an) _____.

6. Circle the letter of each sentence that is true about bringing up groundwater.

a. Most wells are dug with well-digging equipment.

b. A spring is a place where groundwater flows out of cracks in rock.

c. For a well to work, the bottom of the well must reach into the unsaturated zone.

Using Freshwater Resources (pages 412–419)

How People Use Water (pages 413–415)

Key Concept: **People use water for household purposes, industry, transportation, agriculture, and recreation.**

- People need water in homes for many uses.

- Many industries use water to cool hot machinery. Power plants and steel mills also use water for cooling.

- Since ancient times, people have used boats on water to carry people and products.

- Farmers need water to grow crops. **Irrigation** is when water is supplied to areas of land so crops can be grown.

- People use water to have fun, such as for boating and swimming.

Answer the following questions. Use your textbook and the ideas above.

1. The process of supplying water to areas of land so

   crops can be grown is called _____.

2. Circle the letter of each sentence that is true about how people use water.

   a. People use boats on water to carry people and products.

   b. People who farm have no special need for water.

   c. People need water in homes for many uses.

Fresh Water

3. Complete the concept map about how people use water.

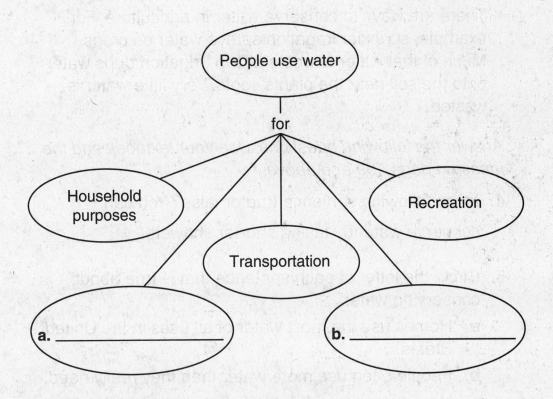

Conserving Water (pages 416–417)

Key Concept: **Reducing water use, recycling water, and reusing water are three ways to conserve water.**

- People often use more water than they really need. You can conserve water at home by doing simple things, such as taking shorter showers.

- New water-saving methods help industries save money and obey environmental laws.

- Some industries conserve water by building cooling pools. That way, the water in the pool can be used over and over.

Fresh Water

- Agriculture, or farming, uses the most water of all uses in the United States.

- There are ways to conserve water in agriculture. For example, sprinkler irrigation sprays water on crops. Much of that water is wasted. Drip irrigation drips water onto the soil near the plants' roots. Very little water is wasted.

Answer the following questions. Use your textbook and the ideas on page 199 and above.

4. Is the following sentence true or false? You can

   conserve water by taking shorter showers. _____

5. Circle the letter of each sentence that is true about conserving water.

   a. Homes use the most water of all uses in the United States.

   b. People often use more water than they really need.

   c. New water-saving methods help industries save money.

6. Is the following sentence true or false? Drip irrigation wastes more water than sprinkler irrigation.

   _____

What Is Pollution? (pages 418–419)

Key Concept: **Scientists classify sources of pollution, in part, by how they enter a body of water.**

- **Water pollution** is adding any substance to water that has a bad effect on the water or the living things that use the water. The substances that cause water pollution are called **pollutants**.

Fresh Water

- A **point source** is a specific source of pollution that can be identified. For example, a pipe pouring polluted water into a river is a point source.

- A widely spread source of pollution is called a **nonpoint source**. For example, pollutants in runoff from a farm field make up a nonpoint source.

- There are many ways to reduce water pollution. For example, never pour paint or motor oil down the drain.

Answer the following questions. Use your textbook and the ideas on page 200 and above.

7. Circle the letter of each sentence that is true about pollution.
   a. Sources of pollution are classified by how they enter a body of water.
   b. Only farms and factories cause water pollution.
   c. A pipe pouring bad water into a river is a nonpoint source.

8. Draw a line from each term to its meaning.

Term	Meaning
water pollution	a. a widely spread source of pollution
pollutant	b. a specific source of pollution that can be identified
point source	c. adding any substance to water that has a bad effect on the water or the living things that use the water
nonpoint source	d. a substance that causes water pollution

Fresh Water

Water to Drink (pages 420–423)

Water Quality (pages 420–421)

Key Concept: **Certain substances, such as iron, can affect the taste or color of water but are harmless unless present at very high levels. Other substances, such as certain chemicals and microorganisms, can be harmful to your health.**

- **Water quality** is a measure of the substances in water other than the water molecules.

- The government sets concentration limits for some substances. A **concentration** is how much there is of one substance in a certain volume of another substance. Concentrations are often measured in parts per million (ppm).

- The pH of water also affects its quality. The **pH** of water is a measure of how acidic or basic the water is.

- **Hardness** is a measure of how much of two minerals there is in a sample of water. The two minerals are calcium and magnesium. Hard water contains high levels of calcium and magnesium.

Answer the following questions. Use your textbook and the ideas above.

1. Is the following sentence true or false? Certain substances in water are harmless unless they are present at very high levels. _____

2. Concentrations are often measured in parts per

_____.

3. Complete the table of terms related to water quality.

Terms Related to Water Quality	
Term	**Meaning**
a. _____	how much there is of one substance in a certain volume of another substance
b. _____	a measure of how acidic or basic the water is
c. _____	a measure of how much calcium and magnesium there is in a sample of water

Treating Drinking Water (pages 422–423)

Key Concept: **Water from both public and private supplies often needs some treatment to ensure that it is clean and safe to drink.**

- Water treatment is a way to make water safe to drink.

- The first step of drinking-water treatment is usually filtration. **Filtration** is when water is passed through a series of screens. The screens do not allow large objects to pass through.

- The second step is coagulation. **Coagulation** is when a chemical is added to water to make particles stick together. The chemical causes sticky globs to form. These globs are then filtered out of the water.

Fresh Water

- The next step is to add chlorine to the water. Chlorine is a chemical that kills organisms that cause disease.

- The next step is to force air through the water. This reduces bad odors and tastes.

Answer the following questions. Use your textbook and the ideas on page 203 and above.

4. Is the following sentence true or false? Water treatment is a way to make water clean and safe to drink.

_____

5. The picture below shows drinking-water treatment. Draw arrows to show the direction that water moves when it is treated.

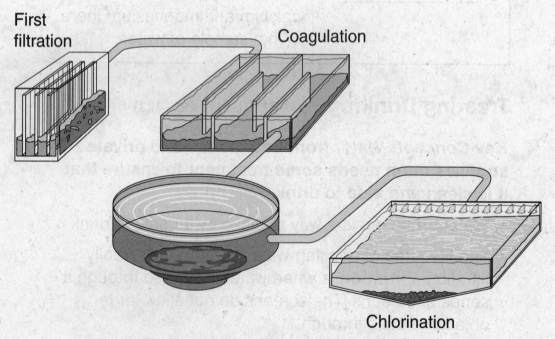

First filtration

Coagulation

Chlorination

6. Draw a line from each term to its meaning.

Term	Meaning
filtration	**a.** the process of particles sticking together
coagulation	**b.** the process of passing water through a series of screens

Ocean Motions

Wave Action (pages 434–441)

What Is a Wave? (pages 435–436)

Key Concept: **Most waves form when winds blowing across the water's surface transmit their energy to the water.**

- A water **wave** is the movement of energy through a body of water.

- The size of a wave depends on two factors:
   1. the strength of the wind
   2. the length of time the wind blows

- Waves do not actually carry water forward. The energy of a wave moves toward a shore, but the water itself stays in place. As a wave passes a place, water particles move in a circle. The particles move forward and down with the energy of the wave and then back to their original positions.

- The highest part of a wave is called the crest. A **wavelength** is the distance from one crest to the next crest.

- Waves are also measured by their frequency. **Frequency** is the number of waves that pass a point in a certain amount of time.

- The lowest part of a wave is called the trough. **Wave height** is the up-and-down distance from a crest to a trough.

Answer the following questions. Use your textbook and the ideas above.

1. Is the following sentence true or false? Waves do not actually carry water forward. _____

Name _____ Date _____ Class _____

Ocean Motions

2. Read each word in the box. In each sentence below, fill in the correct word or words.

> | wave | wavelength | frequency |
> |------|-----------|-----------|
> | wave height | crest | |

a. The distance from one crest to the next crest is a

_____.

b. A water _____ is the movement of energy through a body of water.

c. The up-and-down distance from a crest to a

trough is called the _____.

d. The number of waves that pass a point in a certain

amount of time is the _____ of the waves.

3. The picture below shows a water wave. Draw a line that shows the wavelength of this wave.

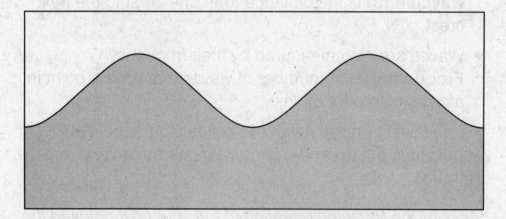

Ocean Motions

How Waves Change Near Shore
(pages 437–438)

Key Concept: **Near shore, wave height increases and wavelength decreases.**

- The white-capped waves that crash onto an ocean shore are often called "breakers." As a wave comes near to shore, the wave slows down. As it slows down, its shape changes. When a wave reaches a certain height, the crest of the wave falls. The wave "breaks" onto the shore.

- A breaker moves up the beach, but gravity stops it. The water then flows back out to sea. This rush of water out to sea is called an undertow. A strong undertow can be dangerous to swimmers.

- A **tsunami** is a wave that forms far below the ocean surface. Earthquakes under the ocean floor cause tsunamis. When a tsunami reaches a coast, it can destroy buildings and bridges.

- A tsunami in deep water may have a long wavelength but a small wave height. When the tsunami reaches shallow water near a coast, the wave height increases as the water "piles up." The tsunami becomes a towering wall of water.

Answer the following questions. Use your textbook and the ideas above.

4. A wave that forms far below the ocean surface is

   a(an) _____.

5. Is the following sentence true or false? The rush of water flowing back out to sea is called an undertow.

   _____

6. Circle the letter of each sentence that is true about how waves change near shore.

    a. When the tsunami reaches shallow water near a coast, the wave height increases.

    b. As waves come near a shore, the waves slow down.

    c. Near shore, wave height decreases and wave length increases.

How Waves Affect the Shore (page 439)

Key Concept: **As waves come into shore, water washes up the beach at an angle, carrying sand grains. The water and sand then run straight back down the beach.**

- Winds far out at sea affect the direction of waves. As a result, waves usually come toward shore at an angle.

- Water flows up a beach at an angle, but the water flows straight back out to sea—not at the angle it flowed in. The result is the movement of sand along the beach. **Longshore drift** is the movement of sand along a beach.

- As waves slow down, they drop the sand they are carrying. The sand forms a long underwater ridge called a sandbar.

- As a sandbar grows, it can trap the water flowing along the shore. In some places, water rushing back out to sea breaks through the sandbar, creating a narrow opening. A **rip current** is a rush of water that flows rapidly back to sea through a narrow opening.

Ocean Motions

Answer the following questions. Use your textbook and the ideas on page 208.

7. Complete the table of terms related to how waves affect a shore.

Terms Related to How Waves Affect a Shore	
Term	**Meaning**
a. _____ _____	the movement of sand along a beach
b. _____	a long underwater ridge of sand
c. _____ _____	a rush of water that flows rapidly back to sea through a narrow opening in a sandbar

8. Circle the letter of what causes longshore drift.
   a. Water flows up a beach at an angle, but the water flows straight back out to sea.
   b. In some places, water rushing back out to sea breaks through the sandbar.
   c. Water flows straight up a beach, but the water flows at an angle back out to sea.

9. Is the following sentence true or false? As waves slow down, they drop the sand they are carrying.

   _____

Name _____ Date _____ Class _____

Waves and Beach Erosion (pages 440–441)

Key Concept: **Waves shape a beach by eroding the shore in some places and building it up in others.**

- The area between the land and an ocean is always changing. Over time, waves break rocks into pebbles and grains of sand. Longshore drift moves sand along a coast. This breaking up of rock and carrying it away is called erosion.

- Long sand deposits called barrier beaches form along a shore. Barrier beaches are separated from the mainland by shallow water. Barrier beaches protect shorelines from the force of waves. Waves break against the barrier beaches instead of against the shore.

- Erosion can wear away beaches. This causes problems for homes and other buildings near beaches. One way to reduce beach erosion is by building groins. A **groin** is a wall of rocks or concrete that is built straight out from a beach. Sand carried by water piles up against the groins instead of moving along a shore.

Answer the following questions. Use your textbook and the ideas above.

10. A wall of rocks or concrete that is built straight out from a beach is a(an) _____.

11. Circle the letter of each sentence that is true about waves and beach erosion.

    a. The process of breaking up rock and carrying it away is called longshore drift.

    b. Barrier beaches protect shorelines from the force of waves.

    c. One way to reduce beach erosion is by building groins.

Tides (pages 442–447)

What Causes Tides? (pages 443–446)

Key Concept: **Tides are caused by the interaction of Earth, the moon, and the sun.**

- **Tides** are the daily rise and fall of Earth's waters on its coastlines.

- As a tide comes in, the level of water rises. High tide is when the water is highest. Then the tide flows out, flowing back toward the sea. Low tide is when the water reaches its lowest point.

- Gravity causes tides. Gravity is the force an object has that pulls other objects toward it.

- The moon's gravity pulls on Earth's waters. The moon's gravity creates a bulge of water on the side of Earth closest to the moon. The water on the other side of Earth forms a second bulge. These are called tidal bulges. In places where there are tidal bulges, high tide occurs.

- In many places, there are two high tides and two low tides each day. In other places, one set of tides is so small that it seems like there is only one high tide and one low tide per day.

Answer the following questions. Use your textbook and the ideas above.

1. Circle the letter of each sentence that is true about tides.

   a. High tide is when the water is highest.

   b. In many places, there are two high tides a day.

   c. In places where there are tidal bulges, low tide occurs.

Ocean Motions

2. The daily rise and fall of Earth's waters on its coastlines are called _____.

3. Is the following sentence true or false? Gravity causes tides. _____

Key Concept: **Changes in the positions of Earth, the moon, and the sun affect the heights of the tides during a month.**

- The sun's gravity also affects Earth's tides. The sun pulls the water on Earth's surface toward it.

- When the sun and the moon are lined up, their gravities combine to produce a spring tide. A **spring tide** is a tide with the greatest difference between high tide and low tide.

- When the sun and the moon are at right angles to each other, the sun's gravity pulls some water away from tidal bulges. The result is a neap tide. A **neap tide** is a tide with the least difference between high tide and low tide.

Answer the following questions. Use your textbook and the ideas above.

4. Complete the table about kinds of tides.

Kinds of Tides	
Kind of Tide	**Description**
a. _____ _____	a tide with the greatest difference between high tide and low tide
b. _____ _____	a tide with the least difference between high tide and low tide

Ocean Motions

5. The picture below shows the Earth, moon, and sun. Circle the letter of the kind of tide that occurs when the Earth, moon, and sun are in line like this.

   a. low tide

   b. spring tide

   c. neap tide

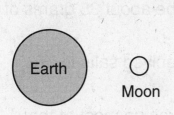
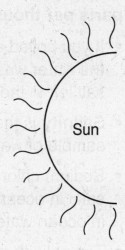

Energy From Tides (pages 446–447)

Key Concept: **The movement of huge amounts of water between high and low tide is a source of potential energy—energy that is stored and can be used.**

- A lot of water moves between high and low tides. In some places, tidal power plants use the energy of tides to produce electricity.

- The energy of tides is used only in places where there is a big difference between high tide and low tide. There are very few places in the world with such a big difference.

Answer the following question. Use your textbook and the ideas above.

6. In some places, tidal power plants use the energy of tides to produce _____.

Ocean Motions

Ocean Water Chemistry (pages 448–453)

The Salty Ocean (pages 449–450)

Key Concept: On average, one kilogram of ocean water contains about 35 grams of salts—that is, 35 parts per thousand.

- If you boiled a kilogram of ocean water in a pot until all the water was gone, there would be about 35 grams of salt left in the pot.

- **Salinity** is the total amount of dissolved salts in a sample of water.

- Sodium chloride—table salt—makes up most of the salts in ocean water. There are also other kinds of salts in ocean water.

- The salinity of ocean water is not always the same. In most parts of the ocean, salinity is between 34 and 37 parts per thousand. Near the mouths of large rivers, salinity is lower because rivers bring fresh water.

- Salinity affects the properties of water. Ocean water freezes at a lower temperature than fresh water. Also, ocean water is denser than fresh water. As a result, you can float more easily in ocean water than in fresh water.

Answer the following questions. Use your textbook and the ideas above.

1. The total amount of dissolved salts in a sample of

   water is _____.

2. Most of the salt in salt water is sodium chloride, or

   _____.

Ocean Motions

3. The circle graph below shows the makeup of ocean water. Circle the letter of what makes up 35 parts per thousand.

   a. water molecules

   b. carbon dioxide and other gases

   c. sodium chloride and other salts

Makeup of Ocean Water

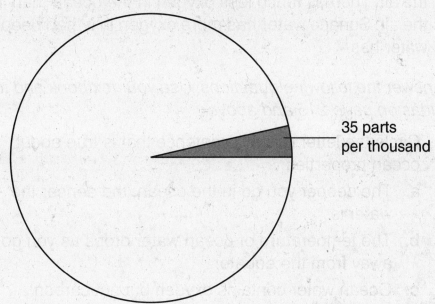

35 parts per thousand

4. Is the following sentence true or false? Near the mouths of large rivers, salinity is higher.

_____

Other Ocean Properties (page 451)

***Key Concept:* Like temperatures on land, temperatures at the surface of the ocean vary with location and the seasons. Gases in ocean water vary as well.**

• The ocean absorbs energy from the sun. Near the equator, the temperature at the surface of the ocean is about 25°C—about room temperature. The temperature drops as you go away from the equator.

- The deeper you go in the ocean, the colder and denser the water is. Cold water is denser than warm water.

- Ocean organisms use gases in ocean water. Two gases that ocean organisms use are carbon dioxide and oxygen. Algae, for example, need carbon dioxide to carry out photosynthesis. Ocean animals need oxygen.

- There is much more carbon dioxide in the ocean than in the air. There is much less oxygen in the ocean than in the air. Surface water has more oxygen in it than deeper water has.

Answer the following questions. Use your textbook and the ideas on page 215 and above.

5. Circle the letter of each sentence that is true about ocean properties.

   a. The deeper you go in the ocean, the denser the water is.

   b. The temperature of ocean water drops as you go away from the equator.

   c. Ocean water contains oxygen but not carbon dioxide.

6. Is the following sentence true or false? Deep water has more oxygen in it than surface water. _____

Changes With Depth (page 452–453)

Key Concept: **As you descend through the ocean, the water temperature decreases. Pressure increases continuously with depth in the ocean.**

- If you could drop from the ocean's surface to the ocean floor, you would pass through a section of the ocean known as the water column. Conditions change as you go from the top of the water column to the bottom.

Ocean Motions

- There are three temperature zones in the water column. The surface zone is warmest. The transition zone begins at about 1 kilometer down. Temperatures drop quickly in the transition zone. Below the transition zone is the deep zone, where the water is very cold.

- Water pressure is the force of the weight of water. Because of high pressure in the deep ocean, divers can go down safely to only about 40 meters.

Answer the following questions. Use your textbook and the ideas on page 216 and above.

7. Is the following sentence true or false? Pressure increases the deeper you go in the ocean. _____

8. Complete the table about the three temperature zones in the ocean water column.

Temperature Zones in the Ocean Water Column	
Zone	**Description**
a. _____ zone	the warmest zone, which goes down to 100–500 meters
Transition zone	the zone that goes from the surface zone down to about 1 kilometer
b. _____ zone	the bottom zone, where temperatures average 3.5°C

Ocean Motions

Currents and Climate (pages 456–461)

Surface Currents (pages 457–459)

Key Concept: **Surface currents, which affect water to a depth of several hundred meters, are driven mainly by winds.**

- A **current** is a large stream of moving water that flows through the oceans. Unlike waves, currents carry water from place to place.

- Surface currents move in circular patterns in the oceans. Most currents flow east or west, and then turn back to complete the circle.

- Earth rotates on its axis. The effect that Earth's rotation has on the direction of winds and currents is called the **Coriolis** (kawr ee OH lis) **effect**. The Coriolis effect causes ocean currents to move in circular patterns.

- The largest and most powerful surface current in the North Atlantic Ocean is called the Gulf Stream. It moves northward along the east coast of the United States.

Answer the following questions. Use your textbook and the ideas above.

1. A large stream of moving water that flows through the oceans is a(an) _____.

2. Circle the letter of each sentence that is true about surface currents.
   a. The Gulf Stream moves northward along the east coast of the United States.
   b. Surface currents are driven mainly by differences in density.
   c. Surface currents move in circular patterns in the oceans.

Ocean Motions

3. The effect that Earth's rotation has on the direction of winds and ocean currents is called the

_____ effect.

Key Concept: **A surface current warms or cools the air above it, influencing the climate of the land near the coast.**

- **Climate** is the pattern of temperature and precipitation that is usual in an area over a long time.

- Currents affect climate by moving cold and warm water around the world. Some currents carry warm water from the equator to the poles. Other currents carry cold water from the poles to the equator. Warm water warms the air above it. Cold water cools the air above.

- Sometimes, changes in wind patterns and currents occur. Such changes can have big effects on oceans and the land nearby.

- One example of a change in wind patterns and currents is El Niño. **El Niño** is an uncommon climate event that happens every two to seven years in the Pacific Ocean. During an El Niño, warm water moves toward the South American coast. This climate event can affect the climate of places far away.

Answer the following questions. Use your textbook and the ideas above.

4. Draw a line from each term to its meaning.

Term	Meaning
climate	a. uncommon climate event that happens every two to seven years in the Pacific Ocean
El Niño	
	b. the pattern of temperature and precipitation that is usual in an area over a long time

5. Is the following sentence true or false? Warm water cools the air above it. _____

Deep Currents (page 460)

Key Concept: **Deep currents are caused by differences in the density of ocean water. Deep currents move and mix water around the world. They carry cold water from the poles toward the equator.**

- The density of water depends on the water's temperature and salinity. When warm water flows toward the poles, the water gets cooler. Some of the water freezes and becomes ice. When water freezes, it leaves its salts behind. That causes the salinity of the remaining water to be higher.

- As the water gets colder and its salinity gets higher, the water becomes denser. Dense water sinks.

- The cold water deep in the ocean flows along the ocean floor toward the equator as a deep current.

- Deep currents flow very slowly.

Answer the following questions. Use your textbook and the ideas above.

6. Cold water that flows along the ocean floor toward the equator is a(an) _____.

7. Circle the letter of each sentence that is true about deep currents.

   a. Deep currents carry cold water from the poles toward the equator.

   b. Deep currents are caused by differences in the density of ocean water.

   c. Deep currents flow very quickly.

Ocean Motions

Upwelling (pages 460–461)

Key Concept: **Upwelling brings up tiny ocean organisms, minerals, and other nutrients from the deeper layers of the water. Without this motion, the surface waters of the open ocean would be very scarce in nutrients.**

- Sometimes, winds cause surface waters to mix with deep ocean waters. Winds blow away the warm surface water. Cold water from the deep ocean rises to replace the surface water.

- When cold water moves upward from the deep ocean, it is called **upwelling**.

- Places where upwelling occurs usually have many fish. This is because the rising water brings nutrients up from the deep ocean.

Answer the following question. Use your textbook and the ideas above.

8. The picture below shows the ocean near the coast of a continent. The arrows show wind, the movement of warm surface water, and upwelling from the deep ocean. Circle the arrows that show upwelling.

Exploring the Ocean (pages 470–476)

Learning About the Ocean (pages 471–473)

Key Concept: **People have studied the ocean since ancient times, because the ocean provides food and serves as a route for trade and travel. Modern scientists have studied the characteristics of the ocean's waters and the ocean floor.**

- People have been using the sea for trade for thousands of years.

- As trade increased in modern times, people needed good maps of the oceans and the lands nearby. In the 1700s and 1800s, most of Earth's coastlines had been mapped.

- Studying the ocean floor is difficult because the ocean is so deep. The deep ocean is dark, and the water is very cold. The pressure is very high in the deep ocean.

- It got easier to map the ocean floor when sonar was invented. Sonar stands for **so**und **na**vigation and **r**anging. **Sonar** is a system that uses sound waves to find the distance to an object.

Answer the following questions. Use your textbook and the ideas above.

1. Circle the letter of each condition that makes exploring the ocean difficult.
   a. The ocean is very deep.
   b. The water is very cold in the deep ocean.
   c. The pressure in the deep ocean is great.

2. Sonar is a system that uses _____ waves to find the distance to an object.

3. Is the following sentence true or false? People only very recently began using the ocean for trade.

   _____

The Ocean Floor (pages 474–475)

Key Concept: **If you could travel along the ocean floor, you would see the continental shelf, the continental slope, the abyssal plain, and the mid-ocean ridge.**

- The ocean floor is not a flat, sandy area. It has mountain ranges, deep canyons, and many other features.

- The **continental shelf** is a gently sloping, shallow area at the edge of a continent.

- The **continental slope** is the steep dropoff at the far edge of the continental shelf.

- On the ocean floor, there are both flat areas and mountains. The **abyssal** (uh BIHS ul) **plain** is a smooth, nearly flat region of the ocean floor. The **mid-ocean ridge** is a very long mountain range that winds around Earth. The mid-ocean ridge passes through all of Earth's oceans.

- A **trench** is a deep canyon in the ocean floor.

Answer the following questions. Use your textbook and the ideas above.

4. Is the following sentence true or false? The ocean

   floor is a sandy, flat area. _____

Ocean Zones

5. Draw a line from each feature to its description.

Feature	**Description**
continental shelf	**a.** a smooth, nearly flat region of the ocean floor
continental slope	**b.** a very long mountain range that winds around Earth
abyssal plain	**c.** a gently sloping, shallow area at the edge of a continent
mid-ocean ridge	**d.** a deep canyon in the ocean floor
trench	**e.** the steep dropoff at the far edge of the continental shelf

6. The picture below shows features of the ocean floor, including the mid-ocean ridge, the abyssal plain, the continental slope, and the continental shelf.

a. Make an X on the continental shelf.

b. Draw a circle around the mid-ocean ridge.

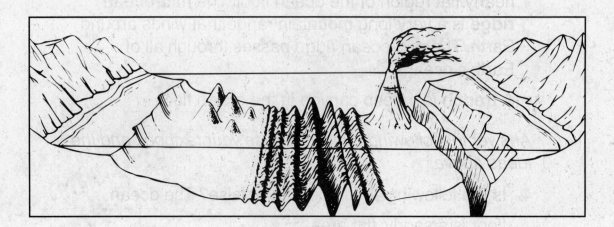

Ocean Zones (page 476)

Key Concept: **Ocean zones include the intertidal zone, the neritic zone, and the open-ocean zone.**

- The ocean is divided into three zones: the intertidal zone, the neritic zone, and the open-ocean zone.

- The **intertidal zone** stretches from the line made by the highest tide on shore to the line on the continental shelf where the lowest low tide ends.

- The **neritic zone** goes from the low-tide line to the edge of the continental shelf.

- The **open-ocean zone** is the vast area beyond the edge of the continental shelf.

- Each of the three ocean zones has its own physical conditions. The physical conditions of a zone determine what kinds of organisms live in that zone.

Answer the following questions. Use your textbook and the ideas above.

7. Draw a line from each ocean zone to its location.

Zone	Location
intertidal zone	**a.** the vast area beyond the edge of the continental shelf
neritic zone	**b.** from the low-tide line to the edge of the continental shelf
open-ocean zone	**c.** stretches from the line made by the highest tide on shore to the line on the continental shelf where the lowest low tide ends

Name _____ Date _____ Class _____

Ocean Zones

8. The picture below shows the three ocean zones. Circle the letter of the neritic zone.

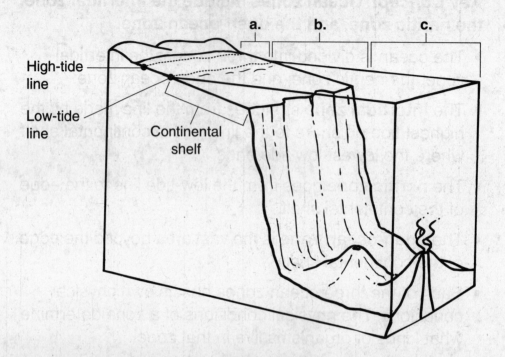

9. Is the following sentence true or false? The physical conditions of an ocean zone determine what kinds of organisms live in that zone. _____

Ocean Habitats (pages 478–489)

Life in the Ocean (pages 479–480)

Key Concept: **Scientists classify marine organisms according to where they live and how they move.**

- There are three main groups of ocean organisms: plankton, nekton, and benthos.

- **Plankton** are tiny organisms that float on the water. Plankton include some kinds of algae, such as diatoms. Plankton also include very tiny fish and shellfish.

- **Nekton** are animals that can swim throughout the water column. Nekton include fishes, whales, seals, and squid.

- **Benthos** are organisms that live on the ocean floor. Benthos include crabs, sea stars, lobsters, and sponges.

- Plantkton, nekton, and benthos are all found in most ocean habitats. Plants and algae produce their own food through photosynthesis. They are called producers. The organisms that eat other organisms are called consumers. The organisms that break down wastes and other dead organisms are called decomposers.

- All the feeding relationships in a habitat make up a **food web**.

Answer the following questions. Use your textbook and the ideas above.

1. All the feeding relationships in a habitat make up a(an)

_____.

2. Complete the table about the main groups of ocean organisms.

Main Groups of Ocean Organisms	
Group of Ocean Organisms	**Description**
a. _____	tiny organisms that float on the water
b. _____	animals that can swim throughout the water column
c. _____	organisms that live on the ocean floor

The Intertidal Zone (pages 481–483)

Key Concept: **Organisms that live in intertidal zones must be able to tolerate changes in both the salinity and temperature of the water, as well as periods of being underwater and periods of being exposed to the air. Some also experience pounding waves.**

- Organisms that live in intertidal zones must be able to live in harsh conditions. The waves pound. The temperature often changes. The salinity of the water can change, too.

- **Estuaries** are inlets or bays where fresh water from rivers mixes with salt water from the ocean. Estuaries contain water that is partly salt water and partly fresh water.

- Mangrove forests are found along the coasts of Florida. Mangroves are short trees that grow in partly salty water. Mangrove forests protect the land by breaking the waves and the wind that comes off the ocean.

Ocean Zones

- A salt marsh is made up of mud, animal and plant matter, and nutrients. Cordgrass is the most common plant in salt marshes. Many ocean animals hatch and grow in salt marshes before going to the open ocean.

- Rocky shores are found along both coasts of the United States. At the top of the rocks is the spray zone. This is where a spray hits from the ocean smashing against rocks below. Some organisms live on the rocks below the spray zone, including barnacles and limpets.

- When the tide goes out, some water stays in large puddles among the rocks. These large puddles are called tide pools. Organisms that can live in tide pools include sea stars, sea urchins, and sea anemones.

Answer the following questions. Use your textbook and the ideas on page 228 and above.

3. Circle the letter of each condition that an organism in the intertidal zone must be able to live with.

   a. The waves pound.

   b. The temperature always stays the same.

   c. The salinity of the water can change.

4. Draw a line from each term to its meaning.

Term	Meaning
estuary	a. large puddle left behind when the tide goes out
mangrove forest	b. inlet or bay where fresh and salt water mix
salt marsh	c. coastal wetland where cordgrass is common
tide pool	d. coastal wetland where short trees grow

Ocean Zones

Conditions in the Neritic Zone (page 484)

Key Concept: **The shallow water over the continental shelf receives sunlight and a steady supply of nutrients washed from the land into the ocean. The light and nutrients enable large plantlike algae to grow.**

- A huge variety of organisms is found in the neritic zone. The algae in the neritic zone serve as food for other organisms.

- In many parts of the neritic zone, upwelling brings nutrients from the bottom up to the surface. These nutrients provide food for large numbers of plankton. The plankton are food for many other larger organisms, including such fish as sardines and herrings.

Answer the following questions. Use your textbook and the ideas above.

5. Circle the letter of each sentence that is true about conditions in the neritic zone.

    a. Nutrients from upwelling provide food for large numbers of plankton.

    b. Plankton are food for many other larger organisms.

    c. Organisms in the neritic zone must live in total darkness.

6. Is the following sentence true or false? Nutrients that provide food for plankton are brought to the ocean surface by upwelling. _____

Ocean Zones

Coral Reefs (pages 484–485)

Key Concept: Coral reefs can form only in shallow, tropical ocean waters.

- Coral reefs are found in the neritic zone. Coral reefs are formed by tiny coral animals. Each animal makes a hard structure that surrounds its body. After the animal dies, the hard structure remains. Over many years, a reef builds up.

- Algae live inside coral animals and provide food for the corals. Algae need warm water and sunlight. So, coral reefs grow where water is warm and shallow.

- An **atoll** is a ring-shaped coral reef that surrounds a shallow pool of water. An atoll begins as a reef that surrounds an island. Over time, the island sinks and the reef keeps growing upward.

- Many animals live in and around a coral reef. Coral-reef animals include octopuses and fishes of all colors.

Answer the following questions. Use your textbook and the ideas above.

7. Is the following sentence true or false? Many animals live in and around a coral reef. _____

8. The pictures show steps in the formation of an atoll. But the steps are not in the correct order. Number the pictures 1 to 3 to show the correct order of how an atoll forms.

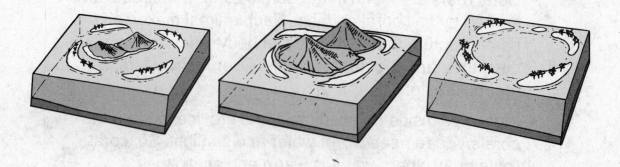

_____   _____   _____

Kelp Forests (page 486)

Key Concept: **Kelp forests grow in cold neritic waters where the ocean has a rocky floor.**

• Kelp are large, heavy algae. A giant kelp can grow up to 30 meters long. Kelp have little bulbs called air bladders that keep them upright in water.

• The kelp use sunlight to produce their own food. Kelp forests provide homes for many living things. Animals that live in kelp forests include sea slugs and snails.

Answer the following questions. Use your textbook and the ideas above.

9. Kelp are large, heavy _____.

10. Is the following sentence true or false? Kelp forests grow in cold neritic waters. _____

Conditions in the Open Ocean (pages 487-489)

Key Concept: The open ocean differs from the neritic zone in two important ways. First, only a small part of the open ocean receives sunlight. Second, the water has fewer nutrients.

- The open ocean has fewer living things than the neritic zone. This is because the open ocean receives less sunlight and has fewer nutrients.

- Few organisms live in the deep zone of the water column, because it is so cold and dark there. Many deep-sea fishes produce their own light. **Bioluminescence** is when living things produce light.

- There is one environment in the deep zone where many different organisms live. A **hydrothermal vent** is a place where hot water rises out of cracks in the ocean floor. Many organisms live around hydrothermal vents.

Answer the following questions. Use your textbook and the ideas above.

11. Draw a line from each term to its meaning.

Term	Meaning
bioluminescence	**a.** when living things produce light
hydrothermal vent	**b.** a place where hot water rises out of cracks in the ocean floor

12. Circle the letter of each way that the open ocean differs from the neritic zone.

    a. The open ocean has more organisms than the neritic zone.

    b. The water of the open ocean has fewer nutrients.

    c. Only a small part of the open ocean gets sunlight.

Resources From the Ocean
(pages 490–496)

Living Resources (pages 491–492)

Key Concept: **People depend heavily on fishes and other ocean organisms for food. Ocean organisms also provide materials that are used in products such as detergents and paints.**

- Many kinds of fish are caught to be eaten. Most fishes are caught near coasts or in areas of upwelling.

- Overfishing causes the number of fish to go down. New tools have helped people catch large numbers of fish quickly. Sometimes the fish are caught faster than they can reproduce. The fish in an area can become hard to find.

- **Aquaculture** is the farming of saltwater and freshwater organisms. In aquaculture, people build the right environment to raise organisms. Oysters, shrimp, and salmon have been successfully raised.

- Algae are used in products such as detergents, shampoos, and paints.

Answer the following questions. Use your textbook and the ideas above.

1. The farming of saltwater and freshwater organisms is called _____.

2. Is the following sentence true or false? Algae are used in some detergents. _____

3. Complete the flowchart about how fish become scarce.

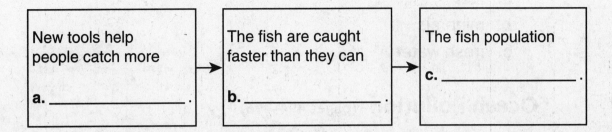

New tools help people catch more

a. _____ .

The fish are caught faster than they can

b. _____ .

The fish population

c. _____ .

Nonliving Resources (pages 493–494)

Key Concept: **Some nonliving ocean resources include water, fuels, and minerals.**

- Fresh water can be made from salt water by desalination.

- The remains of ancient ocean organisms are the source of oil and natural gas underneath the ocean floor.

- Minerals are solid substances that can come from the ground and from water.

- People mine minerals from the ocean floor. In some places, diamonds and gold are mined from sand deposits. Some metals, such as manganese, can be found on the ocean floor. A **nodule** (NAHJ ool) is a black lump formed when a metal builds up around a piece of shell. Nodules are gathered from the deep ocean.

Answer the following questions. Use your textbook and the ideas above.

4. A black lump formed when a metal builds up around a

piece of shell is a(an) _____ .

Ocean Zones

5. Circle the letter of each nonliving ocean resource.

    a. fish

    b. minerals

    c. fresh water

Ocean Pollution (pages 494–496)

Key Concept: **Although some ocean pollution is the result of natural occurrences, most pollution is related to human activities.**

- Some pollution is caused by weather. For example, heavy rains can wash fresh water into an estuary. Fresh water lowers the estuary's salinity, and that can kill some ocean organisms.

- Sewage, chemicals, and trash are dumped into ocean waters. Runoff from fields and roads goes into oceans.

- Oil pollution is a major threat to ocean organisms. An oil tanker or an oil platform may leak oil. Oil is harmful to organisms, and many die.

Answer the following questions. Use your textbook and the ideas above.

6. Circle the letter of each sentence that is true about ocean pollution.

    a. Oil pollution is a major threat to ocean organisms.

    b. Some ocean pollution is caused by weather.

    c. Runoff from fields and roads can pollute the ocean.

7. Is the following sentence true or false? Most ocean pollution is related to human activities. _____

The Air Around You (pages 512–515)

Introduction (page 512)

Key Concept: **Earth's atmosphere is like water on an apple—a thin layer of gases on Earth's surface.**

- Earth's **atmosphere** (AT muh sfeer) is the covering of gases that surrounds Earth. Compared to the size of Earth, the atmosphere is a very thin covering.

- The atmosphere is commonly called the air.

- **Weather** is the condition of Earth's atmosphere at a particular place and time. For example, the weather you have right now is the condition of the atmosphere at your particular place.

Answer the following questions. Use your textbook and the ideas above.

1. Read each word in the box. In each sentence below, fill in one of the words.

weather	atmosphere	climate

    a. The covering of gases that surrounds Earth is called the _____.

    b. The condition of Earth's atmosphere at a particular place and time is called _____.

2. Is the following sentence true or false? The atmosphere is commonly called the air. _____

The Atmosphere

Composition of the Atmosphere

(pages 513–514)

Key Concept: Earth's atmosphere is made up of nitrogen, oxygen, carbon dioxide, water vapor, and many other gases, as well as particles of liquids and solids.

- Nitrogen is the main gas in the atmosphere. Nitrogen gas makes up about 78 percent of the atmosphere.

- Oxygen is the number two gas in the atmosphere. It makes up about 21 percent of the atmosphere.

- Most oxygen molecules in the atmosphere have two oxygen atoms. Another form of oxygen has three atoms instead of two. **Ozone** is a form of oxygen that has three oxygen atoms.

- Carbon dioxide makes up a tiny portion of the atmosphere. But carbon dioxide is needed for life on Earth. Plants need carbon dioxide to make food.

- The amount of water vapor in the atmosphere varies. **Water vapor** is the gas form of water.

- The solids in the atmosphere are referred to as particles. Particles in the air include dust, smoke, and other chemicals.

Answer the following questions. Use your textbook and the ideas above.

3. Draw a line from each term to its meaning.

Term	Meaning
ozone	**a.** the solids in the atmosphere
water vapor	**b.** a form of oxygen that has three oxygen atoms
particles	**c.** the gas form of water

The Atmosphere

4. In circle graph below, identify the gases in the atmosphere by filling in each blank.

Gases in Dry Air

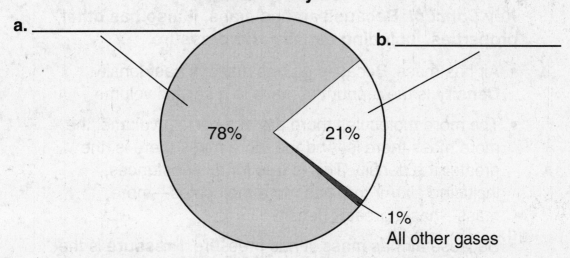

a. _____

b. _____

78%

21%

1%
All other gases

Importance of the Atmosphere (page 515)

Key Concept: **Earth's atmosphere makes conditions on Earth suitable for living things.**

- One reason the atmosphere is important is that it contains oxygen and other gases living things need.

- The atmosphere traps heat energy from the sun. Trapping heat allows living things to live on Earth.

- The atmosphere also prevents Earth form being hit by rocks from outer space.

Answer the following question. Use your textbook and the ideas above.

5. Circle the letter of each sentence that is true about the atmosphere.

   a. The atmosphere contains oxygen that living things need to live.

   b. The atmosphere lets all rocks from outer space hit Earth.

   c. The atmosphere traps energy from the sun.

The Atmosphere

Air Pressure (pages 516–520)

Properties of Air (page 517)

Key Concept: **Because air has mass, it also has other properties, including density and pressure.**

- Air has mass. Because air has mass, it has density. **Density** is the amount of mass in a certain volume.

- The more molecules there are in a certain volume, the more mass there is. And the more mass there is, the greater the density. This is true for all substances, including air. Air that has more molecules—more mass—has a greater density.

- Because air has mass, it has pressure. **Pressure** is the force pushing on an area or a surface.

- Air has pressure because air's mass has weight. The weight of air presses down. **Air pressure** is the pressing down of the weight of air on an area.

- Denser air has more air pressure than less dense air has.

Answer the following questions. Use your textbook and the ideas above.

1. Circle the letter of each sentence that is true about the properties of air.
   a. Air has no density.
   b. Air has mass.
   c. Air that has more mass has a greater density.

2. Is the following sentence true or false? Denser air has more air pressure than less dense air. _____

3. Draw a line from each term to its meaning.

Term	Meaning
density	**a.** the pressing down of the weight of air on an area
pressure	**b.** the force pushing on an area or a surface
air pressure	**c.** the amount of mass in a certain volume

Measuring Air Pressure (pages 518–519)

Key Concept: **Two common kinds of barometers are mercury barometers and aneroid barometers.**

• A **barometer** (buh RAHM uh tur) is an instrument that measures air pressure.

• One kind of barometer is a mercury barometer. A **mercury barometer** is made up of a glass tube that is open at the bottom end. The open end of the tube sits in a dish of mercury. Air pressure causes the mercury to go up the tube.

• An **aneroid** (AN uh royd) **barometer** has a closed space surrounded by metal. Air pressure pushes the metal in and out. As the shape of the space changes, a needle moves to show what the air pressure is.

Answer the following questions. Use your textbook and the ideas above.

4. Circle the letter of each sentence that is true about barometers.

  a. There are two kinds of barometers.

  b. A barometer is used to measure temperature.

  c. In an aneroid barometer, a needle moves to show air pressure.

5. Read each word in the box. In each sentence below, fill in the correct word.

> aneroid   barometer
>
> thermometer   mercury

  a. An instrument used to measure air pressure is a(an) _____.

  b. A(an) _____ barometer has a closed space surrounded by metal.

  c. A(an) _____ barometer has a glass tube that is open at the bottom end.

6. The picture shows a mercury barometer. Draw a line on the glass tube to show where the level of mercury might be if the air pressure falls.

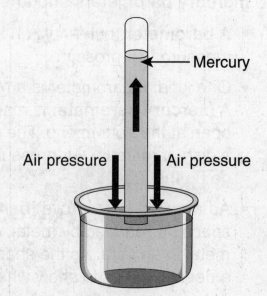

Altitude and the Properties of Air
(pages 519–520)

Key Concept: **Air pressure decreases as altitude increases. As air pressure decreases, so does density.**

• **Altitude** is the distance above sea level. Altitude is also called elevation. Sea level is the average level of the ocean's surface.

The Atmosphere

- Air at sea level carries the weight of all the air above it. As you go higher, the air has less air on top of it, and therefore, it has less weight. So, air pressure at sea level is greater than the air at any place above it.

- Altitude affects density. As you go higher, air becomes less dense. As you go lower, air becomes more dense.

Answer the following questions. Use your textbook and the ideas on page 242 and above.

7. Circle the letter of each sentence that is true about altitude.

    a. Altitude affects density of air.

    b. Altitude is the distance above sea level.

    c. Altitude is also called elevation.

8. The picture shows a mountain. The elevation is higher at altitude A than it is at altitude B. Circle the letter of the altitude where the air is denser.

Layers of the Atmosphere
(pages 522–527)

Introduction (pages 522–523)

Key Concept: **Scientists divide Earth's atmosphere into four main layers classified according to changes in temperature. These layers are the troposphere, the stratosphere, the mesosphere, and the thermosphere.**

- Scientists divide the atmosphere into four layers. They classify these layers by the changes in temperature. As you go from one layer to the next, the temperature changes in a different way.

- The troposphere is the lowest layer of the atmosphere. The stratosphere is the second layer as you go up. The mesosphere is the third layer as you go up. The thermosphere is the top layer.

Answer the following questions. Use your textbook and the ideas above.

1. In the picture below, fill in the blanks.

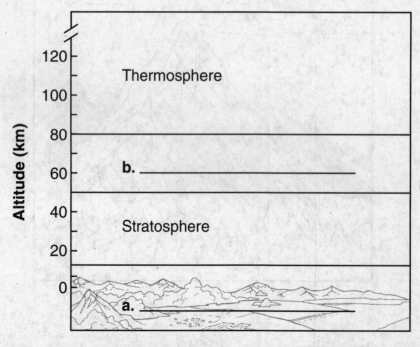

The Atmosphere

2. Is the following sentence true or false? Scientists divide the atmosphere into layers based on thickness.

_____

The Troposphere (page 524)

Key Concept: **The troposphere is the layer of the atmosphere in which Earth's weather occurs.**

- You live in the **troposphere** (TROH puh sfeer). It is the lowest layer of the atmosphere.

- Most weather happens in the troposphere. For example, when it is raining, it is raining in the troposphere.

- The troposphere contains almost all of the mass of the atmosphere.

- In the troposphere, the temperature decreases as the altitude increases. In other words, the higher you go in the troposphere, the colder it gets.

Answer the following questions. Use your textbook and the ideas above.

3. Circle the letter of each sentence that is true about the troposphere.

  a. The troposphere is the lowest layer of the atmosphere.

  b. Most weather happens in the troposphere.

  c. The troposphere contains almost no mass.

4. Is the following sentence true or false? In the troposphere, the temperature increases as the altitude

  increases. _____

The Atmosphere

The Stratosphere (page 525)

Key Concept: **The stratosphere is the second layer of the atmosphere and contains the ozone layer.**

- The **stratosphere** is the layer of the atmosphere just above the troposphere. It is just below the mesosphere.

- The middle portion of the stratosphere contains the ozone layer. The ozone layer is where there is more ozone than in any other part of the atmosphere. The ozone layer blocks harmful energy from the sun.

- In the stratosphere, the temperature increases as the altitude increases. In other words, the higher you go in the stratosphere, the warmer it gets.

Answer the following questions. Use your textbook and the ideas above.

5. The layer just above the troposphere is the

   _____.

6. Circle the letter of each sentence that is true about the stratosphere.

   a. The stratosphere is just below the thermosphere.

   b. The middle portion of the stratosphere contains the ozone layer.

   c. The higher you go in the stratosphere, the warmer it gets.

7. Is the following sentence true or false? In the stratosphere, the temperature decreases as the

   altitude increases. _____

The Atmosphere

The Mesosphere (page 526)

Key Concept: **The mesosphere is the layer of the atmosphere that protects Earth's surface from being hit by most meteoroids.**

- The **mesosphere** is the layer of the atmosphere just above the stratosphere.

- In the mesosphere, the temperature decreases as the altitude increases. So, the higher you go in the mesosphere, the colder it gets.

- A meteoroid is a chunk of rock or metal from space. Most meteoroids heading toward Earth burn up in the mesosphere.

Answer the following questions. Use your textbook and the ideas above.

8. Circle the letter of each sentence that is true about the mesosphere.
   a. Most meteoroids heading toward Earth burn up in the mesosphere.
   b. In the mesosphere, the temperature decreases as the altitude increases.
   c. The mesosphere is the layer just above the thermosphere.

9. A chunk of rock or metal from space is a(n)

   _____.

The Thermosphere (pages 526–527)

Key Concept: **The outermost layer of Earth's atmosphere is the thermosphere.**

- The top layer of the atmosphere is the **thermosphere**. It is above the mesosphere.

The Atmosphere

- In the thermosphere, the temperature increases as the altitude increases. So, the higher you go in the thermosphere, the higher the temperature is.

- The thermosphere is divided into two layers. The lower layer of the thermosphere is called the **ionosphere** (eye AHN uh sfeer). The colorful displays called the Northern Lights take place in the ionosphere.

- The outer layer of the thermosphere is called the **exosphere**. The exosphere gradually blends with outer space.

Answer the following questions. Use your textbook and the ideas on page 247 and above.

10. Circle the letter of each sentence that is true about the thermosphere.

    a. The thermosphere is divided into two layers.

    b. In the thermosphere, the temperature increases as the altitude increases.

    c. The thermosphere is the top layer of the atmosphere.

11. Read each word in the box. In each sentence below, fill in one of the words.

exosphere	mesosphere	ionosphere

    a. The Northern Lights take place in the

    _____.

    b. The _____ gradually blends with outer space.

Air Quality (pages 528–531)

Sources of Pollution (page 529)

Key Concept: Some air pollution occurs naturally. But many types of air pollution are the result of human activities.

- **Pollutants** are harmful substances in the air, water, or soil.

- Many things in nature add pollutants to the air. For example, forest fires and volcanoes add pollutants to the air.

- Most air pollution is caused by burning fossil fuels. Fossil fuels include coal, oil, and natural gas.

- When fossil fuels burn, they release particles and gases. These are pollutants.

Answer the following questions. Use your textbook and the ideas above.

1. Read each word in the box. In each sentence below, fill in one of the words.

pollution	pollutant	polluted

   a. A harmful substance in the air is a

      _____.

   b. A process that makes air polluted is called

      _____.

   c. Air that contains pollutants is said to be

      _____.

2. Is the following sentence true or false? Most air

   pollution is caused by burning fossil fuels. _____

The Atmosphere

Smog and Acid Rain (page 530)

Key Concept: **The burning of fossil fuels can cause smog and acid rain.**

- The term *smog* is a combination of the words *fog* and *smoke*. A smog is a smoky fog.

- The brown haze that forms in sunny cities is called **photochemical** (foh toh KEM ih kul) **smog**. Photochemical smog forms when sunlight hits certain pollutants in the air.

- **Acid rain** is rain that has more acid than normal rain. Acid rain includes all forms of precipitation, such as rain and snow.

- Burning coal releases pollutants into the air. The pollutants combine with water in the air to form acids. Rain carries these acids down to the surface.

Answer the following questions. Use your textbook and the ideas above.

3. Complete the concept map about pollution caused by burning fossil fuels.

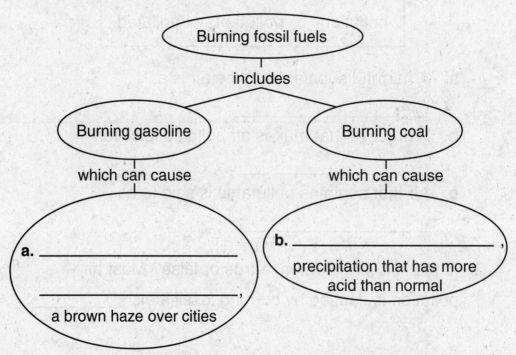

The Atmosphere

4. Read each word in the box. In each sentence below, fill in the correct word or words.

acid rain	photochemical smog	fossil fuels

a. The brown haze that develops in sunny cities is

called _____.

b. Rain that has more acid than normal rain is

called _____.

Improving Air Quality (page 531)

Key Concept: **In the United States, the federal and state governments have passed a number of laws and regulations to reduce air pollution.**

- The EPA watches for air pollutants in the United States. EPA stands for Environmental Protection Agency. The EPA is part of the U.S. government. The EPA enforces laws about air pollution.

- Air quality in the United States has improved over the past 30 years. But, the air in many American cities is still polluted.

Answer the following question. Use your textbook and the ideas above.

5. Circle the letter of each sentence that is true about the Environmental Protection Agency.

a. The EPA enforces laws about air pollution.

b. The EPA is part of the U.S. government.

c. The EPA passes laws about air pollutions.

Name _____ Date _____ Class _____

Weather Factors

Energy in Earth's Atmosphere (pages 542–545)

Energy From the Sun (pages 542–543)

Key Concept: **Most of the energy from the sun travels to Earth in the form of visible light and infrared radiation. A small amount arrives as ultraviolet radiation.**

- Energy from the sun travels to Earth as electromagnetic waves. **Electromagnetic waves** are a form of energy that can travel through space.

- Electromagnetic waves are classified according to their wavelengths.

- **Radiation** is the direct transfer of energy by electromagnetic waves.

- Visible light is the light you can see.

- **Infrared radiation** has wavelengths that are longer than visible light. You cannot see infrared radiation, but you can feel it as heat.

- **Ultraviolet radiation** has wavelengths that are shorter than visible light. Ultraviolet radiation causes sunburn.

Answer the following questions. Use your textbook and the ideas above.

1. Draw a line from each term to its meaning.

Term	Meaning
electromagnetic waves	**a.** the direct transfer of energy by electromagnetic waves
radiation	**b.** a form of energy that can travel through the vacuum of space

2. Is the following sentence true or false? You can feel ultraviolet radiation as heat. _____

Energy in the Atmosphere (page 544)

Key Concept: **Some sunlight is absorbed or reflected by the atmosphere before it can reach the surface. The rest passes through the atmosphere to the surface.**

- Part of the sun's energy is absorbed by the atmosphere. When energy is absorbed, it is taken in by a substance. For example, water vapor and carbon dioxide absorb the some of the sun's energy.

- Part of the sun's energy is reflected back into space. When energy is reflected, it bounces off without being absorbed. Clouds reflect some sunlight back into space.

- Dust particles and gases in the air reflect light in all directions. Reflecting light in all directions is called **scattering**.

- About half of the sun's energy passes through the atmosphere to Earth's surface.

Answer the following questions. Use your textbook and the ideas above.

3. Circle the letter of each sentence that is true about energy in the atmosphere.
   a. About half of the sun's energy passes through the atmosphere to Earth's surface.
   b. Water vapor and carbon dioxide in the atmosphere absorb the some of the sun's energy.
   c. All of the sun's energy is reflected back into space.

4. Reflecting light in all directions is called

_____.

Name _____ Date _____ Class _____

Energy at Earth's Surface (page 545)

Key Concept: When Earth's surface is heated, it radiates most of the energy back into the atmosphere as infrared radiation.

- The energy that reaches Earth's surface heats the land and water.

- The surface of Earth is heated by the sun. The heated surface then radiates the heat back into the atmosphere. The radiation from Earth's surface is infrared radiation.

- Some of the infrared radiation from Earth's surface is taken in by gases in the atmosphere. The gases that take in this heat include carbon dioxide and water vapor. When gases hold heat in the air, it is called the **greenhouse effect**.

- The greenhouse effect is natural. Because of the greenhouse effect, Earth's average temperatures remain about the same.

Answer the following questions. Use your textbook and the ideas above.

5. The process by which gases hold heat in the air is

    called the _____.

6. Complete the flowchart about the greenhouse effect.

The sun's energy reaches the surface of a. _____.	→	Earth's heated surface b. _____ infrared radiation back into the atmosphere.	→	The infrared radiation is absorbed by the c. _____ in the atmosphere.

Weather Factors

Heat Transfer (pages 548–551)

Thermal Energy and Temperature (page 549)

Key Concept: **Air temperature is usually measured with a thermometer.**

- The temperature of something is a measure of the motion of its particles. **Temperature** is the *average* amount of energy in the motion of each particle of a substance.

- **Thermal energy** is the *total* energy of motion of the particles of a substance.

- A **thermometer** is an instrument that measures temperature.

- Temperature is measured in units called degrees. Two temperature scales are the Celsius scale and the Fahrenheit scale. Scientists use the Celsius scale.

Answer the following questions. Use your textbook and the ideas above.

1. Read each word in the box. In each sentence below, fill in the correct word or words.

temperature   thermal energy
thermometer

   a. An instrument that measures temperature is
   called a _____.

   b. The total energy of motion of the particles of a
   substance is the _____ of the
   substance.

Weather Factors

2. Is the following sentence true or false? Scientists use the Fahrenheit scale to measure temperature.

_____.

How Heat Is Transferred (pages 550–551)

Key Concept: **Heat is transferred in three ways: radiation, conduction, and convection.**

• Most of the heat you feel from the sun travels to you as radiation. Radiation is the direct transfer of energy by electromagnetic waves. Radiation does not need matter to travel through. It can travel through empty space.

• **Conduction** is the direct transfer of heat from one thing to another by touching. When you walk on hot sand, your feet get hot by conduction.

• **Convection** is the transfer of heat by the movement of a fluid. A fluid is a liquid or a gas. The particles of a fluid take heat with them as they move. If you heat the air in one room, the air will heat the next room as the air flows from one room to the next. This is heating by convection.

Answer the following questions. Use your textbook and the ideas above.

3. Draw a line from each term to its meaning.

Term	Meaning
radiation	a. the direct transfer of heat from one thing to another by touching
conduction	
convection	b. the direct transfer of energy by electromagnetic waves
	c. the transfer of heat by the movement of a fluid

Weather Factors

4. Read each word in the box. Use the words to complete the table about examples of heat transfer.

radiation	conduction	convection

Examples of Heat Transfer

Type of Heat Transfer	Example of Heat Transfer
a. _____	hot water swirling in a pan
b. _____	warming your hands in front of a campfire
c. _____	putting an electric heating pad on your knee
d. _____	feeling the sun's heat on your face

Key Concept: **Radiation, conduction, and convection work together to heat the troposphere.**

- Sunlight heats Earth's surface by radiation. The warm surface then heats the atmosphere by both conduction and radiation.

- Only the first few meters of the troposphere are heated by conduction. The air closer to the ground is usually warmer than the air above it.

- Heat is transferred by convection through most of the troposphere. Convection currents move heat throughout the troposphere. The upward movement of warm air and the downward movement of cool air form **convection currents**.

Weather Factors

Answer the following questions. Use your textbook and the ideas on page 257.

5. Is the following sentence true or false? Earth's atmosphere is heated by only conduction and radiation.

_____

6. The picture shows all three types of heat transfer working together to heat the troposphere. Draw a circle around heat transfer by convection.

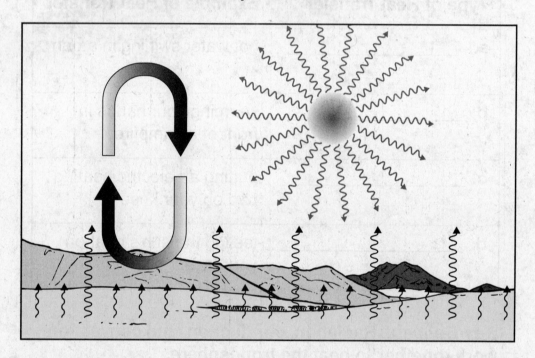

7. The upward movement of warm air and the downward movement of cool air form _____.

Winds (pages 552–558)

What Is Wind? (page 553)

Key Concept: **Winds are caused by differences in air pressure.**

- **Wind** is the sideways movement of air. The air always moves from an area of high pressure to an area of low pressure.

- Differences in air pressure are caused by differences in how places are heated by the sun. Warm air has less pressure than cooler air.

- The name of a wind tells you where the wind is coming from. For example, a west wind blows from the west.

- Wind speed is measured with an **anemometer** (an uh MAHM uh tur).

Answer the following questions. Use your textbook and the ideas above.

1. Read each word in the box. In each sentence below, fill in the correct word or words.

wind   anemometer   air pressure

   a. Wind speed is measured with a(an)

   _____.

   b. The sideways movement of air is called

   _____.

2. Is the following sentence true or false? Air moves from an area of high pressure to an area of low pressure.

   _____

Name _____ Date _____ Class _____

Local Winds (page 554)

Key Concept: **Local winds are caused by the unequal heating of Earth's surface within a small area.**

- **Local winds** are winds that blow over a short distance. A cool breeze blowing in from the water over a beach is an example of a local wind.

- Unequal heating often happens near lakes and ocean coasts.

- A **sea breeze** is a local wind that blows from an ocean. A lake breeze is a local wind that blows from a lake. A sea breeze or lake breeze usually happens during the day.

- A **land breeze** is a local wind that blows from the land over a lake or ocean. A land breeze usually happens at night.

Answer the following questions. Use your textbook and the ideas above.

3. Winds that blow over a short distance are called

   _____.

4. The pictures show two types of local winds. Label the pictures to tell which shows a land breeze and which shows a sea breeze.

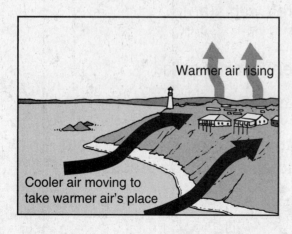

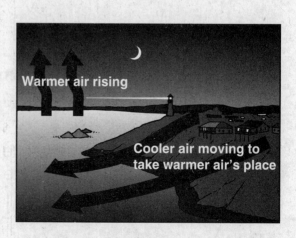

Warmer air rising

Warmer air rising

Cooler air moving to take warmer air's place

Cooler air moving to take warmer air's place

a. _____   b. _____

Global Winds (page 555)

Key Concept: **Like local winds, global winds are created by the unequal heating of Earth's surface. But unlike local winds, global winds occur over a large area.**

- A **global wind** is a wind that blows steadily over long distances. A global wind blows from the same direction every time.

- The sun heats Earth unequally. For example, the sun shines directly over the equator. The sun shines at an angle over the poles.

- Earth rotates from east to west. Earth's rotation makes global winds curve. The way that winds curve is called the **Coriolis** (kawr ee OH lis) **effect**.

- The Coriolis effect makes winds in the Northern Hemisphere curve to the right. It makes winds in the Southern Hemisphere curve to the left.

Answer the following questions. Use your textbook and the ideas above.

5. Read the words in the box. In each sentence below, fill in the correct words.

global wind	local wind	Coriolis effect

    a. The way that winds curve is called the

        _____.

    b. A wind that blows steadily over long distances

        is called a _____.

6. Is the following sentence true or false? The sun

    heats Earth unequally. _____

Weather Factors

Global Wind Belts (pages 556–558)

Key Concept: **The major global wind belts are the trade winds, the polar easterlies, and the prevailing westerlies.**

- A series of wind belts circles Earth. Between the winds belts are calm areas.

- The trade winds are global winds that blow in the Northern Hemisphere toward the equator from 30° north latitude. **Latitude** is the distance from the equator.

- Winds blow from the west to the east between 30° and 60° latitude in both the Northern and the Southern hemispheres. Since these winds always blow from the west, they are called the prevailing westerlies.

- The polar easterlies blow from the poles and curve eastward.

- High-speed winds called **jet streams** blow at the top of the troposphere.

Answer the following question. Use your textbook and the ideas above.

7. Draw a line from each global wind belt to its correct description.

Global Wind Belt	Description
trade winds	**a.** winds that blow from the west to the east between 30° and 60° latitude
prevailing westerlies	
	b. winds that blow in the Northern Hemisphere toward the equator from 30° north latitude
polar easterlies	
	c. winds that blow from the poles and curve eastward

Water in the Atmosphere (pages 560–566)

Introduction (page 560)

Key Concept: **Water is always moving between the atmosphere and Earth's surface.**

- The **water cycle** is the movement of water between the atmosphere and Earth's surface.

- Water vapor enters the air through evaporation. **Evaporation** is when a liquid becomes a gas. Liquid water evaporates to become water vapor.

- The water cycle includes all forms of precipitation, including rain and snow. Water moves from the atmosphere to Earth's surface by precipitation.

Answer the following questions. Use your textbook and the ideas above.

1. Water moves between the atmosphere and Earth's surface through the _____ cycle.

2. Circle the letter of the way that water enters the atmosphere.
   a. evaporation
   b. precipitation
   c. condensation

Humidity (pages 561–562)

Key Concept: **Relative humidity can be measured with an instrument called a psychrometer.**

- **Humidity** is a measure of how much water vapor is in the air. Warm air can hold more water vapor than cold air.

Weather Factors

- Relative humidity is a percentage measurement. **Relative humidity** is the percentage of water vapor in the air compared to how much humidity the air can hold.

- A **psychrometer** (sy KRAHM uh tur) is an instrument that measures relative humidity. A psychrometer has two thermometers. One thermometer has a wet cloth covering it. You can tell the relative humidity of the air by comparing the temperatures on the two thermometers.

Answer the following questions. Use your textbook and the ideas on page 263 and above.

3. Read each word in the box. In each sentence below, fill in the correct word or words.

humidity	psychrometer
water vapor	relative humidity

   a. An instrument that measures relative humidity is

      a(an) _____.

   b. The percentage of water vapor in the air compared to how much humidity the air can hold is

      called _____.

   c. A measure of how much water vapor is in the

      air is called _____.

4. Circle the letter of each sentence that is true about a psychrometer.

   a. A psychrometer has two thermometers.

   b. One thermometer has a wet cloth covering it.

   c. You compare the two thermometers to find out the relative humidity.

Weather Factors

How Clouds Form (page 563)

Key Concept: **Clouds form when water vapor in the air condenses to form liquid water or ice crystals.**

- **Condensation** is when a gas becomes a liquid. For example, water vapor condenses to form liquid water. This happens in the atmosphere when clouds form.

- There are two things needed for condensation to occur in the atmosphere:
    1. There must be cooling of the air.
    2. There must be particles—tiny solids—in the air.

- Cold air holds less water vapor than warm air. When air cools, water vapor condenses into little drops of water or ice crystals. The temperature at which this happens is called the **dew point**.

- Tiny particles must be in the air for condensation of water to take place. Water needs something to condense onto.

Answer the following questions. Use your textbook and the ideas above.

5. The process in which a gas becomes a liquid is

   called _____.

6. Circle the letter of each thing needed for condensation to occur in the atmosphere.
    a. There must be particles in the air.
    b. There must be cooling of the air.
    c. There must be precipitation in the air.

7. Is the following sentence true or false? The temperature at which water vapor condenses into little

   drops of water is called the dew point. _____

Weather Factors

Types of Clouds (pages 564–566)

Key Concept: **Scientists classify clouds into three main types based on their shape: cirrus, cumulus, and stratus. Clouds are further classified by their altitude.**

- **Cirrus** (SEER us) clouds are the wispy clouds that look like feathers in the sky. Cirrus clouds only form high in the sky.

- **Cumulus** (KYOO myuh lus) clouds look like fluffy, rounded piles of cotton. Cumulus clouds can produce thunderstorms. Thunderstorm clouds are called cumulonimbus clouds.

- **Stratus** (STRAT us) clouds are flat layers of clouds. Stratus clouds usually cover most of the sky. Stratus clouds that produce rain are called nimbostratus clouds.

- Clouds that form near the ground are called fog. Fog often forms when the ground cools at night. Fog is common near bodies of water, such as a lake.

Answer the following questions. Use your textbook and the ideas above.

8. Draw a line from each type of cloud to its description.

Type of Cloud	Description
cirrus clouds	**a.** flat layers of clouds
cumulus clouds	**b.** clouds that form at or near the ground
stratus clouds	**c.** clouds that look like fluffy, rounded piles of cotton
fog	**d.** wispy clouds that look like feathers in the sky

Weather Factors

9. Circle the letter of the type of cloud that often produces thunderstorms.
   a. altocumulus
   b. nimbostratus
   c. cumulonimbus

10. The picture shows three types of clouds in the atmosphere. Draw a circle around the cumulus cloud.

Weather Factors

Precipitation (pages 567–571)

Types of Precipitation (pages 568–570)

Key Concept: **Common types of precipitation include rain, sleet, freezing rain, snow, and hail.**

- **Precipitation** (pree sip uh TAY shun) is any form of water that falls from clouds and reaches Earth's surface.

- The most common type of precipitation is rain. Drops of rain must be at least 0.5 millimeter in diameter. Smaller drops are called drizzle.

- Sometimes, ice particles fall. Ice particles smaller than 5 millimeters in diameter are called sleet.

- Sometimes, raindrops do not freeze until they touch a cold surface, such as the ground or a tree. This kind of precipitation is called freezing rain.

- Water vapor in a cloud can become ice crystals called snowflakes.

- Round pellets of ice larger than 5 millimeters in diameter are called hail or hailstones.

- A long period of low precipitation is called a **drought**.

Answer the following questions. Use your textbook and the ideas above.

1. Circle the letter of the most common type of precipitation.
   a. snow
   b. sleet
   c. rain

Weather Factors

2. Read each word in the box. In each sentence below, fill in one of the words.

precipitation	drought	condensation

a. Any form of water that falls from clouds and reaches Earth's surface is called

_____.

b. A long period of low precipitation is called a

_____.

3. Complete the table about types of precipitation.

Types of Precipitation	
Type of Precipitation	
a. _____	drops of water at least 0.5 millimeter in diameter
Drizzle	drops of water smaller than 0.5 millimeter in diameter
Sleet	ice particles smaller than 5 millimeters in diameter
b. _____ _____	raindrops that freeze when they touch a cold surface
Snow	ice crystals that fall all the way to the ground
c. _____	round pellets of ice larger than 5 millimeters in diameter

Measuring Precipitation (pages 570–571)

Key Concept: **Scientists measure precipitation with various instruments, including rain gauges and measuring sticks.**

- Snowfall can be measured using a measuring stick. Snowfall can also be measured by melting the snow and then measuring how much water there is.

- Rain is measured with a rain gauge. A **rain gauge** is a can or tube with an open end that is made to measure rainfall. You can measure the amount of rainfall in a rain gauge either by using a ruler or by reading a scale on the gauge.

Answer the following questions. Use your textbook and the ideas above.

4. Circle the letter of each way that snowfall can be measured.
    a. by using a measuring stick
    b. by using a snow gauge
    c. by melting the snow and measuring how much water there is

5. An open-ended can or tube that collects rainfall is called a(an) _____.

Air Masses and Fronts (pages 578–585)

Types of Air Masses (pages 579–580)

Key Concept: **Four major types of air masses influence the weather in North America: maritime tropical, continental tropical, maritime polar, and continental polar.**

- An **air mass** is a huge body of air. The air at any given height in an air mass all has about the same temperature, humidity, and air pressure.

- A **tropical** air mass forms in the tropics. A tropical air mass has warm air. A **polar** air mass forms near the poles. A polar air mass has cold air.

- A **maritime** air mass forms over an ocean. A maritime air mass has humid air. A **continental** air mass forms over land. A continental air mass has dry air.

- A maritime tropical air mass has warm, humid air. A maritime polar air mass has cool, humid air.

- A continental tropical air mass has hot, dry air. A continental polar air mass has cold, dry air.

Answer the following questions. Use your textbook and the ideas above.

1. Circle the letter of each characteristic scientists use to classify air masses.
   a. cloudiness
   b. temperature
   c. humidity

2. A huge body of air with similar temperature, humidity, and air pressure at any given height is a(an)

   _____.

Weather Patterns

3. Complete the table about air masses.

Air Masses		
Type of Air Mass	**Temperature of Air**	**Humidity of Air**
Maritime tropical	warm	**a.** _____
Maritime polar	**b.** _____	humid
Continental tropical	hot	**c.** _____
Continental polar	**d.** _____	dry

How Air Masses Move (page 581)

Key Concept: **In the continental United States, air masses are commonly moved by the prevailing westerlies and jet streams.**

- Air masses move. Global winds usually move air masses from one part of Earth to another.

- The major wind belts over the United States are the prevailing westerlies. These winds usually push air masses from west to east across the United States.

- Jet streams also push air masses across the United States from west to east.

- As air masses move, they bump into each other. A **front** is a boundary where two air masses meet. Storms and other types of weather develop along fronts.

Weather Patterns

Answer the following questions. Use your textbook and the ideas on page 272.

4. Circle the letter of each wind belt that commonly moves air masses in the continental United States.

   a. prevailing westerlies

   b. trade winds

   c. prevailing easterlies

5. The boundary where two air masses meet is called a(an) _____.

Types of Fronts (pages 582–583)

Key Concept: **Colliding air masses can form four types of fronts: cold fronts, warm fronts, stationary fronts, and occluded fronts.**

- A cold front forms when a cold air mass slides under a warm air mass. Thunderstorms can occur at a cold front.

- A warm front forms when a warm air mass moves over a cold air mass. Light rain or snow may fall.

- Sometimes cold and warm air masses meet, but neither air mass moves over or under the other. The two air masses face each other in a "standoff." This is called a stationary front. A stationary front can bring many days of clouds and precipitation.

- A warm air mass sometimes is caught between two cooler air masses. This forms an occluded front. **Occluded** means to be cut off. In an occluded front, the warm air mass is cut off from the ground. The weather may turn cloudy, and rain or snow may fall.

Answer the following questions. Use your textbook and the ideas on page 273.

6. Draw a line from the type of front to a description of how it forms.

Type of Front	How It Forms
cold front	**a.** A warm air mass moves over a cold air mass.
warm front	**b.** A warm air mass moves between two cold air masses.
stationary front	**c.** A cold air mass slides under a warm air mass.
occluded front	**d.** Two air masses face each other in a "standoff."

7. Circle the letter of the type of front that can result in thunderstorms.

    a. cold front

    b. warm front

    c. occluded front

8. The pictures show two types of fronts. Circle the letter of the cold front.

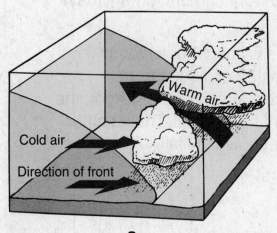

a.

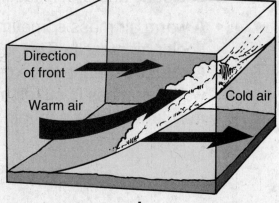

b.

Cyclones and Anticyclones (pages 584–585)

***Key Concept:* Cyclones and decreasing air pressure are associated with clouds, wind, and precipitation.**

- A **cyclone** is a swirling center of low air pressure. The winds in a cyclone spiral around a center. In a cyclone, winds spiral inward towards the low-pressure center.

- The Coriolis effect makes winds spin counterclockwise in a Northern Hemisphere cyclone.

- Air spins upward in a cyclone. The result is clouds, wind, and precipitation.

- Cyclones play a large part in the weather of the United States.

Answer the following question. Use your textbook and the ideas above.

9. Circle the letter of what kind of weather a cyclone brings.

   a. clear, dry weather

   b. wind and precipitation

   c. sunny and hot

***Key Concept:* The descending air in an anticyclone generally causes dry, clear weather.**

- An **anticyclone** is a high-pressure center of dry air. An anticyclone is the opposite of a cyclone. In an anticyclone, winds spiral outward away from the high-pressure center.

- The Coriolis effect makes winds spin clockwise in a Northern Hemisphere anticyclone.

- The air spins down in an anticyclone. The result is dry, clear weather.

Name _____ Date _____ Class _____

Answer the following questions. Use your textbook and the ideas on page 275.

10. Circle the letter of the kind of weather an anticyclone brings.

    a. dry, clear weather

    b. hot, rainy weather

    c. thunderstorms

11. The pictures show a cyclone and an anticyclone. Circle the letter of the anticyclone.

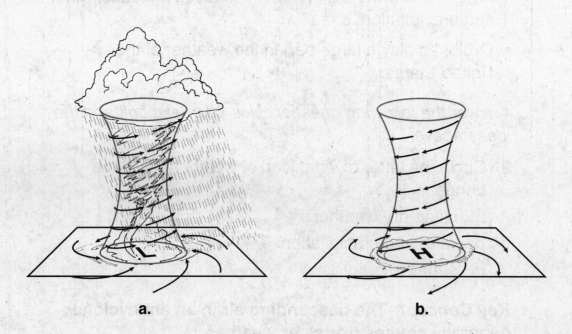

      a.   **b.**

Weather Patterns

Storms (pages 586–595)

Thunderstorms (pages 587–588)

Key Concept: **Thunderstorms form in large cumulonimbus clouds, also known as thunderheads.**

- A **storm** is a violent disturbance in the atmosphere. Storms include thunderstorms, tornadoes, hurricanes, and winter storms.

- A **thunderstorm** is a small storm that often has heavy precipitation and thunder and lightning.

- Cumulonimbus clouds form on hot, humid afternoons. They also form along cold fronts.

- **Lightning** is a sudden spark in the atmosphere. Lightning can cause an explosion of air. Thunder is the sound of that explosion.

Answer the following questions. Use your textbook and the ideas above.

1. Read each word in the box. In each sentence below, fill in one of the words.

storm	lightning	thunderstorm	thunder

   a. A small storm that often has heavy precipitation and thunder and lightning is a

   _____.

   b. A sudden spark in the atmosphere is called

   _____.

   c. A violent disturbance in the atmosphere is a

   _____.

Weather Patterns

2. Complete the concept map about thunderstorms.

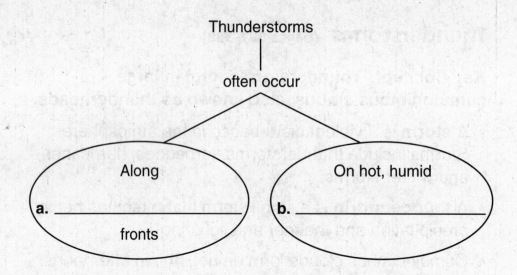

Key Concept: **During thunderstorms, avoid places where lightning may strike. Also avoid objects that can conduct electricity, such as metal objects and bodies of water.**

- The safest place to be during a thunderstorm is indoors.

- Metal objects can conduct electricity. Water also can conduct electricity. Stay away from objects that can conduct electricity during thunderstorms.

Answer the following question. Use your textbook and the ideas above.

3. Is the following sentence true or false? The safest place to be during a thunderstorm is indoors.

_____

Tornadoes (pages 588–591)

Key Concept: **Tornadoes most commonly develop in thick cumulonimbus clouds—the same clouds that bring thunderstorms.**

- A **tornado** is a rapidly spinning cloud that reaches down to Earth's surface.

Weather Patterns

- Tornados usually form in cumulonimbus clouds. A tornado cloud is shaped like a funnel—wide at the top and narrow at the bottom.

- Tornadoes occur more often in the United States than in any other country. They are common on the Great Plains. "Tornado alley" includes parts of Texas, Oklahoma, Kansas, Nebraska, and South Dakota.

Answer the following questions. Use your textbook and the ideas on page 278 and above.

4. A rapidly spinning cloud that touches Earth's

surface is called a(an) _____.

5. Circle the letter of where tornadoes usually form.
   a. over ocean water
   b. in wind belts
   c. in cumulonimbus clouds

Key Concept: **The safest place to be during a tornado is in a storm shelter or the basement of a well-built building.**

- A "tornado watch" is an announcement that tornadoes are possible in your area. A "tornado warning" is an announcement that a tornado has been seen in your area.

- If a building does not have a basement, move to the middle of the lowest floor during a tornado.

Answer the following question. Use your textbook and the ideas above.

6. Draw a line from each term to its meaning.

Term	Meaning
tornado watch	a. a tornado has been seen
	b. a tornado is possible
tornado warning	

Hurricanes (pages 592–593)

Key Concept: **A hurricane begins over warm ocean water as a low-pressure area, or tropical disturbance.**

- A **hurricane** is a tropical cyclone. A cyclone has low pressure. A hurricane has winds that are at least 119 kilometers per hour. Hurricanes form in the Atlantic, Pacific, and Indian oceans.

- A hurricane draws its energy from the warm, humid air at the ocean's surface. The center of a hurricane is called the "eye." The eye is calm.

- Hurricanes last a week or more. Hurricanes that form in the Atlantic Ocean are pushed by easterly trade winds toward the southeastern United States.

Answer the following questions. Use your textbook and the ideas above.

7. Circle the letter of each sentence that is true about hurricanes.
    a. Hurricanes form in the Atlantic, Pacific, and Indian oceans.
    b. The outer edge of a hurricane is called the "eye."
    c. A hurricane is a tropical cyclone.

8. Is the following sentence true or false? A hurricane draws its energy from the warm, humid air at the ocean's surface. _____

Key Concept: **If you hear a hurricane warning and are told to evacuate, leave the area immediately.**

- To **evacuate** means to move away from an area.

- If you have to stay in a house, move away from the windows.

Answer the following question. Use your textbook and the ideas on page 280.

9. To move away from an area is to

_____.

Winter Storms (pages 594–595)

Key Concept: **All year round, most precipitation begins in clouds as snow. If the air is colder than 0°C all the way to the ground, the precipitation falls as snow.**

- In warmer months, the snow that falls from clouds melts and then hits Earth's surface as rain.

- Cities near the Great Lakes can receive a lot of snow.

Answer the following question. Use your textbook and the ideas above.

10. Is the following sentence true or false? The air must be below 0°C all the way to the ground for snow to fall.

_____

Key Concept: **If you are caught in a snowstorm, try to find shelter from the wind.**

- Blowing snow can limit how much you can see.

- The winds in a winter storm can cool your body.

Answer the following question. Use your textbook and the ideas above.

11. Is the following sentence true or false? Blowing snow does not limit how much you can see. _____

Weather Patterns

Predicting the Weather (pages 598–604)

Weather Forecasting (page 599)

Key Concept: **Meteorologists use maps, charts, and computers to analyze weather data and to prepare weather forecasts.**

• A **meteorologist** (mee tee uh RAHL uh jist) is a scientist who studies the causes of weather and predicts the weather. Meteorologists analyze weather data, which means that they organize weather information and try to see trends.

• Most weather information comes from the National Weather Service, a part of the U.S. government. The National Weather Service uses scientific instruments to gather weather data.

Answer the following question. Use your textbook and the ideas above.

1. Circle the letter of a scientist who predicts the weather.
   a. reporter
   b. meteorologist
   c. biologist

Weather Technology (pages 600–601)

Key Concept: **Technological improvements in gathering weather data and using computers have improved the accuracy of weather forecasts.**

• Weather balloons carry scientific instruments up into the atmosphere. The instruments measure temperature, air pressure, and humidity.

Weather Patterns

- Weather satellites orbit Earth in the upper layer of the atmosphere, called the exosphere.

- The National Weather Service has built many weather observation stations. These stations collect data about temperature, humidity, rainfall, and winds.

- Computers are used to process weather data and help weather forecasters make predictions.

Answer the following questions. Use your textbook and the ideas on page 282 and above.

2. Circle the letter of each way weather data is collected.

   a. by weather satellites

   b. by weather balloons

   c. by computers

3. Is the following sentence true or false? Meteorologists use computers in making weather forecasts.

_____

Reading Weather Maps (pages 602–604)

Key Concept: **Standard symbols on weather maps show fronts, areas of high and low pressure, types of precipitation, and temperatures.**

- A weather map is a "snapshot" of weather conditions at a particular time over a large area.

- The National Weather Service collects data from weather stations all over the country. This data can be shown on a weather map.

- Thin lines on a weather map connect places with the same air pressure or temperature. An **isobar** is a line on a weather map that connects places with the same air pressure. An **isotherm** is a line on a weather map that connects places with the same temperature.

Name _____ Date _____ Class _____

Weather Patterns

Answer the following questions. Use your textbook and the ideas on page 283.

4. Read each word in the box. In each sentence below, fill in the correct word or words.

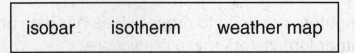

| isobar | isotherm | weather map |

a. A line on a weather map that connects places with the same air pressure is a(an)

_____.

b. A "snapshot" of weather conditions at a particular time over a large area is a(an)

_____.

5. The weather map below shows two fronts stretching across parts of the United States. Circle the warm front shown on the map.

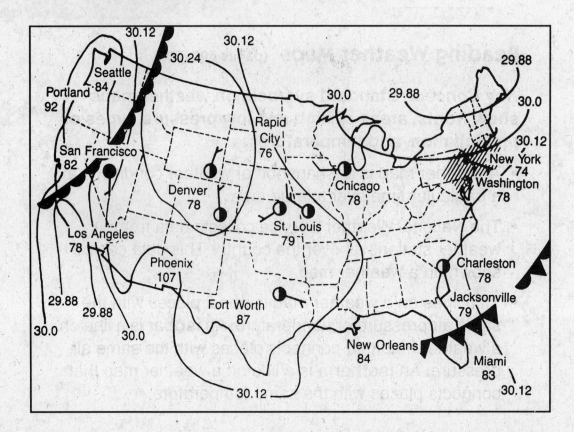

What Causes Climate? (pages 614–621)

Introduction (page 614)

Key Concept: **Scientists use two main factors—precipitation and temperature—to describe the climate of a region.**

- A **climate** is the average, year-after-year weather conditions in an area. Two conditions are most important in describing a climate—temperature and precipitation.

- A climate region is a large area that has similar climate conditions throughout. For example, all of the southwestern United States has a hot, dry climate.

- A small area within a climate region may have climate conditions that are different from the area around it. A small area with different climate conditions is called a **microclimate**.

Answer the following question. Use your textbook and the ideas above.

1. Read each word in the box. In each sentence below, fill in the correct word or words.

climate	weather
microclimate	climate region

    a. A small area with different climate conditions is called a _____.

    b. A large area that has similar climate conditions throughout is called a _____.

    c. The average, year-after-year weather conditions in an area is called _____.

Climate and Climate Change

Factors Affecting Temperature (pages 615–617)

Key Concept: **The main factors that influence temperature are latitude, altitude, distance from large bodies of water, and ocean currents.**

- Earth is divided into three temperature zones based on latitude:
    1. The **tropical zone** is the area near the equator. Climates are warm there.
    2. The **polar zones** are near the North and South poles. Climates are cold there.
    3. The **temperate zones** are between the tropical zone and each of the polar zones. Weather in the temperate zones ranges from warm in the summer to cold in the winter.

- Altitude affects temperatures. Highland areas everywhere have cool climates.

- Oceans and large lakes affect climate. A **marine climate** is the climate of an area near an ocean or large lake. Such an area has mostly mild winters and cool summers.

- **Continental climates** have hotter and colder seasons than do marine climates. Winters are cold, while summers are hot. The central part of the United States has a continental climate.

Answer the following questions. Use your textbook and the ideas above.

2. What are the three temperature zones Earth is divided into? Circle the letter of the correct answer.
    a. marine zones, polar zones, temperate zones
    b. tropical zones, continental zones, polar zones
    c. tropical zones, polar zones, temperate zones

3. Is the following sentence true or false? Highland areas everywhere have cool climates. _____

4. Complete the table about how distance from large bodies of water affects climates.

Climates Near and Far From Large Bodies of Water	
Type of Climate	**Climate Characteristics**
a. _____ climates	winters are cold; summers are hot
b. _____ climates	mostly mild winters and cool summers

Factors Affecting Precipitation (pages 618–619)

Key Concept: **The main factors that affect precipitation are prevailing winds, the presence of mountains, and seasonal winds.**

- Prevailing winds move air masses from one place to another. The amount of water vapor in an air mass influences the amount of precipitation.

- When prevailing winds blow into a mountain range, rain or snow often falls. The rain or snow falls on the windward side of the mountains. The **windward** side of a mountain is the side the wind hits first. The land on the leeward side of mountains remains dry. The **leeward** side of a mountain is the side that is downwind.

- Seasonal winds are wind patterns that change with the seasons over a wide area. Monsoons are seasonal winds. **Monsoons** are large sea and land breezes that change directions with the seasons.

Climate and Climate Change

Answer the following questions. Use your textbook and the ideas on page 287.

5. Complete the concept map about factors that affect precipitation.

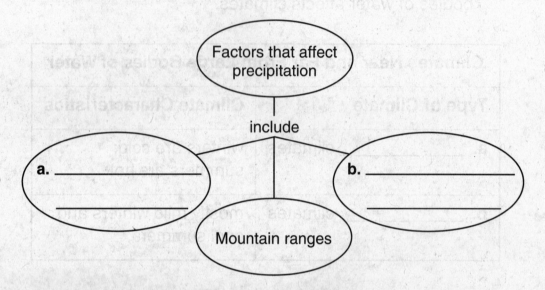

6. Circle the letter of the side of the mountain where rain falls when prevailing winds bring clouds.

   a. leeward side

   b. back side

   c. windward side

7. Large sea and land breezes that change directions with the seasons are called _____.

The Seasons (pages 620–621)

***Key Concept:* The seasons are caused by the tilt of Earth's axis as Earth travels around the sun.**

- The weather changes as the seasons change.

- Earth's axis tilts. As Earth travels around the sun, the axis always points the same way. When Earth is on one side of the sun, Earth tilts toward the sun. When Earth is on the other side, Earth tilts away from the sun.

Climate and Climate Change

- When Earth tilts toward the sun, it is summer in the Northern Hemisphere. When Earth tilts away from the sun, it is winter in the Northern Hemisphere.

- When it is summer in the Northern Hemisphere, it is winter in the Southern Hemisphere. When it is winter in the Northern Hemisphere, it is summer in the Southern Hemisphere.

Answer the following questions. Use your textbook and the ideas on page 288 and above.

8. Circle the letter of each sentence that is true about Earth's axis.

   a. Earth is tilted on its axis.

   b. The axis always points the same way as Earth revolves around the sun.

   c. Earth always tilts toward the sun.

9. The picture shows Earth in its orbit around the sun. Earth is tilted on its axis. Circle the letter of the sentence that is true about the picture.

   a. It is summer in the Northern Hemisphere.

   b. It is winter in the Southern Hemisphere.

   c. It is winter in the Northern Hemisphere.

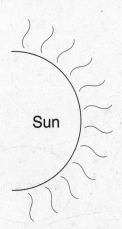

Sun

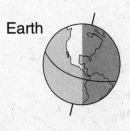

Earth

Climate and Climate Change

Climate Regions (pages 624–633)

Introduction (pages 624, 626–627)

Key Concept: **Scientists classify climates according to two major factors: temperature and precipitation. There are six main climate regions: tropical rainy, dry, temperate marine, temperate continental, polar, and highlands.**

- Scientists mainly use temperature and precipitation to classify different climates. Each kind of climate has a different combination of temperatures and precipitation patterns.

- Scientists identify large regions around the world by climate. Scientists have identified six main climate regions on Earth. Each climate region blends gradually into the next.

- Each climate region is also divided into smaller climate regions.

Answer the following questions. Use your textbook and the ideas above.

1. Complete the concept map about climate regions.

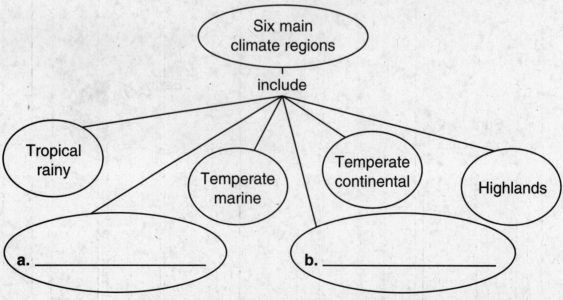

Climate and Climate Change

2. Circle the letter of each factor that scientists use
   to classify climates.

   a. temperature

   b. precipitation

   c. humidity

Tropical Rainy Climates (page 625)

Key Concept: **The tropics haves two types of rainy
climates: tropical wet and tropical wet-and-dry.**

- Tropical wet climates have year-round heat and heavy
  rainfall. Dense rain forests grow in tropical wet climates.
  Rain forests are forests in which large amounts of rain
  fall year-round.

- There are tropical wet climates in parts of South
  America and Africa. Parts of the Hawaiian Islands have
  the only tropical wet climate in the United States.

- Areas with tropical wet-and-dry climates have dry
  seasons and rainy seasons. These areas have
  savannas. A **savanna** is a grassland with
  scattered trees.

- Tropical wet-and-dry climates can be found in India and
  parts of Africa. In the United States, only southern
  Florida has a tropical wet-and-dry climate.

*Answer the following questions. Use your textbook and the
ideas above.*

3. Circle the letter of each sentence that is true about
   tropical wet climates.

   a. There is year-round heat and heavy rainfall.

   b. Dense rain forests grow in tropical wet climates.

   c. Tropical wet climates have savannas.

4. Read each word in the box. In each sentence below, fill in the correct word or words.

rain forest	climate region	savanna

a. A grassland with scattered trees is called a

_____.

b. A forest in which large amounts of rain fall

year-round is called a _____.

Dry Climates (page 628)

Key Concept: **Dry climates include arid and semiarid climates.**

- Humid air masses lose much of their water vapor as they cross mountains. Dry regions are often on the leeward side of mountain ranges.

- The word *arid* means "dry." A **desert** is an arid region. Deserts usually get less than 25 centimeters of rain per year.

- In the United States, there are deserts in California, the Great Basin, and the Southwest.

- The word *semiarid* means "fairly dry." Large semiarid areas are often located on the edges of deserts. A **steppe** is a dry area that gets enough rain for grasses and low bushes to grow.

Answer the following questions. Use your textbook and the ideas above.

5. Is the following sentence true or false? Dry regions are often on the windward side of mountain ranges.

_____

6. Complete the concept map about dry climates.

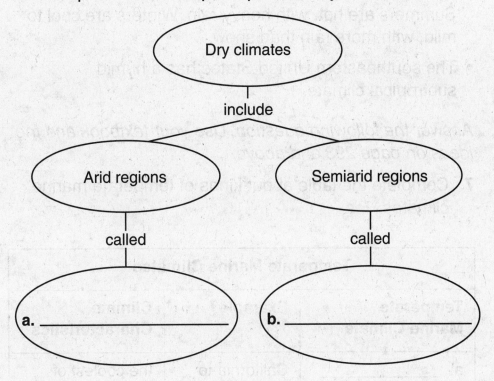

Temperate Marine Climates (pages 629–630)

Key Concept: **There are three kinds of temperate marine climates: marine west coast, humid subtropical, and Mediterranean.**

- All temperate marine climates are humid and have mild winters.

- Marine west coast climates are the coolest of the three kinds of temperate marine climates. Marine west coast climates are found on the west coasts of continents.

- In North America, the marine west coast climate extends from northern California to southern Alaska. In this region, there is heavy precipitation.

- Most areas with a Mediterranean climate are found around the Mediterranean Sea, which is between Europe and Africa. The climate is mild, with two main seasons. Winter is a rainy season. Summer is warm.

Climate and Climate Change

- **Humid subtropical** climates are wet and warm. Summers are hot, with heavy rain. Winters are cool to mild, with more rain than snow.

- The southeastern United States has a humid subtropical climate.

Answer the following question. Use your textbook and the ideas on page 293 and above.

7. Complete the table about kinds of temperate marine climates.

Temperate Marine Climates		
Temperate Marine Climate	**Example**	**Climate Characteristics**
a. _____ _____ _____	California to southern Alaska	the coolest of the temperate marine climates, with heavy precipitation
b. _____	around the Mediterranean Sea	rainy season in winter, warm and dry in summer
c. _____ _____	southeastern United States	hot summers, with heavy rain; cool-to-mild winters, with more rain than snow

Climate and Climate Change

Temperate Continental Climates (page 631)

Key Concept: **Temperate continental climates are only found on continents in the Northern Hemisphere, and include humid continental and subarctic.**

- Temperate continental climates commonly have extreme temperatures in summer and winter. There are no ocean breezes to keep the temperatures moderate.

- Humid continental climates have changing weather because different air masses move through. Summers are hot and rainy. Winters can be very cold with snow.

- In the United States, the Northeast and the Midwest have humid continental climates.

- The **subarctic** climates are north of the humid continental climates. Summers are short. Winters are very cold.

- Much of Alaska and Canada have subarctic climates.

Answer the following questions. Use your textbook and the ideas above.

8. Circle the letter of each climate that is a temperate continental climate.
   a. subarctic climate
   b. humid continental climate
   c. humid subtropical climate

9. Is the following sentence true or false? Temperate continental climates are found only on continents in the Northern Hemisphere. _____

10. The climates north of the humid continental climates are the _____ climates.

11. Circle the letter of each sentence that is true about humid continental climates.

a. Summers are cool and dry.

b. The Midwest has a humid continental climate.

c. Winters can be very cold with snow.

Polar Climates (page 632)

Key Concept: **The polar climate is the coldest climate region, and includes the ice cap and tundra climates.**

• Polar climates are found only near the North Pole and the South Pole. Most polar climates are dry.

• Ice cap climates are found on Greenland and in Antarctica. Average temperatures are always below freezing, and the land is covered with ice and snow. Few plants grow.

• The **tundra** climate region stretches across northern Alaska, Canada, and Russia. The soil in a tundra climate region is permanently frozen. Permanently frozen soil is called **permafrost**. It is too cold on the tundra for trees to grow. Summers, though, are warm. Grasses and shrubs grow quickly.

Answer the following questions. Use your textbook and the ideas above.

12. Read each word in the box. In each sentence below, fill in the correct word or words.

tundra	permafrost	ice cap

a. The _____ climate region stretches across northern Alaska, Canada, and Russia.

b. Permanently frozen soil is called

_____ .

Climate and Climate Change

13. Is the following sentence true or false? In ice cap climates, the land is covered with ice and snow.

_____

Highlands (page 633)

Key Concept: **Temperature falls as altitude increases, so highland regions are colder than the regions that surround them.**

- Increasing altitude produces climate changes similar to increasing latitude. For example, the climate on top of a tall mountain is like the polar climates of the northern latitudes.

- The climate at the bottom of a mountain is the same as the surrounding countryside.

- The climate high on a mountain is like a subarctic climate. Closer to the top of a mountain, it is like tundra climate.

Answer the following question. Use your textbook and the ideas above.

14. Circle the letter of each sentence that is true about highlands climates.

   a. As you go higher up a mountain, temperatures become higher.

   b. The climate at the bottom of a mountain is the same as the surrounding countryside.

   c. The climate at the top of a tall mountain is like a polar climate.

Climate and Climate Change

Long-Term Changes in Climate

(pages 636–640)

Studying Climate Change (page 637)

Key Concept: In studying ancient climates, scientists follow an important principle: If plants or animals today need certain conditions to live, then similar plants and animals in the past also required those conditions.

- Scientists study ancient climates to find out how climates have changed during the history of Earth. Changes in climate may have affected many regions around the world.

- When scientists study ancient climates, they assume that the ancestors of today's plants needed the same conditions to live. For example, if a palm tree needs a hot and rainy climate to live today, scientists assume that palm trees long ago also needed hot and rainy climates.

- One source of information about ancient climates is pollen. Pollen is made by plants. Scientists find pollen in plant material at the bottoms of some lakes.

- Another source of information about ancient climates is tree rings. A tree ring forms every year a tree grows. The size of the ring depends on how much the tree grows.

Answer the following questions. Use your textbook and the ideas above.

1. Is the following sentence true or false? Scientists study ancient climates to find out how climates have changed. _____

2. Circle the letter of the principle scientists follow in studying ancient climates.

   a. If plants or animals today need certain conditions to live, then similar plants and animals in the past required very different conditions.

   b. If plants or animals today need certain conditions to live, then very different plants and animals in the past also required those conditions.

   c. If plants or animals today need certain conditions to live, then similar plants and animals in the past also required those conditions.

3. Circle the letter of each source of information about ancient climates.

   a. tree rings

   b. pollen

   c. tree branches

Ice Ages (page 638)

Key Concept: **During each ice age, huge sheets of ice called glaciers covered large parts of Earth's surface.**

- An **ice age** is a period in Earth's history when glaciers covered large parts of Earth. Over millions of years, warm periods have alternated with ice ages.

- Scientists think we are now in a warm period between ice ages.

- Ice ages can last 100,000 years or more. The last ice age ended about 10,500 years ago. When that ice age ended, the ice melted and the Great Lakes formed.

Answer the following questions. Use your textbook and the ideas above.

4. A period in Earth's history when glaciers covered large parts of Earth is called a(an) _____.

Climate and Climate Change

5. Circle the letter of each sentence that is true about ice ages.

   a. Scientists think we are now between ice ages.

   b. Ice ages can last 100,000 years or more.

   c. Scientists think that we are now in an ice age.

Causes of Climate Change (pages 639–640)

Key Concept: **Possible explanations for major climate changes include variations in the position of Earth relative to the sun, changes in the sun's energy output, major volcanic eruptions, and the movement of continents.**

- Over thousands of years, Earth's orbit around the sun shifts a little. The tilt of Earth's axis also changes slightly. The combined effects of these changes may be the main cause of ice ages.

- **Sunspots** are dark, cooler regions on the surface of the sun. When there are many sunspots, Earth's temperature may increase.

- When volcanoes erupt, they release gases and ashes into the atmosphere. These materials can block sunlight. As a result, huge volcanic eruptions may lower Earth's temperatures.

- About 225 million years ago, there was a single continent on Earth called Pangaea (pan JEE uh). Pangaea broke apart, and the continents have been moving ever since. As the continents have moved, climates have changed.

Climate and Climate Change

Answer the following questions. Use your textbook and the ideas on page 300.

6. Complete the concept map about possible explanations for major climate changes.

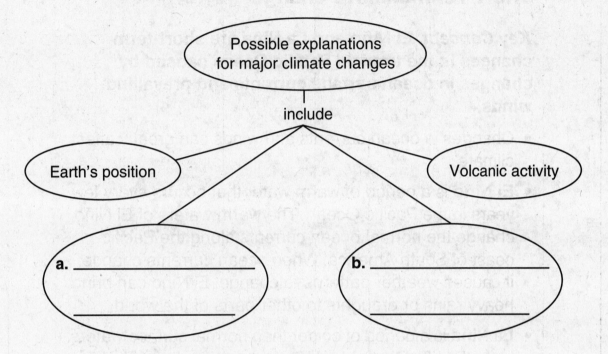

7. Circle the letter of what happens on Earth when there are more sunspots on the sun.

   a. Earth's temperature may increase.

   b. Earth's precipitation may increase.

   c. Earth's temperature may decrease.

8. Circle the letter of the continent that broke apart long ago.

   a. North America

   b. Pangaea

   c. Africa

Name _____ Date _____ Class _____

Climate and Climate Change

Global Changes in the Atmosphere (pages 641–647)

Short-Term Climate Change (page 642)

Key Concept: El Niño and La Niña are short-term changes in the tropical Pacific Ocean caused by changes in ocean surface currents and prevailing winds.

- Changes in ocean currents and winds can greatly affect climate.

- **El Niño** is a period of warm water that occurs every few years in the Pacific Ocean. The warm waters of El Niño change the normal ocean currents along the Pacific coast of South America. When ocean currents change, it causes weather patterns to change. El Niño can bring heavy rains or droughts to other parts of the world.

- **La Niña** is a period of colder than normal surface waters in the Pacific Ocean. La Niña is the opposite of El Niño. La Niña brings cold winters and greater precipitation to the Pacific Northwest of the United States.

Answer the following questions. Use your textbook and the ideas above.

1. Draw a line from the type of short-term climate change to its description.

Climate Change

El Niño

La Niña

Description

a. a period of colder than normal surface waters in the Pacific Ocean

b. a period of warm water that occurs every few years in the Pacific Ocean

2. Circle the letter of each sentence that is true about El Niño.

    a. El Niño brings cold winters to the Pacific Northwest of the United States.

    b. El Niño can bring heavy rains or droughts to other parts of the world.

    c. The warm waters of El Niño change the normal ocean currents along the Pacific coast of South America.

Global Warming (pages 643–645)

Key Concept: **Many scientists have hypothesized that human activities that add greenhouse gases to the atmosphere may be warming Earth's atmosphere.**

- Over the last 120 years, the average temperature of the troposphere has increased. The gradual increase in the temperature of the atmosphere is called **global warming**.

- Earth's surface is heated by energy from the sun. Some of the heat is radiated back into space. Certain gases in the atmosphere hold heat that is radiated from Earth. The process by which the gases trap heat energy is called the greenhouse effect.

- The gases in the atmosphere that trap heat energy are called **greenhouse gases**. Greenhouse gases include carbon dioxide, water vapor, and methane.

- Human activities add carbon dioxide to the atmosphere. For example, burning wood, coal, and oil adds carbon dioxide to the air.

- Adding carbon dioxide to the air increases the greenhouse effect. Increasing the greenhouse effect may be the cause of global warming.

Name _____ Date _____ Class _____

Climate and Climate Change

Answer the following questions. Use your textbook and the ideas on page 303.

3. Read the words in the box. In each sentence below, fill in the correct words.

greenhouse gases   El Niño   global warming

    a. The gases in the atmosphere that trap energy are

      called _____.

    b. The gradual increase in the temperature of the

      atmosphere is called _____.

4. Read each word in the box. In each step of the flowchart about global warming, fill in the correct word or words.

energy   carbon dioxide   atmosphere

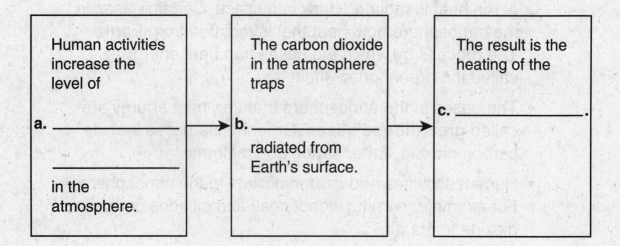

Human activities increase the level of	The carbon dioxide in the atmosphere traps	The result is the heating of the
a. _____ _____ in the atmosphere.	b. _____ radiated from Earth's surface.	c. _____.

Climate and Climate Change

Ozone Depletion (pages 646–647)

Key Concept: **Chemicals produced by humans have been damaging the ozone layer.**

- Ozone in the atmosphere blocks ultraviolet radiation from the sun. The loss of ozone means more ultraviolet radiation reaches Earth's surface. Ultraviolet radiation can cause eye damage and skin cancer.

- In the 1970s, scientists noticed a hole in the ozone layer of the atmosphere.

- A major cause of the ozone hole is a group of chemicals that were used in air conditioners, refrigerators, and spray cans. The chemicals are called **chlorofluorocarbons**, or CFCs. In the atmosphere, CFCs break down ozone into oxygen atoms.

- The United States and other countries have cut down use of CFCs. People will stop using CFCs completely by about 2010.

Answer the following questions. Use your textbook and the ideas above.

5. Circle the letter of the chemicals that have caused ozone depletion in the atmosphere.
   a. CFCs
   b. carbon dioxide
   c. hydrocarbons

6. Is the following sentence true or false? Ozone allows ultraviolet radiation from the sun to reach Earth.

   _____

Earth in Space (pages 660–665)

How Earth Moves (page 661)

Key Concept: **Earth moves through space in two major ways: rotation and revolution.**

- **Rotation** is spinning. Earth rotates on its axis. Earth's **axis** is an imaginary line through the North and South poles.

- Earth's rotation causes day and night. As Earth rotates from west to east, the sun appears to move across the sky. The sun is not really moving. Earth's rotation makes it appear to move. It takes Earth about 24 hours to rotate once.

- Earth also moves around the sun. This movement is called revolution. **Revolution** is the movement of one object around another.

- The path that Earth follows around the sun is called an **orbit**. Earth takes one year to travel all the way around the sun in its orbit.

Answer the following questions. Use your textbook and the ideas above.

1. The picture shows the planet Earth. Draw a line through the picture that shows Earth's axis.

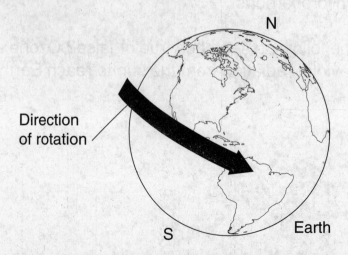

Direction of rotation

N

S   Earth

2. The picture shows Earth's revolution around the sun. Label Earth and the sun.

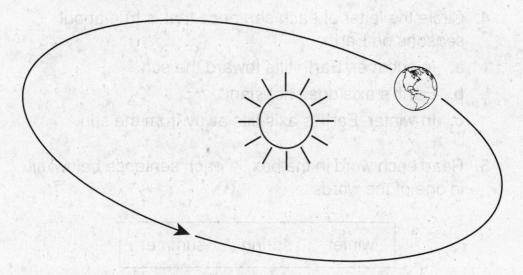

3. Draw a line from each term to its meaning.

Term	Meaning
axis	**a.** the movement of one object around another object
rotation	**b.** the imaginary line that passes through Earth's center and the North and South poles
revolution	**c.** the spinning of Earth

The Seasons on Earth (pages 662–665)

Key Concept: **Earth has seasons because its axis is tilted as it revolves around the sun.**

• Earth's axis is tilted, or slanted.

• Earth is warmer near the equator than near the poles.

• In summer, Earth is tilted toward from the sun. Day is longer than night. Earth's surface is warm.

• In winter, Earth is tilted away from the sun. Night is longer than day. Earth's surface is cold.

Earth, Moon, and Sun

Answer the following questions. Use your textbook and the ideas on page 307.

4. Circle the letter of each sentence that is true about seasons on Earth.

   a. In summer, Earth tilts toward the sun.

   b. Earth's axis does not slant.

   c. In winter, Earth's axis tilts away from the sun.

5. Read each word in the box. In each sentence below, fill in one of the words.

winter	spring	summer

   a. The days are longer in _____.

   b. The days are shorter in _____.

6. Fill in the blanks in the table below about Earth's tilt and the seasons.

Seasons in the Northern Hemisphere		
Season	**Length of Daytime**	**How the Northern Hemisphere Tilts**
Summer	longer than night	**b.** _____
Winter	**a.** _____	away from the sun

Earth, Moon, and Sun

Gravity and Motion (pages 666–669)

Gravity (pages 666–667)

Key Concept: **The strength of the force of gravity between two objects depends on two factors: the masses of the objects and the distance between them.**

- A **force** is a push or a pull.

- **Gravity** is the force that attracts all objects toward each other. Gravity does not need contact between objects. Gravity causes a book to fall if the book is dropped.

- **Mass** is the amount of matter in an object. The more mass an object has, the greater its force of gravity.

- Because of gravity, Earth pulls on the moon. The moon also pulls on Earth. The moon stays in orbit around Earth because of gravity.

- The force of gravity is stronger when two objects are close together. The force of gravity gets weaker if the two objects are farther apart.

Answer the following questions. Use your textbook and the ideas above.

1. Read each word in the box. In each sentence below, fill in one of the words.

force	pull	gravity	mass

   a. The force that attracts all objects toward each other is called _____.

   b. The amount of matter in an object is called

   _____.

   c. A push or pull is called a _____.

2. Circle the letter of each sentence that is true about gravity.

   a. Gravity attracts objects toward each other.

   b. The more mass an object has, the greater its force of gravity is.

   c. The force of gravity is stronger when two objects are farther apart.

3. Is the following sentence true or false? Gravity is a force that pushes all objects away from each other.

_____

Inertia and Orbital Motion (pages 668–669)

Key Concept: **Isaac Newton concluded that two factors—inertia and gravity—combine to keep Earth in orbit around the sun and the moon in orbit around Earth.**

- Objects that are moving tend to stay in motion. Objects that are not moving tend to stay still, or at rest. This tendency of an object to not change its motion is called **inertia**.

- Suppose you are in a car that stops suddenly. You will keep moving forward because of inertia.

- Isaac Newton stated his ideas about inertia as a scientific law. **Newton's first law of motion** says that an object at rest will stay at rest. The law also says that an object in motion will stay in motion.

- Earth's gravity keeps the moon from moving in a straight line. The moon's inertia keeps the moon moving ahead. The two forces combine to keep the moon revolving around Earth.

Name _____ Date _____ Class _____

Earth, Moon, and Sun

Answer the following questions. Use your textbook and the ideas on page 310.

4. Read each word in the box. In each sentence below, fill in one of the words.

| inertia   motion   gravity |

a. A moving object keeps moving because of

_____.

b. The moon keeps moving ahead because of

_____.

c. Earth's _____ keeps the moon from moving in a straight line.

5. Look at the picture below. Draw an arrow to show the direction of Earth's pull of gravity on the moon.

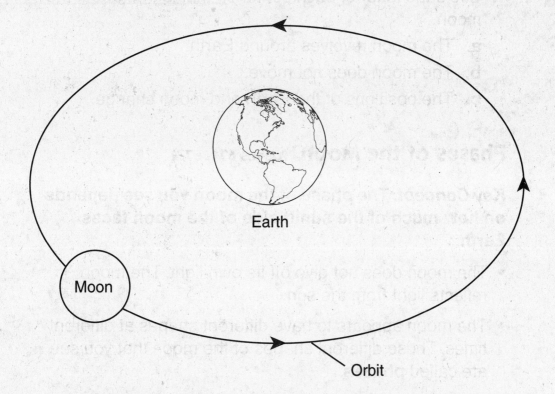

Earth

Moon

Orbit

Phases, Eclipses, and Tides

(pages 670–677)

Motions of the Moon (page 670)

Key Concept: **The changing relative positions of the moon, Earth, and sun cause the phases of the moon, eclipses, and tides.**

- The moon revolves around Earth. It takes the moon about 27.3 days to revolve around Earth.

- As the moon and Earth move, their positions change in relation to each other. Their positions also change in relation to the sun.

Answer the following question. Use your textbook and the ideas above.

1. Circle the letter of each sentence that is true about the moon.
   a. The moon revolves around Earth.
   b. The moon does not move.
   c. The positions of the Earth and moon change.

Phases of the Moon (pages 671–673)

Key Concept: **The phase of the moon you see depends on how much of the sunlit side of the moon faces Earth.**

- The moon does not give off its own light. The moon reflects light from the sun.

- The moon appears to have different shapes at different times. These different shapes of the moon that you see are called **phases**.

- As the moon revolves around Earth, you see the moon from different angles. You cannot always see all of the part of the moon that is lit by the sun.

Answer the following questions. Use your textbook and the ideas on page 312 and above.

2. The different shapes of the moon that you see are

   called _____.

3. Complete the table below to show what you see during the different phases of the moon.

Phases of the Moon	
Phase	**What You See**
New moon	The side of the moon facing Earth is dark.
First quarter	a. _____
Full moon	b. _____
Third quarter	c. _____

Earth, Moon, and Sun

Eclipses (pages 673–675)

Key Concept: **When the moon's shadow hits Earth or Earth's shadow hits the moon, an eclipse occurs. A solar eclipse occurs when the moon passes directly between Earth and the sun, blocking sunlight from Earth.**

- An **eclipse** (ih KLIPS) is when an object in space comes between the sun and another object. For example, an eclipse occurs when the moon comes between the sun and Earth.

- Sometimes the moon moves between Earth and the sun. The moon blocks sunlight from reaching Earth. A **solar eclipse** occurs when a new moon blocks your view of the sun.

Answer the following questions. Use your textbook and the ideas above.

4. A(An) _____ is when an object in space comes between the sun and another object.

5. The drawing below shows the sun, the moon, and Earth during a solar eclipse. Draw lines from the moon to Earth that show the shadow.

Sun

6. Is the following sentence true or false? A solar eclipse occurs when a full moon blocks your view of the sun. _____

Key Concept: **During a lunar eclipse, Earth blocks sunlight from reaching the moon.**

- A **lunar eclipse** occurs when Earth is between the moon and the sun.

- In a lunar eclipse, Earth's shadow hits the moon.

- A lunar eclipse occurs when there is a full moon.

Answer the following questions. Use your textbook and the ideas above.

7. Read each word in the box. In each sentence below, fill in the correct word or words.

solar eclipse	lunar eclipse	umbra

   a. Earth comes directly between the moon and the sun in a(an) _____.

   b. In a(an) _____, the moon's shadow hits Earth.

8. Is the following sentence true or false? A lunar eclipse occurs only when there is a full moon. _____

Tides (pages 676–677)

Key Concept: **Tides are caused mainly by differences in how much the moon's gravity pulls on different parts of Earth.**

- **Tides** are the regular rise and fall of ocean water.

Earth, Moon, and Sun

- The moon's gravity causes tides. The force of the moon's gravity causes ocean water on Earth to move higher in some places and lower in other places.

- The sun's gravity also pulls on Earth's ocean waters.

- During a new moon, the sun, moon, and Earth are lined up in a straight line. The combined forces of the sun and the moon cause spring tides. A **spring tide** is the highest possible high tide.

- Sometimes, the sun, moon, and Earth form a right angle. This arrangement produces a neap tide. A **neap tide** is the lowest possible high tide.

Answer the following questions. Use your textbook and the ideas on the page 315 and above.

9. Read the words in the box. In each sentence below, fill in the correct word or words.

tides   spring tide   neap tide

    a. When the sun, moon, and Earth are lined up in a

    straight line, a _____ occurs.

    b. The regular rise and fall of ocean water are

    _____ .

    c. When the sun, moon, and Earth form a right angle,

    a _____ occurs.

10. Circle the letter of each sentence that is true about tides.

    a. The moon's gravity causes tides.

    b. The sun's gravity also causes tides.

    c. The sun's gravity and the moon's gravity do not combine.

Earth's Moon (pages 680–683)

The Moon's Surface (page 681)

***Key Concept:* Features on the moon's surface include maria, craters, and highlands.**

- A **telescope** makes faraway objects appear closer.

- The moon's surface has dark, flat areas called **maria** (MAH ree uh). Maria are flat areas of hardened rock.

- **Craters** are large, round pits on the moon. Craters were caused when meteoroids crashed into the moon. A **meteoroid** is a chunk of rock or dust from space.

- Highlands are mountains that cover most of the moon's surface.

Answer the following questions. Use your textbook and the ideas above.

1. A scientific instrument that makes faraway objects appear closer is a(an) _____.

2. Draw a line from each term to its meaning.

Term	Meaning
maria	**a.** large, round pits on the moon
craters	**b.** dark, flat areas on the moon
	c. chunks of rock or dust from space
highlands	**d.** mountains on the moon
meteoroids	

Earth, Moon, and Sun

Characteristics of the Moon (page 682)

Key Concept: The moon is dry and airless. Compared to Earth, the moon is small and has large variations in its surface temperature.

- There is no air on the moon. The moon has no atmosphere.
- The moon is about one-fourth the diameter of Earth.
- Temperatures on the moon range from very hot to very cold.
- The moon has no liquid water.

Answer the following questions. Use your textbook and the ideas above.

3. Circle the letter of the size of the moon.
   a. about twice the diameter of Earth
   b. about half the diameter of Earth
   c. about one-fourth the diameter of Earth

4. The moon can get very hot and very _____.

The Origin of the Moon (page 683)

Key Concept: Scientists theorize that a planet-sized object collided with Earth to form the moon.

- Very long ago, big rocks were moving around in space.
- Scientists think that one of these big rocks may have crashed into Earth. Material from Earth broke off. The broken off portion of Earth became the moon.

Answer the following question. Use your textbook and the ideas above.

5. The moon may have formed when a big rock crashed

   into _____.

Earth, Moon, and Sun

Traveling Into Space (pages 684–691)

Introduction (page 684)

Key Concept: **Rocket technology originated in China hundreds of years ago. Modern rockets were first developed about a century ago.**

- A **rocket** is a device that sends gas in one direction to move in the opposite direction. A rocket sends gas out the back, causing the rocket to move forward.

- The first rockets were made in China in the 1100s. These rockets were arrows that could be set on fire and then shot with bows.

- The first modern rockets were built in the early 1900s.

Answer the following questions. Use your textbook and the ideas above.

1. A device that sends gas in one direction to move in the opposite direction is called a(an)

   _____.

2. Circle the letter of where the first rockets were made.
   a. the United States
   b. China
   c. Russia

3. Circle the letter of when modern rockets began to be built.
   a. 1700s
   b. 1800s
   c. 1900s

Earth, Moon, and Sun

How Do Rockets Work? (page 685)

Key Concept: **A rocket moves forward when gases shooting out the back of the rocket push it in the opposite direction.**

- A rocket burns fuel to make hot gases. The gases shoot out the back of the rocket. The force of gases shooting out the back of a rocket is called the action force.

- The gases shooting out the back of a rocket send the rocket forward. This force that moves the rocket forward is called the reaction force. The reaction force that sends a rocket forward is called **thrust**.

- The greater the thrust, the greater the rocket's velocity. **Velocity** is speed one direction.

Answer the following questions. Use your textbook and the ideas above.

4. Draw a line from each term to its meaning.

Term	Meaning
thrust	**a.** speed in one direction
velocity	**b.** the reaction force that sends a rocket forward

5. Circle the letter of the sentence that is true about thrust and the velocity of a rocket.

   a. The less the thrust, the greater the velocity.

   b. Thrust has nothing to do with velocity.

   c. The greater the thrust, the greater the velocity.

6. The picture shows two forces that act on a rocket. Each force is represented by an arrow. Circle the arrow in the picture that represents the thrust of the rocket.

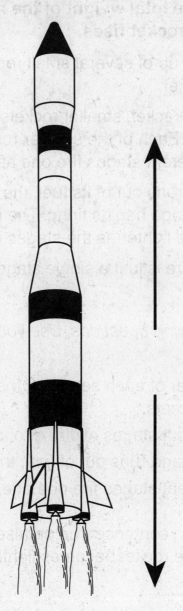

Earth, Moon, and Sun

Multistage Rockets (pages 686–687)

Key Concept: **The main advantage of a multistage rocket is that the total weight of the rocket is greatly reduced as the rocket rises.**

- A rocket made up of several small rockets is called a multistage rocket.

- In a multistage rocket, smaller rockets are placed one on top of another. Each of the smaller rockets is called a stage. The different stages fire one after the other.

- When a stage runs out of its fuel, the stage drops off and the next stage begins firing. The multistage rocket gets lighter and lighter as the stages drop off.

- At the end, there is just a single stage left, which is the spacecraft.

Answer the following questions. Use your textbook and the ideas above.

7. Circle the letter of each sentence that is true about multistage rockets.
   a. The different stages all fire at once.
   b. When a stage runs out of fuel, that stage drops off.
   c. The different stages fire one after another.

8. Is the following sentence true or false? The total weight of a multistage rocket becomes lighter as the rocket rises. _____

9. Each stage of a multistage rocket is a small

   _____.

Earth, Moon, and Sun

The Race for Space (pages 687–688)

Key Concept: **The rivalry between the United States and the Soviet Union over the exploration of space was known as the "space race."**

- In the 1950s, the United States and the Soviet Union (now Russia) began to compete in the exploration of space.

- The space race began in 1957 when the Soviets launched the satellite *Sputnik I* into orbit. The United States responded by speeding up its own space program.

- A **satellite** is an object that revolves around another object in space. The moon is a natural satellite. A spacecraft orbiting Earth is an artificial satellite. "Artificial" means it is made by people.

- In 1957, the Soviet Union launched a satellite into space. The satellite was called *Sputnik I.* In 1958, the United States launched a satellite called *Explorer I.*

- The Soviet Union launched the first human into space in 1961. His name was Yuri Gagarin. The first American launched into space was Alan Shepard later in 1961. The first American to orbit Earth was John Glenn in 1962.

Answer the following questions. Use your textbook and the ideas above.

10. An object that revolves around another object in space

is called a(an) _____.

11. Circle the letter of the correct answer. The space race was between the United States and

   a. China.

   b. the Soviet Union.

   c. Germany.

12. The time line shows important events in the race for space. Read the events listed in the box. On the time line below, fill in the blanks.

Explorer I launched   John Glenn orbits Earth

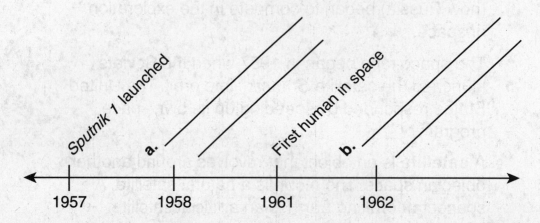

13. Circle the letter of the first human launched into space.
   a. John Glenn
   b. Alan Shepard
   c. Yuri Gagarin

Name _____ Date _____ Class _____

Missions to the Moon (page 689)

Key Concept: **The American effort to land astronauts on the moon was named the Apollo program.**

- President John F. Kennedy set a goal in 1961. He said the United States would send a man to the moon. The effort to put a man on the moon was called the Apollo program.

- Between 1964 and 1972, the United States and the Soviet Union sent many spacecraft to explore the moon. These early spacecraft did not have people in them.

- In 1969, U.S. astronaut Neil Armstrong became the first person to step on the moon. Armstrong and another astronaut named Buzz Aldrin explored the moon. Their flight to the moon was aboard the spacecraft *Apollo II*.

Answer the following questions. Use your textbook and the ideas above.

14. Circle the letter of the first person to step on the moon.
   a. Yuri Gagarin
   b. Neil Armstrong
   c. Buzz Aldrin

15. Circle the letter of the name of the U.S. program to put a man on the moon.
   a. Lunar program
   b. Moon program
   c. Apollo program

Earth, Moon, and Sun

Exploring Space Today (pages 690–691)

Key Concept: **NASA has used space shuttles to perform many important tasks. These include taking satellites into orbit, repairing damaged satellites, and carrying astronauts and equipment to and from space stations. A space station provides a place where long-term observations and experiments can be carried out in space.**

- A **space shuttle** is a spacecraft that can carry people into space. A space shuttle can then return to Earth and land like an airplane. A space shuttle can be used many times.

- A **space station** is a large satellite where people can live and work. The International Space Station is in orbit around Earth.

Answer the following questions. Use your textbook and the ideas above.

16. Read each word in the box. In each sentence below, fill in the correct words.

space station   space shuttle   space orbit

  a. A large satellite where people can live is called a

  _____.

  b. A spacecraft that can carry people into space is

  called a _____.

Earth, Moon, and Sun

17. Circle the letter of each sentence that is true about space shuttles.

    a. They cannot return to Earth.

    b. They return to Earth like an airplane.

    c. They can be used many times.

18. Circle the letter of the picture of the International Space Station.

a.
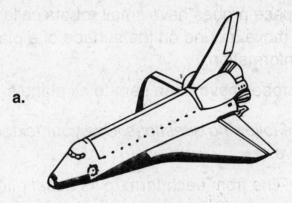

b.
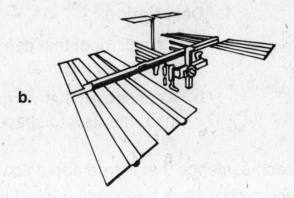

c.

Earth, Moon, and Sun

Key Concept: **Space probes gather data about distant parts of the solar system where humans cannot easily travel.**

- A **space probe** is a spacecraft that carries scientific instruments into space. The instruments collect information. No humans are on board a space probe.

- Some space probes land on other planets. Some space probes fly around other planets.

- Some space probes have small robots called rovers. **Rovers** move around on the surface of a planet and collect information.

- Space probes have been sent to all planets.

Answer the following questions. Use your textbook and the ideas above.

19. Draw a line from each term to its description.

Term	**Description**
space probe	**a.** a small robot that can move around on a planet
rover	**b.** a spacecraft that carries scientific instruments into space

20. Circle each sentence that is true about space probes.

    a. Space probes have been sent to all of the planets.

    b. Some space probes land on planets.

    c. Some space probes fly around planets.

Observing the Solar System
(pages 700–705)

Earth at the Center (page 701)

Key Concept: **In a geocentric system, Earth is at the center of the revolving planets and stars.**

- Most early Greek astronomers believed Earth was the center of the universe.

- A model of the universe in which Earth is at the center is called a **geocentric** (jee oh SEN trik) system. In a geocentric system, planets and stars revolve around Earth.

- The Greek astronomer Ptolemy (TAHL uh mee) developed a complex geocentric model of the universe. Ptolemy's model seemed to explain motions in the sky. Most people believed in Ptolemy's model until the 1500s.

Answer the following questions. Use your textbook and the ideas above.

1. In a geocentric system, planets and stars revolve around _____.

2. Circle the letter of the Greek astronomer who developed a geocentric model of the universe.
   a. Ptolemy
   b. Newton
   c. Copernicus

The Solar System

Sun at the Center (pages 702–703)

Key Concept: **In a heliocentric system, Earth and the other planets revolve around the sun. Copernicus was able to work out the arrangement of the known planets and how they move around the sun. Galileo used the newly invented telescope to make discoveries that supported the heliocentric model. Kepler found that the orbit of each planet is an ellipse.**

- A system in which the sun is at the center is called a **heliocentric** (hee lee oh SEN trik) system. Earth and other planets revolve around the sun in a heliocentric system.

- In 1543, a Polish astronomer named Nicolaus Copernicus developed a good heliocentric model of the universe.

- In the 1600s, the Italian scientist Galileo Galilei made discoveries that supported the heliocentric model.

- In the 1600s, the Danish astronomer Johannes Kepler discovered that the planets orbit the sun in a shape called an ellipse. An **ellipse** is an oval shape.

Answer the following questions. Use your textbook and the ideas above.

3. Circle the letter of the astronomer who developed a heliocentric model in the 1500s.
   a. Ptolemy
   b. Galileo
   c. Copernicus

The Solar System

4. Circle the letter of the picture of a heliocentric model of
the solar system.

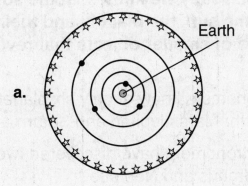

a.

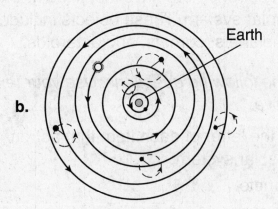

b.

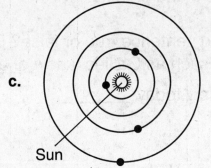

c.

5. Circle the letter of the picture of an ellipse.

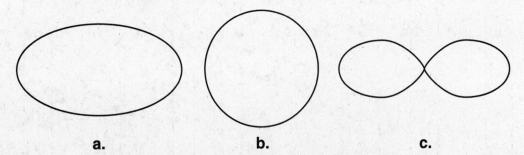

a.   b.   c.

The Solar System

Modern Discoveries (pages 704–705)

Key Concept: **Today we know that the solar system consists of the sun, the planets and their moons, and several kinds of smaller objects that revolve around the sun.**

- Early astronomers knew of only six planets—Mercury, Venus, Earth, Mars, Jupiter, and Saturn.

- Modern astronomers have discovered two more planets—Uranus and Neptune.

- Modern astronomers have identified many more objects in the solar system. These objects include moons around planets, comets, and asteroids.

Answer the following questions. Use your textbook and the ideas above.

6. Circle the letter of each item that astronomers include in the solar system.

   a. planets

   b. the sun

   c. the moons of the planets

7. Is the following sentence true or false? Early astronomers, such as Galileo, knew of all of the

   planets we know today. _____

The Sun (pages 706–710)

The Sun's Interior (page 707)

Key Concept: **The sun's interior consists of the core, the radiation zone, and the convection zone.**

- The sun does not have a solid surface. The sun is a ball of gas that glows. About three fourths of the sun's mass is hydrogen gas. About one fourth of the sun's mass is helium gas.

- The center of the sun is called the **core**. The sun produces energy at its core. The sun's energy comes from nuclear fusion. In **nuclear fusion**, hydrogen atoms join together to form helium.

- The middle layer of the sun is called the **radiation zone**. Gas is tightly packed in the radiation zone.

- The outer layer of the sun is called the **convection zone**. Streams of gas move energy toward the sun's surface.

Answer the following questions. Use your textbook and the ideas above.

1. The sun is a ball of _____ that glows.

2. Circle the letter of the process that gives the sun its energy.
   - **a.** glowing gas
   - **b.** nuclear fusion
   - **c.** streams of gas

The Solar System

3. Read each word in the box. Use the words to fill in the blanks in the table about the sun's interior.

Radiation zone   Core   Convection zone
Atmosphere

The Sun's Interior

Layer of the Sun	Location
a. _____	the center
b. _____	the middle layer
c. _____	the outer layer

The Sun's Atmosphere (page 708)

Key Concept: **The sun's atmosphere includes the photosphere, the chromosphere, and the corona.**

- The inner layer of the sun's atmosphere is called the **photosphere** (FOH tuh sfeer). When you look at a picture of the sun, you see the photosphere.

- The middle layer of the sun's atmosphere is called the **chromosphere** (KROH muh sfeer).

- The outer layer of the sun's atmosphere is called the **corona**. The corona goes out into space for millions of kilometers.

- The corona gradually gets thinner. As the corona gets thinner, it becomes electrically charged particles. The electrically charged particles make up **solar wind**.

The Solar System

Answer the following questions. Use your textbook and the ideas on page 334.

4. Draw a line from each term to its description.

Term	Description
corona	**a.** the inner layer of the sun's atmosphere
photosphere	**b.** the middle layer of the sun's atmosphere
chromosphere	**c.** the outer layer of the sun's atmosphere

5. Is the following sentence true or false? When you look at a picture of the sun, you see the corona. _____

6. As the sun's corona gets thinner, it becomes electrically charged particles. Circle the letter of what these electrically charged particles make up.

a. chromosphere

b. photosphere

c. solar wind

Features on the Sun (pages 708–710)

Key Concept: **Features on or just above the sun's surface include sunspots, prominences, and solar flares.**

- There are dark spots called sunspots on the sun's surface. A **sunspot** is an area of gas that is cooler than the gases around that area.

- A **prominence** is a huge loop of gas that links different areas of sunspots.

- A **solar flare** is an explosion of gas from the sun's surface out into space.

- Solar flares can increase the amount of solar wind from the sun. Solar wind reaches Earth's atmosphere. Solar wind affects Earth's magnetic field.

Answer the following questions. Use your textbook and the ideas on page 335 and above.

7. Read each word in the box. In each sentence below, fill in the correct word or words.

| prominence | sunspot | solar wind |
| solar flare | | |

    a. An area of gas that is cooler than the gases around that area is a _____.

    b. An explosion of gas from the sun's surface out into space is called a _____.

    c. A huge loop of gas that links different areas of sunspots is a _____.

8. Solar flares can increase the amount of _____.

The Inner Planets (pages 712–717)

Introduction (page 712)

Key Concept: **The four inner planets are small and dense and have rocky surfaces.**

- The four planets closest to the sun are called the inner planets. The four inner planets are Mercury, Venus, Earth, and Mars.

- The inner planets are called the **terrestrial planets**.

- The inner planets are more like one another than they are like the outer planets. For example, the inner planets all have rocky surfaces.

Answer the following questions. Use your textbook and the ideas above.

1. The inner planets are called the

   _____ planets.

2. Circle the letter of how many inner planets there are.
   - **a.** 2
   - **b.** 4
   - **c.** 6

Earth (pages 712–713)

Key Concept: **Earth is unique in our solar system in having liquid water at its surface.**

- Earth has three main layers. The surface layer is the crust. Below the crust is the mantle. At Earth's center is the core.

The Solar System

- Most of Earth's surface—about 70 percent—is covered with water. Earth is the only planet with liquid water on its surface.

- Earth's gravity holds onto most gases. The gases around Earth make up Earth's atmosphere.

Answer the following questions. Use your textbook and the ideas on page 337 and above.

3. Is the following sentence true or false? Most of Earth's surface is covered with water. _____

4. Read each word in the box. Then fill in each blank in the picture below with one of the words.

mantle   crust   core

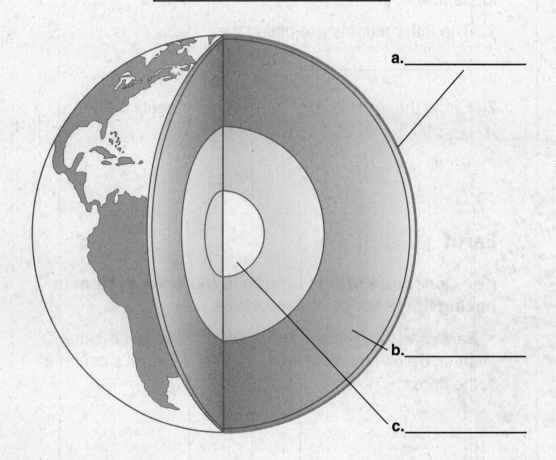

a._____

b._____

c._____

The Solar System

Mercury (page 714)

***Key Concept:* Mercury is the smallest terrestrial planet and the planet closest to the sun.**

- Mercury is the closest planet to the sun. Mercury is the smallest of the inner planets. It is not much larger than Earth's moon.

- Mercury has almost no atmosphere because it has very weak gravity.

- Mercury has extreme temperatures on its surface. It is very hot during the day and very cold at night.

Answer the following questions. Use your textbook and the ideas above.

5. Circle the letter of each sentence that is true about Mercury.
   a. It is the closest planet to the sun.
   b. It has a very thick atmosphere.
   c. It is the smallest of the inner planets.

6. The picture shows the sun and the inner planets. Circle the planet Mercury.

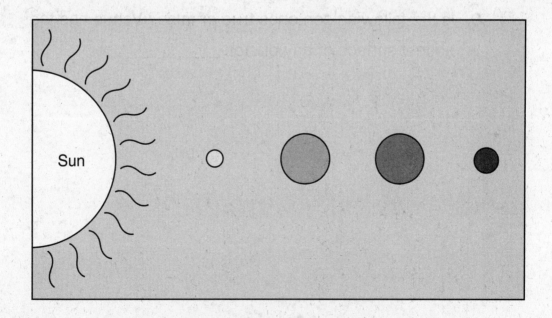

Name _____ Date _____ Class _____

The Solar System

Venus (pages 714–715)

Key Concept: Venus's density and internal structure are similar to Earth's. But, in other ways, Venus and Earth are very different.

- Venus is very much like Earth in size and mass.

- Venus's atmosphere is very thick. It is always cloudy on Venus.

- Venus has the hottest surface of any planet. Venus's atmosphere traps the sun's heat. The trapping of heat by the atmosphere is called the **greenhouse effect**.

Answer the following questions. Use your textbook and the ideas above.

7. Circle the letter of each sentence that is true about Venus.
   a. It is much larger than Earth
   b. It has a very thick atmosphere.
   c. It has no clouds in its atmosphere.

8. The trapping of _____ by Venus's atmosphere is called the greenhouse effect.

9. Is the following sentence true or false? Venus has the hottest surface of any planet. _____

The Solar System

Mars (pages 716–717)

Key Concept: **Scientists think that a large amount of liquid water flowed on Mars's surface in the distant past.**

- Mars is called the "red planet" because it looks red from Earth.

- The surface of Mars has huge canyons and ancient coastlines. Scientists think that liquid water may have formed these features. There is no liquid water on Mars's surface now.

- Mars has two very small moons. They are called Phobos and Deimos.

- Many space probes have been sent to Mars.

Answer the following questions. Use your textbook and the ideas above.

10. Circle the letter of each sentence that is true about Mars.

    a. Mars is called the "red planet."

    b. There are two moons that orbit Mars.

    c. The surface of Mars is covered with water.

11. Is the following sentence true or false? No space probe has been sent to Mars. _____

12. What do scientists think formed some features on the surface of Mars? Circle the letter of the correct answer.

    a. the sun

    b. space probes

    c. water

The Outer Planets (pages 720–727)

Gas Giants and Pluto (page 721)

Key Concept: **The four outer planets—Jupiter, Saturn, Uranus, and Neptune—are much larger and more massive than Earth, and they do not have solid surfaces.**

- The outer planets include Jupiter, Saturn, Uranus, and Neptune.

- The four outer planets—Jupiter, Saturn, Uranus, and Neptune—are called the **gas giants**. They are very large, and they do not have solid surfaces.

- The gas giants are made up mainly of hydrogen and helium.

- All the gas giants have many moons. Each gas giant is also surrounded by rings. A **ring** is a thin circle of small ice and rock particles around a planet.

Answer the following questions. Use your textbook and the ideas above.

1. Circle the letter of the sentence that is true about gas giants.
   a. They have rocky surfaces.
   b. They have no moons.
   c. They do not have solid surfaces.

2. Each of the gas giants is surrounded by circles called

   _____.

3. Complete the concept map about the outer planets.

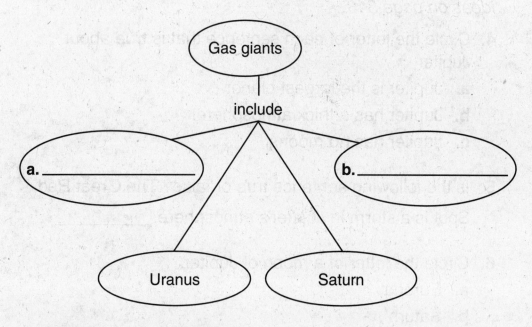

Jupiter (pages 722–723)

Key Concept: **Jupiter is the largest and most massive planet.**

- Jupiter's mass is about $2^{1}/_{2}$ times the mass of all the other planets combined.

- Jupiter has a thick atmosphere made up mainly of hydrogen and helium. A storm in Jupiter's atmosphere is called the Great Red Spot.

- Jupiter has more than 60 moons. The four largest moons are Io (EYE oh), Europa, Ganymede, and Callisto.

The Solar System

Answer the following questions. Use your textbook and the ideas on page 343.

4. Circle the letter of each sentence that is true about Jupiter.
   a. Jupiter is the largest planet.
   b. Jupiter has a thick atmosphere.
   c. Jupiter has no moons.

5. Is the following sentence true or false? The Great Red Spot is a storm in Jupiter's atmosphere. _____

6. Circle the letter of a moon of Jupiter.
   a. Europa
   b. Saturn
   c. Great Red Spot

Saturn (page 724)

Key Concept: Saturn has the most spectacular rings of any planet.

- Saturn is the second-largest planet. Saturn's atmosphere is made up mostly of hydrogen and helium.
- Saturn has many rings. Saturn's rings are broad and thin.
- Saturn has more than 31 moons. Saturn's largest moon is named Titan. Titan is larger than the planet Mercury.

Answer the following questions. Use your textbook and the ideas above.

7. Is the following sentence true or false? Saturn is the second-largest planet. _____

8. The picture shows the sun, the planets, and Pluto. Draw a circle around the planet Saturn.

9. Circle the letter of each sentence that is true about Saturn.

   a. Saturn's rings are broad and thin.

   b. Saturn's largest moon is named Titan.

   c. Saturn's atmosphere is made up mostly of hydrogen and helium.

Uranus (page 725)

Key Concept: **Uranus's axis of rotation is tilted at an angle of about 90 degrees from the vertical.**

- Uranus looks blue-green from Earth because there is methane gas in its atmosphere.

- Uranus is surrounded by a group of thin, flat rings.

- Uranus's axis is different than the axes of other planets. Uranus looks like it is rotating from top to bottom. Other planets look like they are rotating from side to side.

- Uranus has over 25 moons. Uranus's five largest moons have icy surfaces with many craters.

Answer the following questions. Use your textbook and the ideas on page 345.

10. Circle the letter of each sentence that is true about Uranus.

    a. Uranus has no rings.

    b. Uranus has no moons.

    c. Uranus looks blue-green from Earth.

11. Is the following sentence true or false? Uranus looks like it is rotating from top to bottom. _____

Neptune (page 726)

***Key Concept:* Neptune is a cold, blue planet. Its atmosphere contains visible clouds.**

- Neptune is much like Uranus in size and color. Neptune looks blue from Earth. Neptune's atmosphere has clouds.

- Scientists think that Neptune is shrinking.

- Neptune has at least 13 moons. Neptune's largest moon is called Triton.

Answer the following questions. Use your textbook and the ideas above.

12. Is the following sentence true or false? There are no clouds in Neptune's atmosphere. _____

13. Circle the letter of each sentence that is true about Neptune.

    a. Neptune's largest moon is called Triton.

    b. Scientists think that Neptune is shrinking.

    c. Neptune is much larger than Uranus.

The Solar System

Pluto (page 727)

Key Concept: **Pluto has a solid surface and is much smaller and denser than the outer planets.**

- Pluto is very different than the gas giants. For example, Pluto has a solid surface.

- Pluto is smaller than Earth's moon. Pluto has a very elliptical orbit.

- Pluto is no longer considered to be a planet. It is now considered to be a dwarf planet.

Answer the following questions. Use your textbook and the ideas above.

14. Is the following sentence true or false? Pluto is the

nearest planet to the sun. _____

15. Pluto is smaller than Earth's _____.

Comets, Asteroids, and Meteors (pages 730–733)

Comets (page 731)

Key Concept: **Comets are loose collections of ice, dust, and small rocky particles whose orbits are usually very long, narrow ellipses.**

- A comet orbits the sun. A comet is made up of ice, dust, and small rocky particles. You can think of a comet as a "dirty snowball."

- The orbit of a comet is usually an ellipse that is very long and narrow.

- The brightest part of a comet is the head. A comet's head is made up of a nucleus and a coma. The **nucleus** is the solid core of a comet. The **coma** is a fuzzy outer layer made up of clouds of gas and dust.

Answer the following questions. Use your textbook and the ideas above.

1. Read each word in the box. In each sentence below, fill in one of the words.

coma	comet	nucleus	tail

    a. A "dirty snowball" that orbits the sun is a

    _____.

    b. The solid core of a comet is the

    _____.

    c. The fuzzy outer layer of a comet is the

    _____.

2. Is the following sentence true or false? A comet's orbit is usually a very long and narrow ellipse. _____

Asteroids (page 732)

***Key Concept:* Most asteroids revolve around the sun between the orbits of Mars and Jupiter.**

- An asteroid is a rocky object that orbits the sun. Asteroids are too small to be planets.

- Most asteroids are in orbit between Mars and Jupiter. This region of the solar system is called the **asteroid belt**.

- Most asteroids are less than 1 kilometer in diameter. Some are much larger.

- Scientists think that asteroids are leftover pieces of rock from the early solar system.

Answer the following questions. Use your textbook and the ideas above.

3. A rocky object that orbits the sun and is too small to be a planet is a (an) _____.

4. Circle the letter of the location of the asteroid belt in the solar system.
   a. between Earth and Venus
   b. between Jupiter and Saturn
   c. between Mars and Jupiter

5. Is the following sentence true or false? Scientists think that asteroids are leftover pieces of rock from the early solar system. _____

The Solar System

Meteors (page 733)

Key Concept: **Meteoroids come from comets or asteroids.**

- A **meteoroid** is a chunk of rock or dust in space.

- Some meteoroids form when asteroids crash into each other. Other meteoroids form when comets break apart.

- Meteoroids can enter Earth's atmosphere. When one does, friction between the meteoroid and the air produces a streak of light in the sky. A **meteor** is a streak of light in the night sky produced by a meteoroid.

- Most meteoroids burn up completely in Earth's atmosphere. However, some hit Earth's surface. Meteoroids that hit Earth's surface are called **meteorites**.

Answer the following questions. Use your textbook and the ideas above.

6. Circle the letter of each object that a meteoroid can come from.
   a. Earth
   b. comet
   c. asteroid

7. Is the following sentence true or false? Meteoroids never enter Earth's atmosphere. _____

Name _____ Date _____ Class _____

8. Read each word in the box. In each blank in the table below, fill in one of the words.

| Meteor | Meteoroid | Meteorite |

Rocks From Space	
Term	**Description**
a. _____	a streak of light in the night sky
b. _____	a meteoroid that hits Earth's surface
c. _____	a chunk of rock or dust in space

The Solar System

Is There Life Beyond
Earth? (pages 734–737)

Life on Earth (page 735)

Key Concept: **Earth has liquid water and a suitable temperature range and atmosphere for living things to survive.**

- All life that is not Earth life is called **extraterrestrial life**. No one knows if there are living things beyond Earth.

- Scientists talk about "life as we know it." Life as we know it lives on Earth, where there is liquid water, good temperatures, and an atmosphere. These conditions are sometimes called "Goldilocks conditions."

- "Goldilocks conditions" may or may not be necessary for life. No one knows for sure.

Answer the following questions. Use your textbook and the ideas above.

1. All life that is not Earth life is called

   _____ life.

2. Circle the letter of each condition that is included in "Goldilocks conditions."
   a. good temperatures
   b. an atmosphere
   c. liquid water

3. Is the following sentence true or false? No one knows if there are living things beyond Earth. _____

Life Elsewhere in the Solar System?
(pages 736–737)

Key Concept: **Since life as we know it requires water, scientists hypothesize that Mars may have once had the conditions needed for life to exist.**

- Mars is the planet that is most like Earth. Scientists have looked for living things on Mars.

- The surface of Mars looks like it once had water.

Answer the following question. Use your textbook and the ideas above.

4. Circle the letter of why scientists think that life might exist on Mars.

   a. The surface of Mars looks like it once had water.

   b. There is evidence that Mars has the "Goldilocks conditions."

   c. There is evidence that life on Mars came from Europa.

Key Concept: **If there is liquid water on Europa, there might also be life.**

- Europa is a moon of Jupiter. Many scientists think there could be life on Europa.

Answer the following question. Use your textbook and the ideas above.

5. Circle the letter of the planet Europa revolves around.

   a. Mars

   b. Saturn

   c. Jupiter

Stars, Galaxies, and the Universe

Telescopes (pages 744–750)

Electromagnetic Radiation (page 745)

Key Concept: The electromagnetic spectrum includes the entire range of radio waves, infrared radiation, visible light, ultraviolet radiation, X-rays, and gamma rays.

- Energy that travels through space in the form of waves is called **electromagnetic** (ih lek troh mag NET ik) **radiation**.

- Light that you can see is called **visible light**. Visible light is one kind of electromagnetic radiation. There are many other kinds of electromagnetic radiation.

- Visible light has medium wavelengths. A **wavelength** is the distance between the top of one wave and the top of the next wave.

- The range of different wavelengths of electromagnetic waves is called a spectrum. The **spectrum** of all electromagnetic waves is called the electromagnetic spectrum.

Answer the following questions. Use your textbook and the ideas above.

1. Draw a line from each term to its meaning.

Term	Meaning
electromagnetic spectrum	a. the light you can see
	b. the range of different wavelengths
visible light	
	c. energy that travels through space in the form of waves
spectrum	

2. The picture below shows a wave of electromagnetic radiation. Draw a line over the wave to show one wavelength.

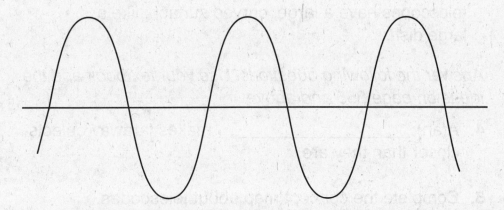

3. Circle the letter of each sentence that is true about electromagnetic radiation.

    a. There are many types of electromagnetic radiation.

    b. Visible light has medium wavelengths.

    c. Energy cannot travel through space.

Types of Telescopes (pages 746–747)

Key Concept: **Telescopes are instruments that collect and focus light and other forms of electromagnetic radiation.**

- A telescope makes faraway objects appear closer than they are.

- A telescope that collects and focuses visible light is called an **optical telescope**. The two major types of optical telescopes are refracting telescopes and reflecting telescopes.

- A **refracting telescope** uses lenses to gather and focus light.

Stars, Galaxies, and the Universe

- A **reflecting telescope** uses a curved mirror to collect and focus light. The largest telescopes are reflecting telescopes.

- A **radio telescope** is a device used to collect radio waves that come from objects in space. Most radio telescopes have a large, curved surface, like a large dish.

Answer the following questions. Use your textbook and the ideas on page 355 and above.

4. A(an) _____ makes faraway objects closer than they are.

5. Complete the concept map about telescopes.

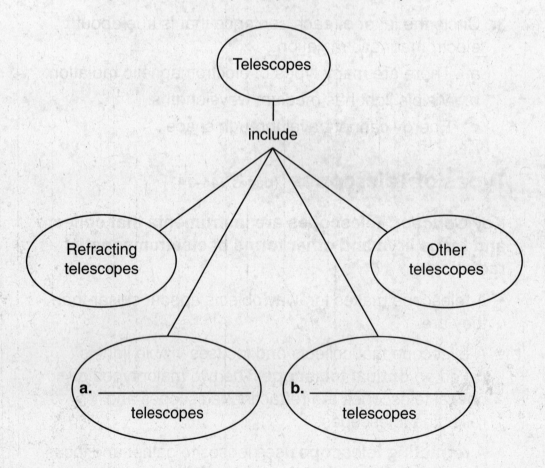

Telescopes

include

Refracting telescopes

Other telescopes

a. _____ telescopes

b. _____ telescopes

Stars, Galaxies, and the Universe

Observatories (pages 748–750)

Key Concept: **Many large observatories are located on mountaintops or in space.**

- An **observatory** is usually a building that has one or more telescopes. Some observatories are not in buildings, because they are located in space.

- Many observatories are on the tops of mountains because the sky is clearer on mountaintops. There are also no city lights on mountaintops. For example, one of the best observatories is on top of Mauna Kea, an old volcano on the island of Hawaii.

- The Hubble Space Telescope is a reflecting telescope in space high above Earth.

Answer the following questions. Use your textbook and the ideas above.

6. A building that has one or more telescopes is called

   a(an) _____.

7. Circle the letter of each sentence that is true about observatories.
   a. Many observatories are on the tops of mountains.
   b. One of the best observatories is on the island of Hawaii.
   c. There are no observatories in space.

8. Is the following sentence true or false? The Hubble Space Telescope is a refracting telescope. _____

Characteristics of Stars

(pages 752–759)

Classifying Stars (pages 753–754)

Key Concept: **Characteristics used to classify stars include color, temperature, size, composition, and brightness.**

* A star's color gives clues about the star's temperature. The coolest stars appear red. The hottest stars appear blue.

* Very large stars are called giant stars or supergiant stars. Our sun is a medium-sized star. Most stars are smaller than the sun.

* Stars differ in their chemical make-ups. Astronomers use spectrographs to find out what elements are in a star. A **spectrograph** (SPEK truh graf) is a device that breaks light into colors. Scientists compare a star's light with the light produced by different elements to find out what elements are in the star.

Answer the following questions. Use your textbook and the ideas above.

1. Is the following sentence true or false? A star's color gives clues about the star's temperature. _____

2. Circle the letter of a device that breaks light into colors.
   a. spectrograph
   b. telescope
   c. observatory

3. Complete the concept map about characteristics used to classify stars.

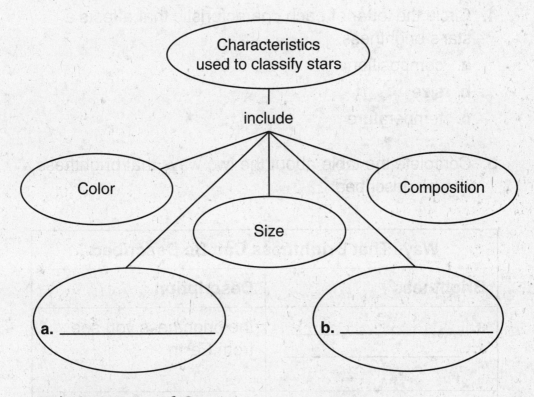

Brightness of Stars (pages 754–755)

Key Concept: **The brightness of a star depends upon both its size and temperature.**

- Stars differ in how bright they are. A hot star shines brighter than a cool star. A large star shines brighter than a small star.

- A star's **apparent brightness** is the brightness you see from Earth. A hot, large star that is very far from Earth does not look very bright. But the sun looks very bright because it is so close to Earth.

- A star's **absolute brightness** is the brightness the star would have if all stars were the same distance from Earth.

Stars, Galaxies, and the Universe

Answer the following questions. Use your textbook and the ideas on page 359.

4. Circle the letter of each characteristic that affects a star's brightness.

   a. composition

   b. size

   c. temperature

5. Complete the table about the two ways that brightness can be described.

Ways That Brightness Can Be Described	
Brightness	**Description**
a. _____ _____	the brightness you see from Earth
b. _____ _____	the brightness a star would have if all stars were the same distance from Earth

Stars, Galaxies, and the Universe

Measuring Distances to Stars (pages 756–757)

Key Concept: **Astronomers use a unit called the light-year to measure distances between the stars.**

- A **light-year** is the distance that light travels in one year. That distance is about 9.5 million million kilometers.

- A light-year is a unit of distance, not time. You could also measure distance on Earth in terms of time. For example, if it takes you 1 hour to ride your bike to the mall, you could say the mall is "1 bicycle-hour" away.

Answer the following questions. Use your textbook and the ideas above.

6. The distance that light travels in one year is a(an)

_____.

7. Is the following sentence true or false? A light-year is a unit of distance, not time. _____

Key Concept: **Astronomers often use parallax to measure distances to nearby stars.**

- **Parallax** is the change in an object's position you seem to see when you change your own position. The object does not really change position. It only seems to change because you change your position.

- Astronomers use parallax. They measure how far a nearby star seems to move when Earth moves from one side of the sun to the other. The distance the star seems to move tells an astronomer how far the star is from Earth.

Answer the following questions. Use your textbook and the ideas above.

8. The change in an object's position you seem to see when you change your own position is

_____.

Stars, Galaxies, and the Universe

9. Circle the letter of what astronomers use parallax for.

   a. to measure distances to nearby stars

   b. to compare the brightness of stars

   c. to determine the elements found in stars

The Hertzsprung-Russell Diagram
(pages 758–759)

Key Concept: **Astronomers use H-R diagrams to classify stars and to understand how stars change over time.**

- The **Hertzsprung-Russell diagram**, or the H-R diagram, shows how the surface temperature of stars is related to their absolute brightness.

- The points on the H-R diagram form a pattern. Most stars on the H-R diagram fall into a band that spreads from the top left corner of the diagram to the bottom right corner. This band is called the main sequence. Stars in the main sequence are called **main-sequence** stars. About 90 percent of all stars are main-sequence stars.

- The brightest stars are located near the top of the H-R diagram. Stars that are not bright are located at the bottom.

Answer the following questions. Use your textbook and the ideas above.

10. The Hertzsprung-Russell diagram shows how the surface temperature of stars is related to absolute

   _____.

11. Most stars are _____ stars.

Name _____ Date _____ Class _____

Stars, Galaxies, and the Universe

12. The picture shows a H-R diagram. The dots represent stars. Draw a line on the diagram to show about where the main sequence is.

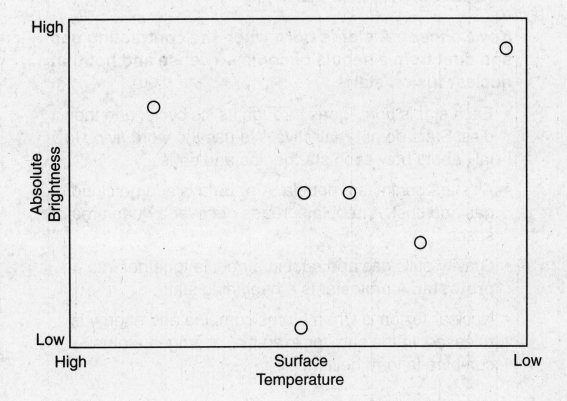

Stars, Galaxies, and the Universe

Lives of Stars (pages 762–766)

The Lives of Stars (page 763)

Key Concept: **A star is born when the contracting gas and dust from a nebula become so dense and hot that nuclear fusion starts.**

- Each star is born, goes through its life cycle, and then dies. Stars do not really live. We use the word *living* to talk about how each star begins and ends.

- All stars begin as a nebula. A **nebula** is a large cloud of gas and dust. A nebula spreads out over a huge area of space.

- Gravity pulls gas and dust in a nebula together into a **protostar**. A protostar is a beginning star.

- Nuclear fusion is when atoms combine and energy is released. In the sun, for example, hydrogen atoms combine to form helium.

Answer the following questions. Use your textbook and the ideas above.

1. Circle the letter of the force that pulls a nebula together into a protostar.
   a. friction
   b. gravity
   c. electricity

2. Circle the letter of what happens when atoms combine in the process of nuclear fusion in a star.
   a. a star dies
   b. gravity pulls a nebula together
   c. energy is released

Stars, Galaxies, and the Universe

3. Read each word in the box. In each sentence below, fill in one of the words.

protostar	supernova	nebula

a. A large cloud of gas and dust in space is called a

_____.

b. A beginning star is called a

_____.

Key Concept: **How long a star lives depends on its mass.**

• Stars with less mass live longer than stars with more mass. Stars with less mass than the sun can live up to 200 billion years.

• Stars with mass equal to the sun live for about 10 billion years.

• A star with a mass 15 times the mass of the sun may live only about 10 million years.

Answer the following questions. Use your textbook and the ideas above.

4. How long a star lives depends on its

_____.

5. Is the following sentence true or false? Stars with more mass live longer than stars with less mass.

6. Circle the letter of how long the sun is likely to live.
   a. 10 million years
   b. 10 billion years
   c. 200 billion years

Stars, Galaxies, and the Universe

Deaths of Stars (pages 764–766)

Key Concept: **After a star runs out of fuel, it becomes a white dwarf, a neutron star, or a black hole.**

- Stars with low mass and medium mass eventually run out of fuel. These stars turn into white dwarfs. A **white dwarf** is the blue-white center of a star that is left after the star cools.

- A star with a high mass has a different life cycle than a star with a low mass. When a supergiant runs out of fuel, it explodes. The explosion of a supergiant star is called a **supernova**.

- After a supergiant explodes, some of the star is left. This material may form a neutron star. A **neutron star** is the leftover remains of a high-mass star.

- A **pulsar** is a rapidly spinning neutron star.

- The stars with the greatest mass become black holes when they die. A **black hole** is an object with very strong gravity that does not give off any light. A black hole has gravity so strong that nothing escapes its pull—not even light.

Answer the following questions. Use your textbook and the ideas above.

7. Draw a line from each term to its meaning.

Term	Meaning
white dwarf	**a.** the blue-white center of a low-mass or medium-mass star that is left after the star cools
supernova	
neutron star	**b.** an object with very strong gravity that does not give off any light
black hole	**c.** the explosion of a supergiant star
	d. the leftover remains of a high-mass star

Name _____ Date _____ Class _____

Stars, Galaxies, and the Universe

8. A black hole has so much _____ that nothing escapes its pull.

9. Read each word in the box. In each blank in the flowchart below, fill in the correct word or words.

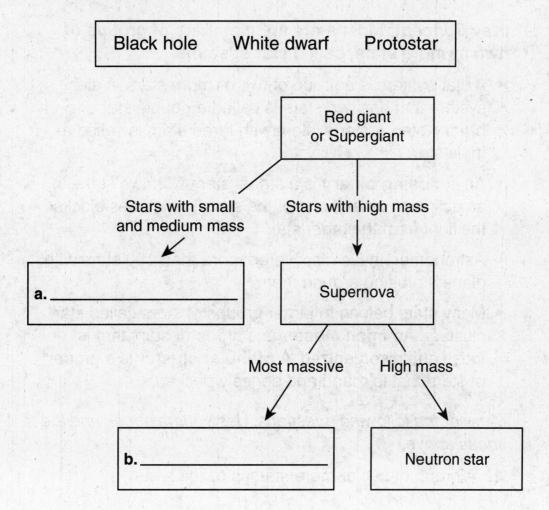

| Black hole | White dwarf | Protostar |

Red giant or Supergiant

Stars with small and medium mass

Stars with high mass

a. _____

Supernova

Most massive

High mass

b. _____

Neutron star

Stars, Galaxies, and the Universe

Star Systems and Galaxies

(pages 767–773)

Star Systems and Clusters (pages 768–769)

Key Concept: **Most stars are members of groups of two or more stars, called star systems.**

- A star system is a group of two or more stars. A star system that has two stars is called a double star or a **binary star**. A star system with three stars is called a triple star.

- An **eclipsing binary** is a star system with two stars. In an eclipsing binary, one of the stars sometimes blocks the light from the other star.

- Astronomers have discovered more than 100 stars with planets orbiting around them.

- Many stars belong to larger groups of stars called star clusters. An **open cluster** is a group of stars that is loose and disorganized. A **globular cluster** is a group of stars that is round and densely packed.

Answer the following questions. Use your textbook and the ideas above.

1. A group of two or more stars is called a star

   _____.

2. Is the following sentence true or false? Astronomers have discovered planets around some stars.

   _____

Name _____ Date _____ Class _____

Stars, Galaxies, and the Universe

3. Complete the table about star systems.

Star Systems	
Type of Star System	**Description**
Binary star	two stars
a. _____	two stars with one star blocking the light of the other
b. _____	loose and disorganized group of stars
c. _____	round and densely packed group of stars

Galaxies (page 770)

Key Concept: **Astronomers classify most galaxies into the following types: spiral, elliptical, and irregular.**

- A galaxy is a huge group of stars that are held together by gravity. A **galaxy** contains single stars, star systems, star clusters, dust, and gas.

- A **spiral galaxy** has a bulge in the middle and arms that curve outward. Most new stars in a spiral galaxy are found in its spiral arms.

- An **elliptical galaxy** looks like a round or flattened ball. Most elliptical galaxies contain only old stars.

- An **irregular galaxy** does not have any certain shape. Irregular galaxies are usually smaller than other types of galaxies. Most irregular galaxies contain many young stars.

Stars, Galaxies, and the Universe

Answer the following questions. Use your textbook and the ideas on page 369.

4. A huge group of stars that is held together by gravity is

a(an) _____.

5. Look at the picture below. Then circle the letter of the kind of galaxy the picture shows.

    a. spiral galaxy

    b. elliptical galaxy

    c. irregular galaxy

Name _____ Date _____ Class _____

Stars, Galaxies, and the Universe

6. Draw a line from each term to its meaning.

Term	Meaning
spiral galaxy	**a.** galaxy that does not have any certain shape
elliptical galaxy	**b.** galaxy with a bulge in the middle and arms that curve
irregular galaxy	**c.** galaxy that looks like a round or flattened ball

The Milky Way (page 771)

Key Concept: **Our solar system is located in a spiral galaxy called the Milky Way.**

- Earth, the sun, and the rest of the solar system are all part of the Milky Way galaxy.
- The Milky Way is a spiral galaxy. Earth is inside one of the galaxy's spiral arms.
- The center of the Milky Way galaxy is about 25,000 light-years from Earth.

Answer the following questions. Use your textbook and the ideas above.

7. Earth is in the galaxy called the

_____.

8. Circle the letter of the type of galaxy that the Milky Way is.

   a. spiral galaxy

   b. elliptical galaxy

   c. irregular galaxy

Stars, Galaxies, and the Universe

The Scale of the Universe (pages 772–773)

Key Concept: **Since the numbers astronomers use are often very large or very small, they frequently use scientific notation to describe sizes and distances in the universe.**

- The **universe** is all of space and everything in space.

- Astronomers study very large things, such as galaxies. Astronomers also study very small things, such as atoms within stars.

- **Scientific notation** is a way of writing large numbers in a short way. Scientific notation uses powers of 10. Each number is written as a number times 10 and a power of 10. For example, consider the number 1,200. Using scientific notation, that number is written like this: 1.2×10^3.

Answer the following questions. Use your textbook and the ideas above.

9. All of space and everything in space is the

   _____.

10. Circle the letter of a number written in scientific notation.
    a. 3.43578
    b. 1.2×10^3
    c. $1.2 \div 10^5$

Stars, Galaxies, and the Universe

The Expanding Universe (pages 774–779)

How the Universe Formed (pages 774–776)

Key Concept: According to the big bang theory, the universe formed in an instant, billions of years ago, in an enormous explosion.

- Astronomers' explanation for the start of the universe is called the big bang theory.

- According to the big bang theory, the universe was at first very hot and very small. It was no larger than a period at the end of a sentence. The universe then exploded. That explosion is called the **big bang**. The big bang happened billions of years ago.

- Since the big bang, the universe has been expanding—growing in size.

- Astronomers estimate that the universe is about 13.7 billion years old.

Answer the following questions. Use your textbook and the ideas above.

1. The explosion that formed the universe is called the

   _____.

2. Circle the letter of each sentence that is true about the big bang theory.
   a. The universe was at first very cool and very large.
   b. The big bang happened billions of years ago.
   c. The universe was at first very hot and very small.

3. Is the following sentence true or false? Since the big bang, the universe has been expanding. _____

Formation of the Solar System (page 777)

Key Concept: **About five billion years ago, a giant cloud of gas and dust collapsed to form our solar system.**

- A **solar nebula** is a large cloud of gas and dust in space. A solar nebula was the beginning of our solar system.

- Gravity pulled the solar nebula together. The sun was born.

- Gas and dust gathered together in the outer parts of the disk to form planetesimals. A **planetesimal** was like an asteroid. Over time, planetesimals joined together and became the planets.

Answer the following questions. Use your textbook and the ideas above.

4. Read each word in the box. In each sentence below, fill in the correct word or words.

planetesimals	solar flare	solar nebula

a. A _____ is a large cloud of gas and dust in space.

b. Asteroid-like bodies that joined together and
became planets were _____.

5. Circle the letter of what the solar nebula formed.
a. the solar system
b. the Milky Way galaxy
c. the universe

Stars, Galaxies, and the Universe

The Future of the Universe (pages 778–779)

Key Concept: **New observations lead many astronomers to conclude that the universe will likely expand forever.**

- No one knows what will happen to the universe in the future. Many astronomers think that the universe will continue to expand.

- Astronomers think that about 23 percent of the universe is dark matter. **Dark matter** is matter that does not give off electromagnetic radiation. Because visible light is part of electromagnetic radiation, dark matter cannot be seen.

- Galaxies seem to moving apart faster than they used to move. Astronomers think that the force moving the galaxies is called **dark energy**.

- Most of the universe is made up of dark matter and dark energy.

Answer the following questions. Use your textbook and the ideas above.

6. Is the following sentence true or false? Dark matter cannot be seen. _____

7. Read each word in the box. In each sentence below, fill in the correct words.

dark energy	dark matter	dark hole

   a. Matter that does not give off electromagnetic radiation is called _____.

   b. Astronomers think that the force moving the galaxies is called _____.

Stars, Galaxies, and the Universe

8. Circle the letter of what many astronomers think the universe will do in the future.
   a. expand
   b. explode
   c. shrink